MICROECONOMIC ANALYSIS

THE IRWIN SERIES IN ECONOMICS

Consulting Editor
Lloyd G. Reynolds
Yale University

MICROECONOMIC ANALYSIS

by

CLIFF LLOYD

Department of Economics
Purdue University

1967
RICHARD D. IRWIN, INC.
Homewood, Illinois

TO ANAMARIA

who recognizes a wall

when she sees one.

PREFACE

To write a textbook is to publicly admit to the sins of vanity, greed and incompetence, for who but a vain man would presume to present well known results more clearly than those who developed them, who but a greedy man would choose to profit financially by expounding the ideas of others and who but an incompetent would busy himself in writing out the findings of his predecessors when there is so much left to be discovered? I suppose that I began this work because of a strong conviction that something better could be offered than had been in the textbooks of microeconomics. As the work progressed it became obvious that this conviction was based more upon ignorance of the high quality of texts in existence than it was upon a unique ability to expose the subject matter of microeconomic theory myself. For good or ill a fourth sin became important along the way, that of pride. One finishes that which one has begun. Besides, if the truth were known I have enjoyed writing this book. It has occupied my hands, and, in my eyes at least, it is significantly different from other books in the field. It is the only one written by me.

Even that is an overstatement. A vast number of people have aided me one way and another. Numerous students at Purdue University, Oxford University and the University of Khartoum have been subjected to all or part of the lecture notes on which the book is based. Many of these students have made comments which have later proven valuable. In addition, numerous friends and colleagues have read portions of the manuscript and been kind enough to give me the benefit of their comments. Particular thanks are due to Douglas Beebe, James Behr, John Carlson, R. W. Clower, Charles Howe, Rene Manes, Frank Orlando, William B. Palmer, Charles Plott, James Quirk, Stanley Reiter, Robert Rohr, Paul Rubin, Hugo Sonnenschein, Mark Walker, and Gerhard Wollan. Mrs. Frances Teeling has seen to it that I have always had first rate secretarial assistance from Mrs. Melody Shaffer, Mrs. Rachel Hill and Miss Jean Powell. Mrs. Rae Korson, head of the Archive of Folk Song of the Library of Congress helped me to find the sources of several of the quotes that lead the various chapters. The Krannert Graduate School of Purdue University has provided the finest academic environment in which to work on the book. Finally my family has put up with unmown lawns, unsaddled ponies, untended cows and a surly and unshaven father, all that Kathryn and I might finish the vanity of this work. We are most grateful.

CLIFF LLOYD

Lafayette, Indiana
November, 1966

TABLE OF CONTENTS

INTRODUCTORY COMMENT

It is the purpose of this book to provide an exposition of the foundations of traditional microeconomic theory. Thus, this is a book about economics—not about economies. We make no attempt whatever to describe or even to discuss the workings of any actual economic system. We shall try very hard to aid the student in understanding certain economic *models*. We shall try not at all to convince him of their truth. Indeed it would be counter to our purposes to instill in the student belief in our models. Belief is appropriate to theology. Science requires understanding of the theoretical system that one employs coupled with skepticism as to its validity. We shall attempt to provide the reader with the understanding. We trust that he will provide himself with the skepticism.

Basically we will be concerned with the customary notions of the way in which prices and quantities traded are determined. There will be a good deal of emphasis on the formal empirical implication of traditional microeconomic theory regarding the behavior of individual economic units. Moreover the discussion will be fairly technical. Nonetheless a great many interesting and valuable modern developments will be ignored, as will almost all of policy-oriented economics. Neither the evils of monopoly nor the virtues of linear programming will concern us, but the reactions of a firm to a change in the price of an input will concern us very much.

Our purpose then is the usual textbook one, to "cast one's bread upon the waters without unduly watering one's bread." Our subject matter is very specific, decidedly theoretical and decidedly traditional. We do try to cover our limited field rather more thoroughly than it is covered elsewhere, and since this entails the utilization of some fairly technical mathematics we do utilize (in appropriately isolated sections) this mathematics. Such mathematics, beyond ordinary differential calculus, as we employ is fully and prosaically developed in the text. Clarity is emphasized to the detriment of brevity, and only the most obvious steps and those which would require lengthy digressions on pure mathematics are omitted. Accordingly, any student combining a knowledge of differential calculus with a certain elementary courage should meet with no insurmountable mathematical obstacles anywhere in our discussion.

1

The reader will find that our mathematical appendixes are not simply mathematical restatements of what has been said in words in the chapters. We confine to mathematics those topics which we feel are better discussed mathematically. Such topics as can just as well be presented in words are so presented, and we have not habitually repeated ourselves. Finally, extreme care has been taken wherever mathematical argument is employed to show that the manipulations utilized are appropriate to the problems under consideration.

We include mathematical analysis out of a conviction that any student fully trained in a field should be conversant with the tools of that field. For good or ill, in traditional microeconomics, these tools include certain sorts of mathematical analysis. Accordingly we have tried to instruct the student in the use of this mathematics. At the same time some students may have estimable reason for wishing to learn microeconomics without undertaking a complete study of the mathematics employed in microeconomic research— they might, for example, be enrolled in a course in intermediate price theory. For the purposes of such students and of such courses we have kept our mathematical analysis suitably confined to appendixes, footnotes, and Chapter 9. The content of the remainder of the book is suitable to a nonmathematical undergraduate course in price theory and has been so employed by the author many times. In the very few places (outside Chapter 9) where mathematical arguments do creep into the text they are used to prove statements which the mathematically untrained may safely accept on faith. Anyone who wishes to use the book for a nonmathematical course in intermediate price theory may do so, simply ignoring the mathematical appendixes along with Chapter 9 and perhaps the last few pages of Chapter 10.

As the book progresses the reader will find more and more frequently that he is asked to establish the proof of some proposition for himself. He will find that attempting these proofs will greatly increase his understanding of the subject matter. It is accordingly suggested that he attempt them.

A final note of apology. The reader may be disturbed to find that some of the most abstract (but not mathematical) going of the entire book comes at the very outset. This section is both brief and quite simple, and the reader should have no trouble with it. It is somewhat axiomatic because it is the beginning of our study, and that is the way with beginnings. We are told in the first chapter of Genesis that even God began his work by stating his assumptions, "Let there be light," and, as it is with assumptions, "there was light." We seek no higher precedent.

PART I

Consumer Equilibrium and the Theory of Exchange

Chapter 1

THE THEORY OF
CONSUMER EQUILIBRIUM

Prices are rising everyday
Says my wife Miranda
I don't believe a word of it
It's Russian propaganda.
—*"Put It on the Ground"**

Introduction

We begin our exposition of traditional microeconomic theory with a discussion of the behavior of the smallest economic decision-making unit, the consumer. In our discussion of this and other topics we will make certain suppositions about the goals of economic decision-making units. These suppositions we will call "behavioral assumptions." In addition to these we will make certain assumptions about the environment in which the economic unit works to achieve these goals. A situation in which relevant economic units achieve their supposed goals within the assumed environment we will call an *equilibrium* situation. In this chapter we will present the traditional theory of consumer equilibrium. This theory attempts to describe the way in which the consumer decides what he will buy.

It seems likely that the consumer's decision to purchase a given group of articles will depend upon a vast array of things—fashions, the consumer's social position and family status, his ethnic background, etc. Systematic work on the effects of such things on consumer purchases has been done and is certainly not without interest; however, traditionally economists have concentrated their attention on the effects of "economic" variables on consumer purchases. Accordingly the traditional theory of consumer equilibrium takes such "noneconomic" factors as those mentioned above and the effects of them as given and proceeds from them. The above factors affect consumer's preferences, and in traditional consumer equilibrium theory, consumer's preferences are considered given.

The Commodity Space

We will suppose that the reader knows what a commodity is. The dictionary describes a commodity as an article of trade or commerce which is of use or advantage. This description does not seem to be at variance with the use we will make of the term. Our procedure will be to define concepts in terms of commodities on the assumption that, roughly speaking, we all know what a commodity is. Be that as it may, as the discussion progresses we will acquire a more developed notion of what we mean by the term commodity, and if the above definition becomes either uncomfortably constraining or unfashionably slack we shall simply shed it without notice.

The reader is also presumably familiar with the concept of two-dimensional Cartesian space, the X, Y axes introduced in ordinary high school algebra. Thus, in Figure 1–1, we have two

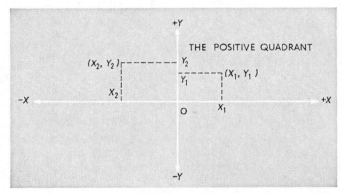

FIGURE 1–1

perpendicular lines, along one (the horizontal) we measure the quantity of X and along the other (the vertical) we measure the quantity of Y. We define the point at which the two axes cross (the origin) as the point at which both X and Y take on zero values. To the left of the origin X has negative values, and to the right it has positive values. Similarly, above the origin Y has positive values, and below it Y has negative values. Every point on the plane on which the X and Y axes are defined corresponds to a single value of X and a single value of Y. Thus the point (X_1, Y_1) in Figure 1–1 corresponds to a quantity X_1 of X and Y_1 of Y, both of which are positive. Similarly the point (X_2, Y_2) corresponds to X_2, a negative quantity of X, and Y_2, a positive quantity of Y.

The plane on which the X axis and the Y axis are defined is a two-dimensional space. If the X values are quantities of some commodity and the Y values are quantities of another commodity, then the X, Y plane is a two-dimensional commodity space.

It is possible to define spaces of greater dimensionality than two, but it is not possible to draw them accurately. A point in two-dimensional space is completely specified by the ordered pair of numbers (X_1, Y_1), as shown above. The pair of numbers is ordered in that the number representing distance along the horizontal axis is written first. In an exactly similar way the ordered set of numbers (X_1, Y_1, Z_1) may represent a point in three-dimensional space. One cannot draw pictures of this space but it is possible to build physical models of it. Indeed it is the space in which we live. It is not possible to represent physically spaces of higher dimensionality than three, but one may work with such spaces and represent points in them by ordered sets of numbers. Let X_i denote distance along the ith axis and X_i^0 denote a particular distance. Then a point in n dimensional space may be specified by

$$(X_1^0, X_2^0, \ldots, X_n^0) ,$$

we need only designate which axis is 1, which is 2, etc. In particular suppose that there are n commodities and that we give each of them a number. Let X_i designate quantity of commodity i, $i = 1, \ldots, n$, then the ordered set of numbers

$$(X_1^0, X_2^0, \ldots, X_n^0) ,$$

represent a point in an n dimensional commodity space just as the ordered pair of numbers (X_1, Y_1) may represent a point in a two-dimensional commodity space like Figure 1–1. We will work in this chapter with two-dimensional commodity spaces. This is for the reader's comfort only. The theorems that we shall prove can be shown to hold for spaces of greater dimensionality than two, and by and large the proofs that we will offer will apply directly to the n dimensional case.

All economic quantities are *not* intrinsically positive. One might sell one's own bonds (promissory notes) and thereby be said to hold a negative quantity of them; however, we will limit our analysis to situations involving positive quantities of commodities. Thus we will confine our attention to the positive (northeast) quadrant (quarter) of the space, as identified in Figure 1–1. We refer to this positive portion as *the commodity space.*

The commodity space is a continuum. That is to say that there are no holes in it. *Every* point in the commodity space corresponds to exactly one quantity of the X commodity and one quantity of the Y commodity. We suppose that all such points are defined, i.e., that each commodity is infinitely divisible. If one wishes to purchase π

units of any commodity one can do so. The notion of the purchase of one-seventh part of an automobile, for example, may disturb the reader's sense of reality, but it needn't. The quantity of any commodity that the consumer purchases may be given a time dimension. Rather than discussing his lifetime purchases of, say, commodity i we will let X_i denote his purchase of commodity i, *per period*. If the period is a week it may make little sense to consider the purchase of one-seventh of an automobile, but the consumer may clearly buy a whole automobile, use it for one-seventh of a week, and then sell it, which comes to the same thing.

Designate by K^n the n *dimensional commodity space.*

In order that we may illustrate our arguments with graphs we shall work with K^2.

We will work with order relationships between points in the commodity space K^2. In particular let APB be read "*A* is preferred to *B*." Similarly, let AIB be read "*A* is indifferent to *B*." *A* and *B* are taken to be points in the commodity space K^2. Thus when we write APB we are saying that the consumer prefers those quantities of the two commodities X and Y that make up the bundle A to those that comprise the bundle B. In order to tie our notion of indifference to our notion of preference we write:

Definition 1: *A is indifferent to B if and only if A is not preferred to B and B is not preferred to A.*

In terms of our symbols we may write this

$$AIB \text{ if and only if } A\not{P}B \text{ and } B\not{P}A \,,$$

where the lines through the *P*'s indicate that the relationship *P* does not hold. We may also define the *indifference class associated with a point A in K^2* as the set of points in K^2 indifferent to A.

The Nature of Consumer Preferences

The reader presumably has some preconceived notion of what consumers' preferences are like. We, however, are concerned with defining *exactly* the notion of a preference ordering on a commodity space. Since this preference ordering will serve as foundation for a large part of economic theory, it is important that we be fairly careful in defining it and its properties. Accordingly, any hairs that present themselves will be judiciously split. The reader is reminded that while the words "preferred" and "indifferent" may have sufficiently unambiguous meanings to make their use outside economics safe, their meanings *in* economics must be confined to what is imputable from whatever definitions and assumptions we make concerning them. To paraphrase Humpty Dumpty the words mean just what we imply that they mean, neither more nor less.

The more that we are able to say about a consumer's preferences, the more will be the implications regarding his behavior. The traditional exposition of the theory of consumer equilibrium embodies four assumptions concerning individual preferences.

Assumption 1—Monotonicity: *Given any bundle (X_1, Y_1), any other bundle (X_2, Y_2) such that $X_2 > X_1$ while $Y_2 \geqq Y_1$, or such that $Y_2 > Y_1$, while $X_2 \geqq X_1$, is preferred to (X_1, Y_1).*

This assumption says simply that the commodities that we are discussing are "goods" as opposed to "bads" in the eyes of the consumer. He prefers having more of them to having less of them. Notice that the assumption goes one way only. If the consumer were confronted with two bundles one of which contained more of one commodity and *less* of the other commodity than did the alternative bundle, the consumer might well prefer one bundle to the other. If, however, some bundle has more of one commodity and no less of the other than does an alternative bundle, then the consumer *certainly will* prefer the former to the latter. Assumption 1 tells us something about consumers' preferences. It does not tell us everything. In particular it is not a definition of preference.

We have said that APB means "A is preferred to B." We will consider this exactly equivalent to the statement "B is inferior to A" and employ whichever is the most convenient statement.

Assumption 2—Continuity: *Any continuous curve in the commodity space connecting a bundle A, which is inferior to the bundle B, with a bundle C, which is preferred to the bundle B, must pass through a bundle D which is indifferent to the bundle B.*

The emphasis in this assumption is on the word *any*. Every possible continuous curve in the commodity space which connects A to C must pass through a point indifferent to B. This assumption, as its name indicates, implies that the consumer's preference ordering possesses certain continuity properties. In particular it implies that if we have points A, B, and C as in the assumption, then by starting with A and varying continuously the commodity bundle so as to approach bundle C we will ultimately locate a bundle indifferent to B.

A further assumption which will be useful to us is:

Assumption 3—Transitivity of the Indifference Class: *If A is indifferent to B and B is indifferent to C then A is indifferent to C.*

Here A, B, and C are points in the commodity space K^2. Assumption 3 may be written

$$AIB \text{ and } BIC \text{ implies } AIC.$$

This assumption imposes consistency on the consumer's indifference class.

Our notions of preference and indifference would seem rather lacking if it could be shown that, for example, a bundle A was preferred to a bundle B and at the same time B was preferred to A. Multiple relationships of this sort would be cumbersome at best —so would the existence of commodity bundles which could not be ordered under our assumptions. Accordingly, it is comforting that we can prove Theorem 1.

Theorem 1: *For any points A and B in the commodity space K^2 either APB or BPA or AIB. The combined ordering P, I is unique and exhaustive.*

Proof: If there were two points A, B in K^2 such that no ordering existed between them, then, in particular, neither of them would be preferred to the other. Then $A\not PB$ and $B\not PA$, but this implies AIB by Definition 1. Thus all points are ordered. If two different orderings existed between two points, neither ordering could be indifference by Definition 1. To complete our proof of Theorem 1 we need only show that APB and BPA together imply a contradiction. Suppose APB and BPA, then by Assumption 2 any continuous curve connecting point A with itself must contain a point indifferent to B. Notice, however, that the point A is itself such a curve. Thus AIB, but this contradicts APB, by Definition 1. The theorem is proved.

Let us examine more closely the notion of indifference.

Theorem 2: *Indifference is a symmetric relation. If A is indifferent to B then B is indifferent to A.*

Proof: This follows directly from Definition 1. AIB if and only if $A\not PB$ and $B\not PA$, but then $B\not PA$ and $A\not PB$ which is true if and only if BIA.

Theorem 2 permits us a bit of laxity in use of the notion of an indifference class. Thus, if A is in the indifference class associated with B, then B is in the indifference class associated with A. We may further show—

Theorem 3: *Indifference is a reflexive relation. If A is any point in the commodity space then A is indifferent to itself.*

Proof: Clearly some relationship holds between the point A and itself, for suppose that none held, then in particular $A\not{P}A$. Since A is A we may turn this last statement around if we wish. Thus if $A\not{P}A$ then $A\not{P}A$ so that by Definition 1, AIA. If no preference relation holds between A and itself then an indifference relation must. Proof of the theorem now requires only that we show that A may not be preferred to itself. Let APA. Turning this around we have

$$APA \text{ and } APA.$$

According to Assumption 2 then any continuous curve connecting A to itself must pass through a point indifferent to A. Notice that, as in the proof of Theorem 1, the point A is such a continuous curve. This continuous curve "passes through" only one point, A itself. Accordingly if APA then AIA, but that is a contradiction. Thus it is not permissible that APA. Accordingly AIA.

The reader has probably heard of indifference curves. It is possible to prove that in K^2 our indifference classes are curves. Because it would take a great deal of space to do so we will not *prove* this statement. Instead of offering a formal proof we will sketch out an explanation.

Theorem 4: *If AIB then there exists a continuous curve passing through A and B, every point on which lies in the indifference class of A and B.*

In a two-dimensional commodity space this curve *is* the indifference class and is called the indifference curve through A and B.[1] The indifference class in K^2 is clearly some kind of negatively sloped curve as may be seen by examination of Figure 1–2. We label the regions of the commodity space by geographical analogy relative to some arbitrary point, A. By Assumption 1 no point to the northeast, east, or north may be indifferent to A, nor may any point to the southwest, the south, or the west. Points indifferent to A must lie to the northwest or southeast of A. By passing continuous curves from the southeast to the northwest of A we generate such points. Since the points so generated may only be indifferent to points lying to the southeast or northwest of themselves, the indifference class of A cannot be "thick." Thus it is some sort of negatively sloped curve. Suppose that it is discontinuous like the negatively sloped curve through A in Figure 1–2. Then one could pass a continuous curve from the southwest of A to the northeast of

---

[1] In a commodity space of dimensionality greater than 2 this curve would lie on a multidimensional indifference surface.

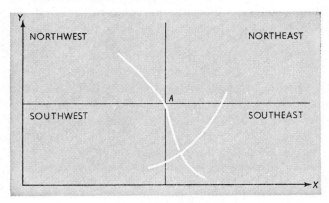

Figure 1–2

A, as shown, without passing through a point indifferent to *A*. Since this is counter to Assumption 2, indifference classes in K^2 must be continuous curves.

The indifference curves (classes), being continuous, cannot end in the commodity space, for such an end point would be a point of discontinuity. Thus they must either intersect an axis or go on forever in the commodity space continuing to be negatively sloped.

Theorem 5: *If A, B, and C are points in the commodity space and if A is preferred to B and B is indifferent to C then A is preferred to C; i.e., if APB and BIC then APC.*

Proof. By Theorem 1, one and only one of the following relationships hold between points *A* and *C*:

$$AIC$$
$$CPA$$
or $$APC.$$

a) Suppose that *AIC*. Then, since, by hypothesis, *BIC*, we have *AIC* and *BIC* which implies *AIB* by Assumption 3, but *AIB* contradicts *APB*. Thus it cannot be true that *AIC*.

b) Next suppose that *CPA*. Then we have *CPA* and *APB*, so that, by Assumption 2, any continuous curve connecting *C* and *B* must pass through a point indifferent to *A*. By hypothesis, *BIC*, so that, by Theorem 4, the indifference curve through *B* and *C* is a continuous curve connecting *B* and *C*. Thus the indifference curve through *B* and *C* must contain a point, *D*, such that *DIA*. However, *DIB*, by Theorem 4. *DIB* with *DIA* implies *AIB*, by Assumption 3. This contradicts *APB*. Thus it cannot be true that *CPA*. By Theorem 1 then *APB* and *BIC* imply *APC*.

What Theorem 5 says is that if a point is preferred to *any* point on a given indifference curve then it is preferred to *every* point on the indifference curve. By a proof exactly similar to that of theorem 5 it is possible to show—

Theorem 6: *If A, B, and C are points in the commodity space and if A is preferred to B and A is indifferent to C then C is preferred to B;* i.e., if *APB* and *AIC* then *CPB*.

The reader should take the proof of Theorem 5 as a model and work out a proof of this theorem. Theorem 6 says that if some point is inferior to any point on a given indifference curve then it is inferior to every point on the indifference curve.

Consider Figure 1–3. Choose a particular point *A* in the

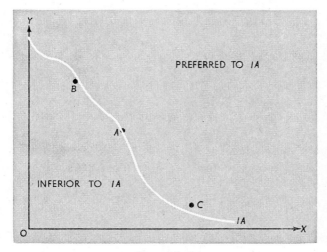

FIGURE 1–3

commodity space shown. By Theorem 3 every point in the commodity space is on some indifference curve. Hence *A* is, and we call the curve *IA*. By Theorem 4 *IA* is continuous and negatively sloped as shown. Finally, by Theorems 5 and 6 and Assumption 1 every point in the region below[2] *IA* is inferior to *IA* and every point in the region above[2] *IA* is preferred to *IA*. Through every point in the commodity space (except the origin) there passes an indifference curve which divides the commodity space into three regions: the indifference curve itself, the region inferior to the indifference curve, and the region preferred to the indifference curve.

---

[2] By "below" we mean to the south, the west, or the southwest of *any* point on *IA*. By above we mean to the north, the east, or the northeast of *any* point on *IA*.

One question remains. Are all the points in the region inferior to *IA* in Figure 1–3 also inferior to all the points in the region preferred to *IA?* For example, is the point *B* in Figure 1–3 inferior to point *C?* We will now prove that it is.

Theorem 7: *For any three points, A, B, and C in the commodity space, if A is preferred to B and B is preferred to C then A is preferred to C, i.e., APB and BPC implies APC.*

This theorem asserts that the preference relation is transitive.

Proof: Assumption 1 implies that point *A* must not be the origin since there exists a point, *B*, to which *A* is preferred. Accordingly construct a continuous straight line from the origin to *A* as in Figure 1–4. Similarly point *B* may not be the origin. Thus

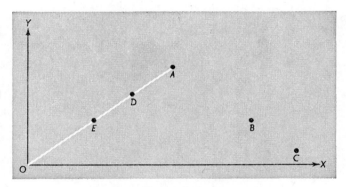

FIGURE 1–4

APB and *BPO* so that, by Assumption 2, the continuous curve *OA* in Figure 1–4 must pass through a point, *D*, indifferent to *B*. Moreover, *APB* and *BID* so that *APD* by Theorem 5, and given the monotonic nature of line *OA*, this implies (by Assumption 1) that *D* lies to the left of *A* on line *OA* as shown.

If point *C* is the origin then the theorem is trivial; accordingly, we suppose that it is not. Now, *DIB* and *BPC* implies by Theorem 6 that *DPC*. *DPC* and *CPO* implies by Assumption 2 that there exists a point *E* on line *OD* such that *CIE*. *DPC* and *CIE* implies by Theorem 5 that *DPE*. The monotonic form of *OD* then implies by Assumption 1 that *E* is to the left of *D* on *OD*. Notice, however, that *OD* is simply part of *OA* so that *D* being to the left of *A* on *OA* and *E* being to the left of *D* on *OD* implies that *E* is to the left of *A* on *OA*. Then Assumption 1 implies that *APE*. Theorem 5 then yields *APE* and *EIC* implies *APC*, which is what we set out to prove. The preference relation is transitive.

The reader should now have a fairly clear notion of what the indifference curve through any given point, A, does. It separates two regions of the commodity space, the region preferred to A and the region inferior to A. In separating these two regions the indifference curve itself forms a third region, the region indifferent to A. The preferred region is the set of all points to the northeast, the north, or the east of *any* point on the indifference curve through A. This region is completely covered with indifference curves, each one of which is *higher* than the indifference curve through A (we will call an indifference curve *higher* than the indifference curve through A if it connects bundles which are indifferent to each other, but each one of which is preferred to A). Similarly, the set of all points to the southwest, the south, or the west of any point on the indifference curve through A is inferior to A (indifference curves in this region are said to be *lower* than the indifference curve through A). We are able to characterize indifference curves as lower and higher without ambiguity because by Theorem 7 every point in the region inferior to the indifference curve through A is inferior to every point in the region preferred to the indifference curve through A.

One further assumption will insure that indifference curves have all the properties that we require of them in this chapter. In the mathematical appendix that follows we will need a bit more.

Assumption 4—Diminishing Marginal Rate of Substitution: *Along any given indifference curve, the quantity of X necessary to substitute for the loss of a given quantity of Y increases continuously[3] as X increases.*

This implies that the indifference curves are convex to the origin. Consider Figure 1–5. As we move along a given indifference curve from a to b to c to d to e decreasing Y by a constant amount each time, the size of the increase in the quantity of X necessary to keep us on the given indifference curve will always increase. A smooth curve connecting points like a, b, c, d, and e will be convex to the origin as shown. We are justified in discussing smooth curves since our assumption is that the substituting quantity of X increases *continuously* as X increases. Thus indifference curves are convex to the origin.

The commodities space is completely covered with continuous, convex to the origin, indifference curves. What is more, as we move to the east, the north, or the northeast in the commodities space we

---

[3] The word "continuously" here means that we can make the necessary quantity of X as small as we like by choosing a sufficiently small decrease in Y.

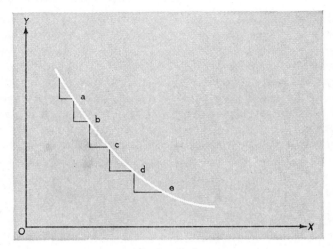

FIGURE 1–5

will pass to higher and higher indifference curves. To insure these properties of the preference ordering we have used four fairly strong assumptions. We could equally well have used more assumptions which were weaker, or fewer assumptions which were stronger. Traditional consumer equilibrium theory requires these properties of the preference ordering. Somehow we must insure that they hold. Our four assumptions are sufficient to do this.

The Consumer's Budget Set

The reader, if he has living grandparents, has probably already been informed that he cannot get something for nothing. If he intends to buy something he must pay for it. One must remain within one's budget.

Definition 2: *The consumer's budget set is defined on the commodity space as the set of commodity bundles that the consumer can afford.*

For the time being we will assume that the consumer has a given amount of money and that all the commodities under discussion have positive prices. Throughout our discussion of consumer equilibrium, we will suppose that the consumer is a "price taker," one who is unable to influence the prices of commodities. So far as the consumer is concerned prices are given constants.

On the basis of these three assumptions we may determine the nature of the consumer's budget set. Suppose that the consumer has money holdings of $80. Let the price of commodity X be $10 per unit and the price of commodity Y be $8 per unit. If the consumer were to spend all his money holdings on X he could buy 8 units of it. If he were to spend all his money on Y he could buy 10 units of it. Accordingly the boundary of the budget set will cut the X axis at 8 units and the Y axis at 10 units as in Figure 1–6. Call this boundary the *budget line*. Since the commodities have positive prices and the budget line represents a given amount of money holdings, whenever the consumer buys more of one good along the budget line, he must give up some of the other good. Thus the boundary of the budget set must be negatively sloped. Finally, since the prices are constant,

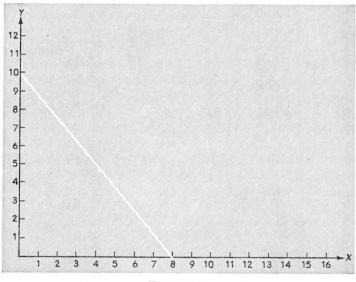

FIGURE 1–6

whenever, along the budget line, the consumer adds to his purchases a certain amount of one commodity, he must forgo a *constant* amount of the other (in our example to purchase an additional unit of Y one must give up .8 units of X). Thus the budget line will be a negatively sloped straight line. In our example it will be the straight line in Figure 1–6 connecting the point representing 8 units of X and none of Y to the point representing no units of X and 10 units of Y.

The slope of the budget line is, as we will see below, important to the theory of consumer equilibrium. Such being the case we may as well see at the outset what the slope of the budget line is. Let M represent the consumer's money holdings and P_x and P_y represent respectively the prices of commodity X and commodity Y. Then the budget line may be written

$$M = XP_x + YP_y .$$

thus

$$YP_y = M - XP_x$$

and

$$Y = \frac{M}{P_y} - \frac{P_x}{P_y} X .$$

Moving along the budget line, whenever X increases by one unit Y must therefore change by $-P_x/P_y$ units. The slope of the budget line is thus $-P_x/P_y$. In our example, Figure 1–6, the slope of the budget line is $-10/8$. Thus by moving 8 units in the X direction, along the budget line, we move -10 units in the Y direction.

The Behavior of Consumers

Behavioral Assumption 1: *The consumer in equilibrium chooses that bundle of commodities that he most prefers from the set of bundles that he is able to afford.*

This assumption determines our approach to consumer equilibrium theory. Because of it we have thus far concerned ourselves with the nature of consumer preferences and consumer purchasing power. Because of it and our assumptions about consumer preferences and purchasing power we will be able to make definite statements about consumer behavior, classifying certain modes of action as inconsistent with traditional consumer equilibrium theory. For these reasons it may be called the fundamental assumption of the theory of consumer equilibrium. The burden of the assumption is this. However complex the consumer may be, however esoteric may be the forces governing his behavior, so far as traditional microeconomic theory is concerned, he is simply a machine choosing a preferred bundle of commodities. True, the consumer's preference function, within the confines of our four assumptions, may cover any number of complexities, perversities, or social forces; these however we will take as externally given. This is not to imply that economists may not, or even should not, concern themselves with consumer behavior alien to the maximization of given preferences; traditionally, however, they have not done so.

The consumer is able to choose any point in his budget set. That is to say that he can afford any bundle of commodities that lie on or below his budget line. We suppose (Behavioral Assumption

1) that from this feasible set he will choose that bundle that ranks highest in his preference ordering. It is easy to see that the bundle that he chooses will always lie *on* his budget line. Consider any point in the interior of the budget set (the region of the commodity space that lies below the budget line) in Figure 1–6. Any such point lies to the southwest of some point on the budget line. Thus, by Assumption 1 for any point in the interior of the budget set there exists a point on the budget line which is preferred to the interior point. The consumer may buy any bundle (X^0, Y^0) such that

$$M \geqq P_x X^0 + P_y Y^0 ,$$

he *will* buy a bundle (X^0, Y^0) such that

$$M = P_x X^0 + P_y Y^0 ,$$

a point on the budget line. In what follows we will use the term budget restraint interchangeably with the term budget line.

Our behavioral assumption implies that in equilibrium the consumer will choose a point on the highest indifference curve that his budget line reaches. This can easily be seen in Figure 1–7. Since the indifference curve separates the commodity space into two regions the "northeastern" of which is entirely preferred to all points on the indifference curve, any time the budget line crosses an indifference curve it enters a region preferred to the indifference curve. Thus no point at which the budget line crosses an indifference curve may be a position of consumer equilibrium (i.e., neither of points A nor either of points B in Figure 1–7 may be positions

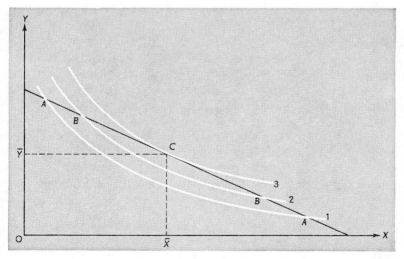

FIGURE 1–7

of consumer equilibrium). The budget line crosses indifference curves 1 and 2 in Figure 1–7. It continues to cross indifference curves until, at point C, it touches but does not cross (i.e., it is tangent to) indifference curve 3. The budget restraint reaches indifference curve 3, but does not reach any point preferred to indifference curve 3. Thus the point C on indifference curve 3 is the preferred point on the budget line and hence a position of consumer equilibrium.

Since the budget restraint is a straight line and the indifference curves are everywhere convex to the origin, the only way for the budget line to touch a given indifference curve more than once is for it to cut that curve as it does indifference curves 1 and 2 in Figure 1–7. As noted above, however, any point at which the budget line cuts an indifference curve may not be a position of consumer equilibrium. Consequently, the budget line can only touch the highest indifference curve it reaches at a single point (i.e., it cannot touch it at more than one point). Thus the position of consumer equilibrium is unique. The unique equilibrium consumption bundle associated with the prices and money holdings that give rise to the budget restraint in Figure 1–7 is $\bar{X}$ of X and $\bar{Y}$ of Y.

Static Analysis and Comparative-Static Analysis

In the foregoing we have been concerned with defining the conditions of consumer equilibrium given the consumer's money holdings and the prices of the commodities. An inquiry of this sort —one which attempts to define the conditions of equilibrium for given values of the parameters[4]—is called "statics" or "static analysis." In the above we have been concerned with the statics of consumer equilibrium. Static analysis might equally well be called equilibrium-defining analysis. Another form of inquiry, and one which we will now take up, is called "comparative statics" or "comparative-static analysis." This is the study of the changes in the equilibrium values of the variables under consideration (in the above case the equilibrium consumption bundle) which results from changes in the parameters (in the above case, prices and money holdings). Thus the comparative statics of consumer equilibrium is the study of the change in the equilibrium consumption bundle which results from a change in the consumer's money holdings or from a change in commodity prices. In pursuing comparative-static analysis we attempt to discover what our theory implies about the

---

[4] Parameters are symbols which may take on various values, the particular values that they do take being determined outside the discussion at hand. In the current discussion the parameters are the consumer's money holdings and the commodity prices.

behavior of economic units confronted with certain changes in their surroundings.

The Consumer's Demand for Commodities

For any individual a given set of prices and a given level of money holdings determines, as shown above, a unique equilibrium bundle of commodities. Accordingly for any level of P_x, P_y, and M, one and only one quantity of X and one and only one quantity of Y will be such that the consumer will prefer them to any other bundle that he can afford. These quantities of X and Y represent the equilibrium quantities demanded by the consumer at the given prices and level of money holdings. As the prices and/or the level of money holdings vary, the equilibrium quantity demanded of each commodity by the consumer will vary. At any permissible (i.e., positive) values for the price and money variables, however, a unique quantity of each commodity will be demanded in consumer equilibrium. Thus we may write demand functions for each individual as follows:

$$D_x = D_x(P_x, P_y, M)$$

and

$$D_y = D_y(P_x, P_y, M).$$

These functions associate with each permissible set of prices and money holdings the quantity of X (called D_x) and of Y (called D_y) that the consumer will purchase in equilibrium at those prices and that money holding. These demand functions for the individual consumer embody the results of the static analysis of consumer equilibrium. Comparative-static analysis of consumer equilibrium is neither more nor less than analysis to discover more about the nature of these demand functions. In particular the comparative statics of consumer equilibrium, since it is analysis of the variations in the equilibrium values of the dependent variables (i.e., D_x and D_y) that result from changes in the parameters (P_x, P_y, and M), is simply examination of the partial derivatives of the individual's demand functions. We will now turn to such analysis and see what, if anything, we are able to ascertain about the nature of the individual's demand functions.

The Effect of a Change in Money Holdings (the Income Effect)

We will first consider the changes in equilibrium consumption which result from changes in consumer money holdings. Because much of traditional theory abstracted from saving phenomena, the only holdings of money which the consumer was supposed to have had was his income. Accordingly the effect on equilibrium consumption of a change in holdings of money has come to be called the income effect.[5] The reader may have noticed that in our discussion of consumer's *preferences* we made no mention either of the consumer's income or of commodity prices. The reason is perfectly straightforward: in traditional microeconomic theory the consumer's preferences are assumed to be independent both of the level of his income and of commodity prices. Since the consumer's preferences are unchanged by changes in his income, any change in equilibrium consumption which follows from a change in income must be the result of changes in his budget restraint.

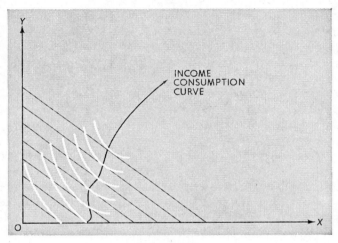

FIGURE 1–8

The level of consumer income determines the intercepts of the budget restraint. As we pointed out above, the slope of the budget line is determined by the ratio of the prices of the two commodities. As the consumer's income changes, prices constant, the budget line will shift, its slope remaining unchanged. Each new budget line will be tangent to a different indifference curve, as in Figure 1–8. The line that the point of equilibrium traces out as income varies in this way is called the *income consumption curve*. It is so labeled in Figure 1–8. We can see from this curve how consumption of each commodity varies as income changes. Notice that this line is the locus of all possible positions of consumer equilibrium at the given

---

[5] The *Locus Classicus* of discussions of the income effect is *Value and Capital* written by Sir John Hicks (2d ed.; Oxford: Clarendon Press, 1946). Hereafter, we will use the word income as the name for the parameter M. Note however, that the form of our analysis would not be changed if one commodity, say X, was money savings and M was taken to include past savings.

set of prices. So long as both commodities are being purchased it is the locus of all points such that the slopes of the indifference curves are equal to the given slope of the budget line.

The income consumption curve may have almost any shape. In Figure 1–8 the consumer purchases only commodity X up to a certain level of income. As income increases the consumer begins purchasing Y, actually decreasing his equilibrium purchases of X over a certain range. As income increases still more, he increases his purchases of both commodities. Since with no money holdings the individual could buy no commodities, the income consumption curve must pass through the origin. Since the indifference curves cover the commodity space and are strictly convex[6] to the origin, the income consumption curve must be continuous. However, over any particular range of income variations we can say almost nothing about it. Traditional consumer equilibrium theory tells us nothing about how the consumption of any single commodity will change when income changes. As income increases, prices constant, the consumption of *some* commodity must increase, because the consumer will be able to buy more commodities, but about any *particular* commodity we cannot say.

The Effect of a Change in the Price of a Commodity

The quantity of a commodity that an individual will purchase in equilibrium depends upon the set of prices that he is confronted with as well as upon the level of his income. The ratio of the prices determines the slope of his budget restraint, and the intercepts are respectively M/P_x and M/P_y. Since the consumer's preferences do not depend upon prices, any change in consumption which results from a change in a price alone must be traceable to changes in the budget line. In particular it must be traceable to changes in one intercept of the budget line. Suppose that the price of commodity X were to fall. Since neither the consumer's income nor the price of commodity Y has changed, the Y intercept of the budget line will be unaffected by any such change. The X intercept of the budget line will shift to the right because at the new lower price the consumer's fixed income will buy more of commodity X. Thus if the price of X falls, the budget line will get flatter, the Y intercept of the budget line remaining unchanged.

In Figure 1–9 (i) when the price of X falls moving the X intercept of the budget line from A to B, the equilibrium consumption of commodity X increases from X_1 to X_2. In Figure 1–9 (ii)

---

[6] By which we mean that they are convex over their entire range and do not have any flat portions.

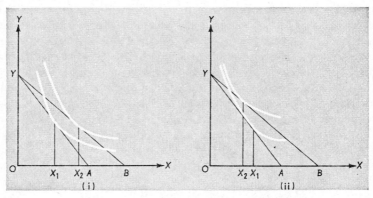

FIGURE 1–9

when the price of X falls moving the budget line as in Figure 1–9 (i), the equilibrium consumption of commodity X decreases from X_1 to X_2. These two examples illustrate the fact that our theory has no formal implications regarding the sign of the change in the consumption of a commodity that results from a change in its price alone. If the price of a commodity falls the consumer may buy more of it or he may buy less of it.[7]

The Income Effect and the Substitution Effect of a Price Change

We are unable to say anything about the effect on consumption of a change either in income or in a price. By examining the latter more extensively, however, we will be able to see what the formal implications of traditional consumer equilibrium theory are. To begin with, notice that if the price of a commodity falls, the consumer's fixed income will buy a larger bundle of commodities. In particular he could buy the previous equilibrium bundle and still have money left over with which to buy more of one or of both of the commodities in addition. Thus one result of a price fall is that *with a constant income* the consumer's purchasing power increases. The effect of this purchasing power change on consumption has been called the *income effect of a price change*.[8] A second result

---

[7] One may define a *price consumption curve* analogous to the income consumption curve defined above. This curve is the locus of all equilibrium consumption bundles that arise for a given set of indifference curves and a given amount of purchasing power as one price varies, all other prices being held constant. It may be either positively or negatively sloped over any given range of price variations. Note that it is not a demand curve as it plots equilibrium quantity of X against equilibrium quantity of Y rather than against price.

[8] This is not merely casual wording. As will be seen in the mathematical appendix to this chapter, the consumption change that follows from a price change is the weighted sum of two terms, one of which is *identical* with the rate of change of consumption with respect to income, prices held fixed.

from a fall in the price of (say) commodity X would be that commodity X would be cheaper relative to other commodities. In our simple two good model the consumer would have to forego consumption of fewer units of commodity Y for each unit of commodity X that he bought. The effect on consumption of this change in the ratios of exchange between the commodities has been called the *substitution effect* of a price change.

There are several ways in which one can show graphically these two effects of a price change on consumption. Historically the results have been discussed two ways, and accordingly we will graph the results in two different ways.[9]

The Substitution Effect as a Movement Along an Indifference Curve

Consider Figure 1–10. When the price of X falls shifting the X intercept of the budget line from A to B, the equilibrium consumption of commodity X changes from X_1 to X_3. Part of this change— the movement from X_1 to X_2—is equivalent to a movement along an income consumption curve, *ICC*. Accordingly this is taken to illustrate that part of the change in the consumption of X that arises because the fall in the price of X leaves the consumer with more purchasing power. Thus the movement from X_1 to X_2 is the income effect on the consumption of X of the change in the price of X shown. The remainder of the change in the equilibrium consumption of commodity X—the change from X_2 to X_3—corresponds to a movement along an indifference curve. This change in X is called the substitution effect on X of the price change. Thus the income effect is the result of the movement along the income consumption curve through the original consumption bundle from point C to point D where the income consumption curve cuts the new indifference curve, i.e., from X_1 to X_2. The substitution effect is the

---

[9] The reader is to be warned that our two graphs will look different. In particular it will appear that by using the two different methods for depicting the income and substitution effects we are measuring different things. Thus it will appear that for a given set of indifference curves, a given set of prices, a given level of income, and a given price change, the two different ways of depicting the income and substitution effects will lead to different values for the income and substitution effects. In drawing our two graphs we will show finite changes in prices. These will lead to finite changes in consumption made up of finite income effects and finite substitution effects. The actual income effect and substitution effect that we want to illustrate are not finite changes at all but rates of change. When we illustrate these rates of change with finite changes, in one way our results look different than when we illustrate them with finite changes in another way. In fact, both graphical representations are quite correct. They are equivalent. For a brief discussion of this point, see Jacob L. Mosak, "On the Interpretation of the Fundamental Equation of Value Theory," in *Studies in Mathematical Economics and Econometrics*, edited by O. Lange, F. McIntyre, and T. O. Yntema (Chicago: The University of Chicago Press, 1942), pp. 69–74.

variation in X that corresponds to the movement along the new indifference curve from point D to point E. Clearly we could also draw in the income effect and the substitution effect of this price change on the equilibrium consumption of commodity Y. We will not do this since Figure 1–10 is quite cluttered enough as it is.

The total effect of the change in the price of X on the consumption of X is the sum of the income effect and the substitution effect. Nothing can be said about the sign of the income effect nor can anything be said about the relative sizes of the income and substitution effects. As we said above about movements along the

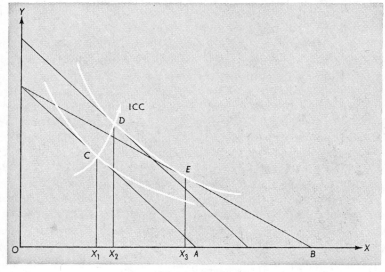

FIGURE 1–10

income consumption curve, the income effect may be positive or negative (X_2 may be on either side of X_1) and it may be so small as to be insignificant or so large as to dwarf the substitution effect.[10] Once again, our theory does not imply anything about the income effect of a price change.

About the substitution effect we can say something. In fact we can say several things. Most of these we will save until the mathematical appendix, but one can be seen from our diagrammatic

---

[10] It has been argued that since the consumer spends a small portion of his income on any one commodity the income effect of a change in the price of such a commodity cannot be very significant. For a comment on this point, see the appendix to this chapter.

discussion. The substitution effect of a price fall is a movement from the point on the new indifference curve which is tangent to a line parallel to the old budget restraint to the point on the new indifference curve tangent to the new budget line. Both these lines are tangent to the new indifference curve, but the new budget line is the flatter of the two. Now lines tangent to each other have the same slope. Accordingly the substitution effect must be a movement from a point on the indifference curve having the same slope as the old budget line to a "flatter" point. By our Assumption 4 on consumer's preferences (diminishing marginal rate of substitution) the indifference curve flattens as X increases. Thus the substitution effect of a price fall will *always* lead to an increase in the equilibrium consumption of the commodity, the price of which has fallen. Similarly, the substitution effect of a price rise will *always* lead to a decrease in the equilibrium consumption of the commodity, the price of which has risen. Since the income effect may be of either sign and may swamp the substitution effect, this result does not enable us to say anything about the sum of the income and the substitution effects. In spite of this we can use our income effect substitution effect discussion to get observable results. To make these clearer we will now derive the income effect and the substitution effect in a slightly different way.

The Substitution Effect as a Residual

Suppose that when the price of X fell we took just enough money away from the consumer to keep his purchasing power constant. The resulting change in his consumption of X would be a substitution effect alone and, as was shown above, it would be positive. His consumption of X would increase. Consider Figure 1–11. The consumer is initially in equilibrium on budget line AA consuming X_1 of X and Y_1 of Y. The price of X falls moving the X intercept of the budget line to B. As a result of this price change the equilibrium consumption rate of X changes to X_3. Now if we took money away from the consumer so that he *could* buy exactly as much after the fall in the price of X as he *did* buy before it, the resultant budget line would pass through (X_1, Y_1) and be parallel to AB. This is line CC in the diagram. Since the line CC cuts the indifference curve through $(X_1, Y_1,)$ it reaches points preferred to (X_1, Y_1). What is more, all such points lie to the right of (X_1, Y_1). Accordingly the equilibrium consumption of X which follows this combination of a price change and an income change must be greater than X_1. This is just another way of isolating the income effect and the substitution effect of a price change. The change from X_1 to X_2 is a substitution effect and the change from X_2 to X_3 is a

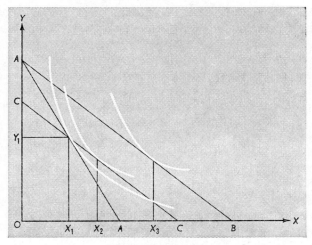

FIGURE 1–11

movement along an income consumption curve, an income effect.[11]

Figure 1–10 shows us that if the consumer were to vary his consumption as a result of a price fall and if he were constrained to move along an indifference curve, he would buy more of the commodity the price of which had fallen. Figure 1–11 shows us that if the consumer confronted with a price fall were also confronted with a change in income such that he could just afford his old consumption bundle at the new prices, he would buy more of the commodity the price of which had fallen. It is not likely that we will ever be able to observe events of either of these sorts. Thus we have not yet said anything about consumption that will enable us to describe consumer behavior.

Fortunately Figure 1–11 admits to a different interpretation than the above. One which we are able to observe. The movement from X_1 to X_3 in Figure 1–11 is the result of a fall in the price of X; the movement *back* from X_3 to X_2 is the result of a certain fall in income. The movement from X_1 to X_2 *which must be positive* is the sum of the effect of the price change and the income change. Now the effect of the income change, as will be shown in the mathematical appendix to this chapter, is, in the limit, simply X_1 times the rate of change of the equilibrium consumption of X with respect to a change in income. What Figure 1–11 illustrates is that the sum of the rate of change of the equilibrium consumption of X with

---

[11] The reader who is disturbed by the difference between Figure 1–10 and Figure 1–11 is referred back to footnote 9. Notice also that in the limit the movement from X_1 to X_2 would approach a movement along an indifference curve.

respect to a fall in price plus X_1 times the rate of change of the equilibrium consumption of X with respect to a fall in income must be positive.[12] *By observing how consumption changes when income changes and how consumption changes when price changes and then forming the sum described in the previous sentence we can tell if our theory describes observed consumer behavior.* In the mathematical appendix further empirical ramifications of traditional consumer equilibrium theory will be stated.

A further comment on the relation between Figures 1–10 and 1–11 may be helpful. For reasons explained in footnote 9 there is an approximation factor in each diagram. It can be shown that the substitution effect that we are trying to draw is equal to the variation in X that corresponds to a movement along an indifference curve as in Figure 1–10. Thus Figure 1–10 shows the substitution effect correctly, and the approximation is compounded upon the income effect. Similarly it can be shown that the income effect that we are trying to draw is exactly equal to the change in consumption that we have compensated away in Figure 1–11. In that diagram the income effect is accurately drawn and the approximation is compounded upon the substitution effect. Because we are drawing finite changes to depict rates of change, the most that we can do in a single diagram is correctly show either the income effect or the substitution effect, not both. Accordingly, in Figure 1–10 the substitution effect is correct and in Figure 1–11 the income effect is correct.

Market Demand for Commodities

Consider individual i's demand functions for commodities X and Y,

$$D_{x_i} = D_{x_i}(P_x, P_y, M_i) ,$$
$$D_{y_i} = D_{y_i}(P_x, P_y, M_i) .$$

The i subscripts tell us that these are the demand functions of the ith individual. If we hold P_y and M_i constant we may draw two demand curves, one showing the variation in the equilibrium quantity purchased of X and one showing the variation in the equilibrium quantity purchased of Y as P_x varies. Traditionally more attention has been paid to the curve showing the variations in the equilibrium consumption of X as P_x varies. In Figure 1–12 we show such a demand curve.

It is conventional to suppose that these curves are negatively

---

[12] In symbols, $\dfrac{\partial X}{\partial P_x} + X\dfrac{\partial X}{\partial M} < 0$. This sum is less than zero because these symbols refer to *rises* in P_x and in M.

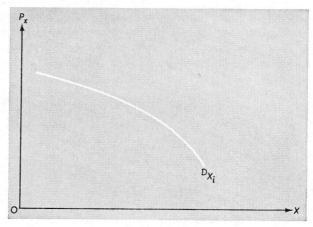

FIGURE 1–12

sloped. As we pointed out above, traditional theory does not imply that as the price of X falls the equilibrium quantity of X purchased will increase. It is perfectly clear that since the consumer has a finite purchasing power, if we set the price of X high enough he will eventually be forced to cut his purchases of it. Over any particular range, however, there is no need to suppose that the curve in Figure 1–12 must be negatively sloped. Because it is conventional to do so we will usually draw demand curves with a negative slope, but we remind ourselves that this is only a convention.[13]

For each individual we can define demand functions. Then, supposing that each individual, i, has a fixed amount of income, M_i, we can at each level of P_x and P_y add up all individual equilibrium quantities demanded to get the total equilibrium quantity demanded. This is simply a matter of adding together several functions. Supposing that there are L persons and that D_x is as defined above, then the market demand for commodity X is given by

$$D_x = \sum_{i=1}^{L} D_{x_i}(P_x, P_y, M_i) .$$

This yields

$$D_x = D_x(P_x, P_y, M_1, \ldots, M_L) ,$$

---

[13] The quantity demanded of X depends upon several things. In Figure 1–12 we show how it might vary when one of those things varies. Thus a change in P_x, other things constant, will lead to a *movement along* the demand curve in Figure 1–12. A change in another relevant variable, say P_y, will lead to a *shift in the curve* in Figure 1–12. A change in some variable other than P_x, P_y, M_i, or consumer preferences will have no effect on D_x at all.

which simply states that the market demand for commodity X depends upon the set of prices and the distribution of purchasing power between consumers. Note that it does not depend upon "national income," $\sum_{i=1}^{L} M_i$, alone. Market demand for each commodity will vary not only with the level of total income accruing to all consumers but with the distribution of that income as well. By similar arguments

$$D_y = D_y(P_x, P_y, M_1, \ldots, M_L) .$$

Summary

The theory of consumer equilibrium is concerned with the determination of the quantities that consumers will purchase. There is no doubt that these quantities will depend upon a great many things. The traditional notion is that the most important *economic* variables are commodity prices and consumer incomes (purchasing powers). Thus the traditional theory of consumer equilibrium tells us how, given *preferences, prices,* and *the set of individuals' purchasing powers,* the equilibrium quantity demanded of each commodity is determined.

On the basis of our four assumptions about the consumer's preferences we constructed his indifference curves. On the basis of the set of prices ruling in the market and the consumer's income we constructed his budget restraint. We then assumed that the consumer would choose to consume that bundle of commodities that he most preferred among the set of bundles that he could afford. This implied that he would purchase that unique bundle of commodities on the highest indifference curve that his budget restraint touched. We next examined the changes in equilibrium consumption that would result from changes in prices and from changes in purchasing power. We found that our theory did not imply anything at all about such changes, taken individually, but that we were able to establish the sign of a certain *sum* of the effects of prices and income changes on consumption.[14] We also noted that in the mathematical appendix to follow we will establish further results regarding this sum.

Supplementary Note: Income as a Variable

Throughout the above discussion we have treated the consumer's income as given. The consumer was supposed to have a fixed amount of purchasing power, independent of the quantities of

---

[14] In particular that $\dfrac{\partial X}{\partial P_x} + X \dfrac{\partial X}{\partial M} < 0$.

the goods that he chose to purchase. If we assume that the individual gains his income by selling some commodity (his labor perhaps), then the amount of purchasing power that he has will depend, given prices, upon the quantity of this commodity that he supplies to the market. Possibly the simplest way of introducing this alteration is to assume that the individual does not have any fixed income, but is able to earn money by working (which he dislikes doing). We will not completely develop the analysis of this case since the interested reader will be able to do so on his own. We will introduce the rudiments of the analysis only. To this end consider Figure 1–13. Along the X axis we measure quantities of

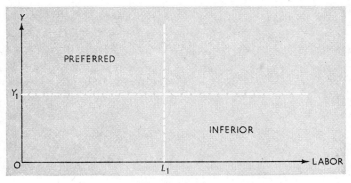

FIGURE 1–13

the commodity "labor," which the consumer dislikes supplying; i.e., so far as he is concerned labor is a "bad." Along the Y axis we measure quantities of a "good," Y, which the individual likes to consume. Consider the point, (L_1, Y_1). To the southeast of this point the consumer supplies more labor and consumes less Y, thus this segment of the commodity space must be inferior to (L_1, Y_1). To the northwest of point (L_1, Y_1) the consumer works less and consumes more, so that all points in this region are preferred to (L_1, Y_1). The reader should establish for himself how the monotonicity assumption, Assumption 1 above, would be written in this case where one of the commodities is something that the consumer dislikes.

From Figure 1–13 it can be seen that the consumer's indifference curves must be positively sloped. We now alter our Assumption 4 above to fit this case by saying that along a given indifference curve, as labor increases continuously the amount of commodity Y necessary to bring forth an additional unit of labor increases continuously. Thus the indifference curves will be convex downward. For practice the reader may combine Assumptions 1 and 4 as restated for this case, with Assumptions 2 and 3 as given above, and establish the existence of a continuous, unique, and exhaustive preference ordering having the property that each indifference curve completely divides the commodity space into two regions every point in one of which (the northwesterly one) is preferred to every point on the indifference curve, and every point in the other of which (the southeasterly one) is inferior to every point on the indifference curve, etc. We will leave this task to the reader and make free use of the preference ordering described. Thus in Figure 1–14 we have sample indifference curves from this ordering. As we move to the northwest we go to higher and higher indifference curves.

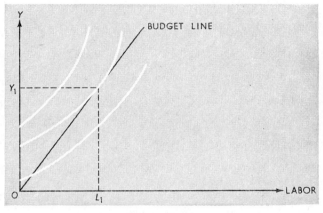

FIGURE 1–14

The amount of Y that the individual can buy will depend upon the amount of labor that he supplies. In particular, if labor is paid a positive wage, W, and if Y costs a positive price, P, the consumer's budget restraint will be given by the equation

$$P \cdot Y = W \cdot L$$

which is to say

$$Y = \frac{W}{P} L .$$

This will be a straight line through the origin and will have a slope of W/P. Such a budget line is shown in Figure 1–14. The consumer will be in equilibrium in the case illustrated in Figure 1–14 supplying L_1 units of his labor and consuming Y_1 units of commodity Y. The reader may amuse himself by ascertaining the effects on consumption and the supply of labor of a change in wages or in the price of Y.[15]

Throughout the rest of our discussion in Part I we will treat the consumer's income as given. The reader should note, however, that following the analysis of this section it is possible to derive the labor supply function from consumer equilibrium theory.

---

[15] From examination of the above budget restraint it is clear that if both prices W and P were to, say, double, nothing would happen to the quantities demanded and supplied by the consumer. Neither his budget line nor his utility function would be changed if both prices were multiplied by some constant, α. The only parameters facing the individual here are the prices, thus his demand function for Y may be written

$$D_y = D_y(P, W).$$

Similarly his supply function of labor is

$$S_L = S_L(P, W).$$

Since multiplying both P and W by α would not change the quantities supplied and demanded,

$$D_y = D_y(P, W) = D_y(\alpha P, \alpha W)$$

and

$$S_L = S_L(P, W) = S_L(\alpha P, \alpha W).$$

Functions having this property are said to be *homogeneous of degree zero*. For a more complete discussion of homogeneity, see Chapter 3 and the mathematical appendix to Chapter 8. For a brief discussion of the homogeneity of demand functions when income is a parameter, see the mathematical appendix to this chapter.

MATHEMATICAL APPENDIX TO CHAPTER 1

> *From here on up the hills don't get any higher*
> *From here on up the hills don't get any higher*
> *But the valleys get deeper and deeper.*
> —*"From Here on Up"**

Introductory Comment

The mathematically inept student should not feel that this section of our discussion is out of his reach. We shall explain what we are about as we go along. The mathematics that we shall employ are such that any reader can master them with a little study. Since the mathematics of traditional microeconomic theory are quite simple, quite specific, and rarely presented, the reader will find it well worth his time to pursue carefully the arguments that follow. We shall be quite shameless in attempting to keep these arguments clear. As we progress from chapter to chapter the pace will pick up a bit, but only very slowly. The reader may rest assured that if the author has mastered this stuff, so can he. If any apologies are called for regarding this section, they must needs be apologies to the mathematically adroit reader who may find our discussion rather detailed and perhaps a bit intuitive.

Section 1: Special Mathematical Topics

Much of the mathematics employed in traditional microeconomic theory is very old-fashioned. So much so, in fact, that it is not safe to assume that even the mathematically trained student is familiar with all that we shall use. Moreover it is difficult to find modern textbooks which deal with these subjects. Where such treatments exist in the mathematical literature they are normally either too advanced for the student of elementary mathematics or are presented in such a way that the student would need to master a prohibitive quantity of material in order to avail himself of them. Accordingly, before beginning a mathematical development of the theory of consumer equilibrium we offer the reader discussion of certain mathematical topics to be employed later.

Differentials and Total Derivatives

We suppose that the reader is sufficiently familiar with the differential calculus to be comfortable in the presence of derivatives

---

* "From Here on Up," words and music by Earl Robinson. Copyright, Earl Robinson. USED BY PERMISSION.

and partial derivatives. We shall feel free to make use of these notions, all-be-it rather prosaically, and advise the student who is not familiar with them to become so.

In the usual classroom presentation of differential calculus the reader is introduced to the notion of a derivative and made familiar with the symbol,

$$\frac{dy}{dx},$$

to designate the rate of change of y with respect to x when $y = f(x)$. It is repeatedly impressed upon him that this is a symbol and not a ratio until he ultimately comes to believe it. No sooner is his faith in this statement sufficiently established to prevent him from attempting to multiply through by dx than the instructor informs him that really, if one is properly cautious, one can split the symbol dy/dx up into the symbols dy and dx which are called *differentials*. Since differentials will be used frequently in what follows it is important to our purpose that the reader have a fairly clear notion of what they are about. Accordingly we shall begin this appendix with a brief discussion of them.

Suppose that we have a differentiable function,

$$y = f(x) .$$

We *define* the differential dy as follows:

(1) $$dy \equiv f'(x) \, dx ,$$

here $f'(x)$ is the derivative of the function f and dx is an *arbitrary* increment in x. Consider the differential dy at the point x^0

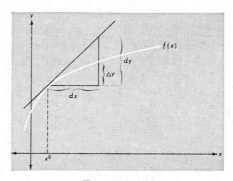

FIGURE 1–15

in Figure 1–15. The derivative $f'(x^0)$ is equal to the slope of the line tangent to $f(x)$ at x^0. Multiplying this slope by dx yields the quantity designated dy in the picture. Thus dy is equal in value to a certain change in y. The first thing to notice is that in order to ascertain the size of this change we must know not only x^0, but the size of the arbitrary dx as well,

$$dy = g(x, dx) .$$

Notice also that if we denote by Δy the change in y along the function $f(x)$ as x increases by dx from x^0, so that

$$\Delta y = f(x^0 + dx) - f(x^0) ,$$

then, for nonlinear functions,

$$\Delta y \neq dy .$$

Thus, what we have defined as dy is not the same thing as Δy. It is clear, however, from consideration of Figure 1–15 that, as we choose smaller and smaller values of dx, Δy and dy approach equality. In fact

$$\operatorname*{Lim}_{dx \to 0} dy = \Delta y .$$

In the limit as dx tends to zero dy may be identified with Δy. In any case, limit or no, it is clear that we may legitimately divide both sides of (1) by dx to get

$$(2) \qquad\qquad \frac{dy}{dx} = f'(x) .$$

Utilizing the notion of differentials we may freely consider dy/dx as a ratio. We may refer to large changes in y and x as dy and dx where dy is defined as in (1), and in the limit as dx tends to zero dy will tend to Δy. Note that (2) follows directly from (1) and does not require equality of dy with Δy. In fact dy is defined in (1) so as to make (2) true, and it is from that definition that we established that Δy need not equal dy. Were they identical, (2) would be false for some (i.e., nonlinear) functions.

It will be to our advantage to be familiar with certain rules for manipulating differentials. These follow very simply from the definition, identity (1). Suppose

$$y = af(x)$$

then

$$dy = af'(x)\, dx ,$$

so that

$$dy = adf ,$$

where df is the differential of the function $f(x)$. Similarly let

$$y = f(x) + g(x)$$

then

$$dy = (f'(x) + g'(x))\, dx = f'(x)\, dx + g'(x)\, dx$$

and

$$dy = df + dg .$$

Finally, let

$$y = f(x) \cdot g(x)$$

then

$$dy = [f'(x) \cdot g(x) + g'(x)\, f(x)]\, dx$$
$$= f'(x)\, dx\, g(x) + g'(x)\, dx\, f(x) ,$$

and

$$dy = df\, g(x) + dg\, f(x) .$$

Other such formulas will no doubt arise, but the above should enable the reader to understand the use of differentials in the discussion that follows.

Just as we are able to define a second derivative so are we able to define a second differential, the differential of a differential. Thus

$$d^2y = d(dy) = \left\{ \frac{d}{dx} [f'(x)\, dx] \right\} dx .$$

Since dx is an arbitrary constant,

$$d^2y = f''(x)\, dx^2 .$$

In similar vein higher-order differentials may be written.

Consider now a differentiable function of several variables,

$$y = f(x, w, z) .$$

We *define* the total differential of y as

$$(3) \qquad dy \equiv \frac{\partial f}{\partial x}\, dx + \frac{\partial f}{\partial w}\, dw + \frac{\partial f}{\partial z}\, dz ,$$

where dx, dw, and dz are arbitrary. Accordingly

$$dy = g(x, w, z, dx, dw, dz) .$$

Just as the differential of a function of a single variable is a linear approximation to the variation in the function as x changes by dx (see Figure 1–15), so the total differential of a function of several variables is a linear approximation to the variation in the value of the function as the independent variables change. According to (3) dy is equal to the rate of change of y with respect to x weighted by the change in x plus the rate of change of y with respect to w weighted by the change in w, etc., a linear approximation to the variation in y. Not only is the interpretation of the differential of a function of several variables the same as that of a function of one variable, the manipulations are similar as well. Thus, if

$$y = f(x, w, z) + g(x, w, z) .$$

Then

$$dy = df + dg , \quad \text{etc.}^{16}$$

In connection with functions of one variable we employed differentials to establish the derivative of the function. A function of several variables does not always possess a unique single derivative, rather has it several partial derivatives. In order to gain a better understanding of the relationship between the differential of a function of several variables and the derivative or partial derivatives of such a function, consider the case in which a function of several variables is possessed of a unique nonpartial derivative. Let

$$y = f(x, w, z)$$

and

$$x = F(r) , \quad w = g(r) , \quad \text{and} \quad z = h(r) .$$

Applying definitions (1) and (3) yields

$$dy = \frac{\partial f}{\partial x} F'(r) \, dr + \frac{\partial f}{\partial w} g'(r) \, dr + \frac{\partial f}{\partial z} h'(r) \, dr .$$

Dividing through by dr this yields

$$(4) \qquad \frac{dy}{dr} = \frac{\partial f}{\partial x} \frac{dx}{dr} + \frac{\partial f}{\partial w} \frac{dw}{dr} + \frac{\partial f}{\partial z} \frac{dz}{dr} ,$$

which is called the *total derivative* of y.

In principle a total derivative is different from a partial derivative. Suppose that

$$y = f(x, z)$$

and

$$z = g(x) .$$

Consider an increment dx in x. Applying definitions (1) and (3)

$$dy = \frac{\partial y}{\partial x} dx + \frac{\partial y}{\partial z} g'(x) \, dx$$

which yields

$$\frac{dy}{dx} = \frac{\partial y}{\partial x} + \frac{\partial y}{\partial z} \frac{dz}{dx} .$$

---

[16] The reader should show that this follows from (3).

Notice that two similar symbols appear here. dy/dx, the total derivative, is the rate of change of y with respect to x. It includes the effect of variations in x upon the variable z. The partial derivative, $\partial y/\partial x$, is the rate of change of the function $f(x, z)$ with respect to its first variable. It is the slope of this function in the direction of the x axis for given levels of z. Thus it does not take into account the effect upon z of variations in x.

It is possible for a total derivative to be equal to a partial derivative, and in what follows we will frequently develop partial derivatives through total differentials. Suppose that

$$y = f(x, w, z)$$

and that x, w, and z are independent. Consider an increment, dx, in x. Then, by definitions (1) and (3),

$$dy = \frac{\partial y}{\partial x} dx + \frac{\partial y}{\partial w} \frac{dw}{dx} dx + \frac{\partial y}{\partial z} \frac{dz}{dx} dx ,$$

however, x, w, and z are independent so that

$$\frac{dw}{dx} = \frac{dz}{dx} = 0 .$$

Thus

$$dy = \frac{\partial y}{\partial x} dx$$

and

$$\frac{dy}{dx} = \frac{\partial y}{\partial x} .$$

Just as we could define the second differential of a function of a single variable so we can define the second differential of a function of several variables. Consider in particular the function

$$y = f(x, w, z) .$$

By definition (3)

$$dy = \frac{\partial f}{\partial x} dx + \frac{\partial f}{\partial w} dw + \frac{\partial f}{\partial z} dz .$$

The second differential of this function will be the differential of dy. Before writing this out we introduce a convenient notation which will be much used in what follows. In particular let

$$f_x = \frac{\partial f}{\partial x}, \qquad f_w = \frac{\partial f}{\partial w}, \qquad \text{etc.,} \qquad \text{and} \qquad f_{xw} = \frac{\partial^2 f}{\partial x \, \partial w}, \qquad \text{etc.}$$

Then

$$dy = f_x dx + f_w dw + f_z dz$$

and

$$d^2y = d(dy) = \frac{\partial}{\partial x} (f_x \, dx + f_w \, dw + f_z \, dz) \, dx$$

$$+ \frac{\partial}{\partial w} (f_x \, dx + f_w \, dw + f_z \, dz) \, dw + \frac{\partial}{\partial z} (f_x \, dx + f_w \, dw + f_z \, dz) \, dz$$

$$= f_{xx} \, dx^2 + f_{xw} \, dxdw + f_{xz} \, dxdz + f_{wx} \, dwdx + f_{ww} \, dw^2$$

$$+ f_{wz} \, dwdz + f_{zx} \, dzdx + f_{zw} \, dzdw + f_{zz} \, dz^2 \, .$$

If $f(x, w, z)$ has continuous second partial derivatives so that $f_{ij} = f_{ji}$, $i, j = x, w, z$, then we may collect terms and write

$$d^2y = f_{xx}dx^2 + 2f_{xw}dxdw + 2f_{xz}dxdz$$

$$+ f_{ww}dw^2 \quad + 2f_{wz}dwdz$$

$$+ f_{zz}dz^2 \, .$$

The Theory of Determinants

In sharp distinction with the recent past it is now far safer to suppose that a reader is familiar with the rudiments of matrix algebra than it is to expect him to be knowledgeable about the manipulation of determinants. On the grounds that it is not really safe to expect either of these things of him, we will develop enough of the theory of determinants to fill our needs. Because we will be able to derive all that we need of the theory of determinants, the reader who is unfamiliar with matrix algebra will be at no disadvantage.

A matrix is an ordered rectangular array of numbers such as

$$A = \begin{bmatrix} a_{11} & a_{12} & \cdots & a_{1n} \\ a_{21} & a_{22} & \cdots & a_{2n} \\ \cdots\cdots\cdots\cdots\cdots\cdots \\ a_{m1} & a_{m2} & \cdots & a_{mn} \end{bmatrix}.$$

The symbol A denotes this entire array. There is a well-developed algebra of matrices, and a great many operations may be performed with and on them. The terms

$$a_{i1}, a_{i2}, \ldots, a_{in} \, , \qquad i = 1, \ldots, m$$

comprise the ith *row* of A. The terms

$$a_{1i}$$
$$a_{2i}$$
$$\vdots$$
$$a_{mi} \, , \qquad i = 1, \ldots, n \, ,$$

comprise the ith column. The individual terms a_{ij}, $i = 1, \ldots, m$, $j = 1, \ldots, n$, are called elements. Associated with any square matrix, that is with any matrix having the same number of columns as it has rows, there is a particular number called the determinant of the matrix. This determinant is *the algebraic sum of all the products which can be formed by taking exactly one element from each column and one element from each row of the matrix and attaching an appropriate sign to each such product.* Associated with the matrix

$$A = \begin{bmatrix} a_1 & b_1 & \ldots & n_1 \\ a_2 & b_2 & \ldots & n_2 \\ \ldots\ldots\ldots\ldots\ldots \\ a_n & b_n & \ldots & n_n \end{bmatrix}$$

is the determinant, written[17]

$$(1) \qquad |A| = \begin{vmatrix} a_1 & b_1 & \ldots & n_1 \\ a_2 & b_2 & \ldots & n_2 \\ \ldots\ldots\ldots\ldots\ldots \\ a_n & b_n & \ldots & n_n \end{vmatrix} = \sum_{nPn} \pm a_1 b_2 c_3 \ldots n_n \, ,$$

where the sum is taken over all possible permutations of the n subscripts taken n at a time, the letters remaining in alphabetical order. We shall discuss below the sign to be attached to each term of this sum. According to our definition of a determinant we could just as well take the sum above over all possible permutations of the letters $abc \ldots n$ keeping the number subscripts in their natural order. The product written out above, $a_1 b_2 c_3 \ldots n_n$, is that of the terms of the *principal diagonal* of $|A|$, the diagonal of elements running from the upper left-hand corner of $|A|$ to the lower right-hand corner.

We shall refer to the above sum as the *development* of the determinant. The determinant is equal to its development. Suppose that we rewrote the determinant $|A|$ writing its rows as columns and its columns as rows. The principal diagonal of the resulting determinant would be the same as that of $|A|$. Moreover, the development of $|A|$ would be that of the new determinant with the permutation being taken over columns rather than rows. As noted above, however, we may take the permutations over columns rather than rows. This brings us to our first theorem.

---

[17] Notice the difference between the notation

$$\begin{bmatrix} a_1 & b_1 & \ldots & n_1 \\ a_2 & b_2 & \ldots & n_2 \\ \ldots\ldots\ldots\ldots\ldots \\ a_n & b_n & \ldots & n_n \end{bmatrix}$$

which denotes a matrix, and

$$\begin{vmatrix} a_1 & b_1 & \ldots & n_1 \\ a_2 & b_2 & \ldots & n_2 \\ \ldots\ldots\ldots\ldots\ldots \\ a_n & b_n & \ldots & n_n \end{vmatrix}$$

which denotes the determinant of the matrix.

Theorem 1: *The value of a determinant is unchanged if its rows and columns are interchanged.*

According to Theorem 1 we need only establish theorems for rows (or columns) and they will follow for columns (or rows).

Notice that in the development of $|A|$ there is one product for each permutation of n things taken n at a time. A determinant having n rows and n columns, like $|A|$, is said to be *of order n*. Thus

Theorem 2: *Any determinant of order n has n! terms in its development.*

Consider what would happen to the value of $|A|$ if we multiplied each element of one column (or row) by a constant M. Since each term of the development of $|A|$ contains exactly one element from each column (or row), each term of the development will be multiplied by M so that the new determinant has the value

$$\sum_{nPn} \pm Ma_1b_2 \ldots n_n = M \sum_{nPn} \pm a_1b_2 \ldots n_n = M \cdot |A| .$$

Theorem 3: *If the elements of any row or column of a determinant are multiplied by a constant, M, the value of the determinant is multiplied by M.*

We are now prepared to attach signs to the products in the development of the determinant. Consider the sequence 1, 2, 4, 3. The numbers 4 and 3 have been reversed from their natural order. We shall refer to such an event as a reversal. Thus the sequence 1, 4, 3, 2, we shall say, contains three reversals, for 4 comes before 3, 4 comes before 2, and 3 comes before 2. When the development of a determinant is written as in (1) each of the products will be given a plus sign if the number of reversals in its subscripts is even and a minus sign if the number of reversals is odd (zero is taken to be an even number). This rule completes our definition of the determinant associated with a square matrix.

Suppose that we were to write a determinant $|B|$ identical to $|A|$ in (1) in every respect save that the first two columns were interchanged. The principal diagonal of $|B|$ would be $b_1a_2c_3, \ldots, n_n$. Thus, employing the notation of (1),

$$|B| = \sum_{nPn} \pm b_1a_2c_3 \ldots n_n .$$

According to our definition each term would be given a plus sign if, with the letters in the order shown, there is an even number of reversals in the subscripts, a minus sign if there is an odd number. Each term of the development of $|B|$ will also appear in the development of $|A|$, however, in the development of $|A|$ a comes before b so that if a term has an even number of reversals in the development of $|B|$ it will have an odd number in the development of $|A|$ hence, a term with a plus sign in $|B|$ will have a minus sign in $|A|$ and vice versa, so that

$$|B| = -|A|.$$

The only difference between $|A|$ and $|B|$ will be the interchange of two subscripts in each term of their developments. In general, if we interchange two columns (rows) having k columns (rows) between them there will be $2k + 1$ additional reversals of subscripts in each term after the interchange. An odd number of additional reversals will result in each term of the development. Thus each term of the development will change signs and the determinant will change signs.

Theorem 4: *If two columns (rows) are interchanged then the sign of the determinant is changed.*

Consider a determinant $|B|$ having two columns (rows) identical. Interchanging these two columns (rows) will change the sign of $|B|$. Since the two columns (rows) are identical, however, it does not change $|B|$ to interchange them. Hence

$$|B| = -|B| = 0.$$

Theorem 5: *If a determinant has two columns (rows) identical, then its value is zero.*

As a corollary to this statement, if any column (row) is M times any other column (row) the value of the determinant is zero. To prove this statement we combine the arguments underlying Theorem 5 with those underlying Theorem 3 to show that if $|B|$ is such a determinant then

$$|B| = -M|B| = 0.$$

An additional property of determinants which we shall not employ, and hence not prove, is that if any column (row) is increased by M times any other column (row) then the value of the determinant is unchanged.

Each of the elements of a determinant is in exactly one column and one row. We may unambiguously associate with each element a subdeterminant formed by deleting both the column and the row in which the element appears. The subdeterminant so formed is called the *minor* of the element.

It will be convenient at this point to introduce a notation far more common than that employed above. Write

$$(2) \qquad |B| = \begin{vmatrix} b_{11} & b_{12} & \cdots & b_{1n} \\ b_{21} & b_{22} & \cdots & b_{2n} \\ \cdots\cdots\cdots\cdots\cdots \\ b_{n1} & b_{n2} & \cdots & b_{nn} \end{vmatrix} = \sum_{nPn} \pm\, b_{11}b_{22} \ldots b_{nn}$$

where the permutations are over either the first subscripts, the second kept in order, or over the second, the first kept in order. This conforms to our definition above. Similarly our rule for establishing the signs of terms in the development of the determinant holds for whichever set of subscripts permutations are taken over. The advantage of this notation is that the first subscript denotes row and the second denotes column of the element. Thus b_{ij} is in the ith row and j^{th} column.

Let $|B_{ij}|$ be the minor of b_{ij} in $|B|$. Then we call

$$(-1)^{i+j}\,|B_{ij}| = B_{ij}$$

the *cofactor* of b_{ij} in $|B|$.

Theorem 6: B_{ij} *is the coefficient of* b_{ij} *in the development of* $|B|$.

Proof: The development of $|B|$ is a sum of all the terms that can be formed by taking exactly one element from each row and column. Thus, in this development, b_{ij} will never be multiplied by any element of the ith row or j^{th} column, rather will it be multiplied by all terms which can be formed by taking one element from each row other than the ith and each column other than the jth. Now B_{ij} is a signed subdeterminant of $|B|$ formed by deleting row i and column j. The development of B_{ij} is precisely a sum of all those terms which we have just described as multiplying b_{ij}.

B_{ij} contains all the terms by which b_{ij} is multiplied in the development of $|B|$. What about the signs of these terms? Each of the terms of $b_{ij} \cdot |B_{ij}|$ will have a certain sign in the development of $|B|$. If we can attach the appropriate sign to one such term the sign of all the others will vary according to whether they contain an odd or even number of reversals relative to the signed term, just as in the development of $|B|$. We thus seek a term in $b_{ij} \cdot |B_{ij}|$ to which we can attach the sign that it has in the development of $|B|$. Forming B_{ij} by attaching this sign to $|B_{ij}|$ will then insure that every term of $b_{ij}B_{ij}$ has the same sign that it has in $|B|$.

Let P_{ij} denote the principal diagonal of $|B_{ij}|$. In the development of $|B_{ij}|$ this term is positive. Thus if $b_{ij}P_{ij}$ is positive in the development of $|B|$ we attach a plus sign to $|B_{ij}|$ to form B_{ij}, etc. To establish the sign of $b_{ij}P_{ij}$ in $|B|$ consider how many interchanges of rows and columns would be required to make $b_{ij}P_{ij}$ the principal diagonal of $|B|$ because each such interchange represents 1 reversal.

It would take $i-1$ row interchanges plus $j-1$ interchanges of columns. Thus $b_{ij}P_{ij}$ has the sign $(-1)^{i+j}$ in the development of $|B|$. Accordingly

$$(-1)^{i+j}|B_{ij}| = B_{ij}$$

is the coefficient of b_{ij} in the development of $|B|$.

This leads to a most useful result,

Theorem 7:

$$|B| = \sum_{i=1}^{n} b_{ij}B_{ij} = \sum_{j=1}^{n} b_{ij}B_{ij},$$

the proof of which is quite simple. We establish the proof of the first equality (sum over rows). That of the second follows from exactly similar considerations. The first term of the sum includes all permissible permutations of other elements with b_{1j}. The second includes all permissible permutations of other elements with b_{2j}, etc. Thus all permissible permutations with elements of the jth column are included. But every term in the development of $|B|$ contains some element of the jth column. Thus every permissible permutation in the development of $|B|$ is included in the sum; moreover, no term of the jth column appears in more than one term of the sum so that every term in the development of $|B|$ appears exactly once. By Theorem 6 they are appropriately signed. Thus Theorem 7.

Now consider, not the sum in Theorem 7 but a new determinant formed from the elements of $|B|$ thusly

$$|D| = \sum_{i=1}^{n} b_{ir}B_{is}.$$

Suppose that $r \neq s$. Then we have the elements of one column multiplying the cofactors of another. We may write $|D|$ out, inserting the elements of column r of $|B|$ in place of those of column s. Column r would still be in place, however, so that $|D|$ would have two columns identical. By Theorem 5 then

$$|D| = \sum_{i=1}^{n} b_{ir}B_{is} = 0, \qquad r \neq s.$$

Similarly

$$\sum_{j=1}^{n} b_{rj}B_{sj} = 0, \qquad r \neq s.$$

These are called *expansions by alien cofactors* (the cofactors are alien to the terms they multiply), and expansions by alien cofactors equal zero.

Theorem 8:

$$\sum_{i=1}^{n} b_{ir}B_{is} = \sum_{j=1}^{n} b_{rj}B_{sj} = 0 , \qquad r \neq s .$$

Below we employ an additional theorem on reciprocal determinants which we state here but do not prove. Consider a determinant

$$H = \begin{vmatrix} h_{11} & h_{12} & \ldots & h_{1n} \\ h_{21} & h_{22} & \ldots & h_{2n} \\ \cdots\cdots\cdots\cdots\cdots \\ h_{n1} & h_{n2} & \ldots & h_{nn} \end{vmatrix} .$$

Let H_{ij} denote the cofactor of h_{ij} in H. Let $H_{11,22}$ denote the cofactor of h_{22} in H_{11}. Let $H_{11,22,33}$ denote the cofactor of h_{33} in $H_{11,22}$, etc. Then

$$(H^{k-1})(H_{11,22,33} \ldots , _{kk}) = \begin{vmatrix} H_{11} & H_{12} & \ldots & H_{1k} \\ H_{21} & H_{22} & \ldots & H_{2k} \\ \cdots\cdots\cdots\cdots\cdots \\ H_{k1} & H_{k2} & \ldots & H_{kk} \end{vmatrix} .$$

This result will be employed below and following what appears to be standard usage in mathematical writing will be said to be *well known*.[18]

Second-Order Conditions for an Extremum of a Function of Several Variables

We suppose that the reader is familiar with the theory of relative maxima and relative minima of a function of a single variable. The necessary or first-order condition for a differentiable function,

$$y = y(x) ,$$

to be a relative maximum or a relative minimum is that

$$y'(x) = 0 .$$

This implies that

$$dy = y'(x) \, dx = 0 .$$

If $y = f(x)$ is at a maximum or minimum then $dy = 0$. The second-order condition for y to be a relative maximum is that

$$y''(x) < 0 ,$$

so that

$$d^2y = y''(x) \, dx^2 < 0 .$$

---

[18] The reader who feels that this result is not so well known as it might be may look it up in Burnside and Panton, *The Theory of Equations* (3d ed.; Dublin University Press, 1892), pp. 283–85.

The second-order condition for y to be a relative minimum is that

$$y''(x) > 0$$

so that

$$d^2y = y''(x) \, dx^2 > 0 \, .$$

If $y = f(x)$, $dy = 0$, and $d^2y < 0$, then $f(x)$ is a maximum. If $dy = 0$ and $d^2y > 0$ then $f(x)$ is a minimum.

Now consider the function

(1) $$f = f(x_1, x_2, x_3) \, .$$

The values of x_1, x_2, and x_3 such that this function is either a relative maximum or a relative minimum will be those such that the first-order conditions for an extrema are met, i.e., such that

$$\frac{\partial f}{\partial x_1} = 0 \, ,$$

$$\frac{\partial f}{\partial x_2} = 0 \, , \quad \text{and}$$

$$\frac{\partial f}{\partial x_3} = 0 \, .$$

For notational convenience we will write these in the following ways, for

$$\frac{\partial f}{\partial x_i} \, , \quad \text{we write } f_i \text{ or } f_i(x_1, x_2, x_3) \, , \quad \text{where } i = 1, 2, 3.$$

We will use the longer form when we wish to remind ourselves that the partial derivative of f with respect to x_i is a function of x_1, x_2, and x_3. Similarly, for

$$\frac{\partial^2 f}{\partial x_1 \partial x_2} \text{ we write } f_{12} \text{ or } f_{12}(x_1, x_2, x_3), \text{ etc.}$$

The first-order condition for f to be an extrema implies that

$$df = f_1 \, dx_1 + f_2 \, dx_2 + f_3 \, dx_3 = 0 \, .$$

The second-order condition for f to be a maximum is that

$$d^2f < 0 \, .$$

The second-order condition for f to be a minimum is that

$$d^2f > 0 \, .$$

The reader may have seen these second-order conditions referred to as "sufficient" conditions for a maximum or a minimum. This is a misnomer. The second-order conditions alone are certainly not sufficient to insure a maximum. For example, consider the function $f(x)$ in Figure 1–15 (p. 36), as drawn, $d^2f < 0$ for all values of x shown. Yet $f(x)$ does not achieve a maximum in the domain depicted. The first- and second-order conditions for a maximum *together* are sufficient to insure a maximum, as the appropriate first- and second-order conditions are *together* sufficient to insure a minimum.

It is true that if $df = 0$ and $d^2f < 0$ (for arbitrary dx_1, dx_2, and dx_3 not all zero) then $f(x_1, x_2, x_3)$ is at a maximum. It is *not* true that if $f(x_1, x_2, x_3)$ is at a maximum point then $d^2f < 0$ (for all dx_1, dx_2, and dx_3 not all zero). We shall suppose, however, that this is true. A maximum may be flat like the top of a table or round like the top of a ball. A tabletop maximum would not be unique. Any point on top of the table would be just as maximal. A balltop maximum *would* be unique. Any movement away from it would be a downward movement. For a tabletop maximum

$$d^2f \leq 0$$

(i.e., some movements from the maximum point are *not* downward movements). We will say that an extremum is a *regular maximum* if at that extremum

$$d^2f < 0 \,.$$

Similarly we shall call an extremum a *regular minimum* if at that extremum

$$d^2f > 0 \,.$$

We will assume that the maxima and minima that we work with are *regular* in this sense.[19]

The second-order conditions for a particular sort of extrema are sometimes called "stability conditions" by economists. This too is a misnomer. Stability conditions are quite other than second-order conditions. The notion of stability is taken up briefly in Chapter 7.

For functions having continuous second partial derivatives

(2) $$d^2f = f_{11}dx_1{}^2 + 2f_{12}dx_1dx_2 + 2f_{13}dx_1dx_3$$
$$+ \ f_{22}dx_2{}^2 \quad + 2f_{23}dx_2dx_3$$
$$+ f_{33}dx_3{}^2 \,.$$

If f is to be a *regular* maximum, this sum must be negative for any values of dx_1, dx_2, and dx_3, provided that not all of them are equal to zero. If f is to be a *regular* minimum, this sum must be positive for

---

[19] Second-order conditions are related to the second differentials of the functions under consideration. A distinction is sometimes made between second-order *necessary* conditions which are implied by a function's being (say) a maximum (i.e., $d^2f \leq 0$) and second-order sufficient conditions which, with the appropriate first-order conditions, insure (say) a maximum (i.e., $d^2f < 0$). We will use the term "second-order conditions" to mean second-order *sufficient* conditions.

any values of dx_1, dx_2, and dx_3 such that not all of them are equal to zero. Now d^2f is a quadratic form because every term in the sum is of the second (quadratic) degree in the variables dx_1, dx_2, and dx_3. A quadratic form that is negative for all values of its variables provided that they are not all zero is called a *negative definite quadratic form*. One that is positive for all such values is said to be a *positive definite quadratic form*. If d^2f is a negative definite quadratic form at an extremum then f is a maximum. If d^2f is positive definite at an extremum then f is a minimum.

Equation (2) may be rewritten[20] in such a way as to express d^2f as a sum of squares,

$$(3) \qquad d^2f = f_{11}\left(dx_1 + \frac{f_{12}}{f_{11}}dx_2 + \frac{f_{13}}{f_{11}}dx_3\right)^2$$
$$+ \frac{f_{11}f_{22} - f_{12}{}^2}{f_{11}}\left(dx_2 - \frac{f_{13}f_{12} - f_{11}f_{23}}{f_{11}f_{22} - f_{12}{}^2}dx_3\right)^2$$
$$+ \frac{f_{11}f_{22}f_{33} + 2f_{23}f_{13}f_{12} - f_{11}f_{23}{}^2 - f_{22}f_{13}{}^2 - f_{33}f_{12}{}^2}{f_{11}f_{22} - f_{12}{}^2}dx_3{}^2 .$$

If an extrema of equation (1) is to be a *regular* maximum, the sum in equation (3) must be negative for all values of dx_1, dx_2, dx_3 not all zero. If the coefficients of the squared terms were all negative then since the squared terms are all necessarily positive, d^2f would be a sum of negative terms and would thus be negative. A sufficient condition for d^2f to be negative definite is thus that all these coefficients be negative. Examination of the coefficients of the squared terms in equation (3) reveals that they are made up of ratios of three determinants. Replacing the developments of these determinants by the determinants themselves, we have

$$(4) \qquad d^2f = f_{11}\left(dx_1 + \frac{f_{12}}{f_{11}}dx_2 + \frac{f_{13}}{f_{11}}dx_3\right)^2$$
$$+ \frac{\begin{vmatrix} f_{11} & f_{12} \\ f_{12} & f_{22} \end{vmatrix}}{f_{11}}\left(dx_2 - \frac{f_{13}f_{12} - f_{11}f_{23}}{f_{11}f_{22} - f_{12}{}^2}dx_3\right)^2$$
$$+ \frac{\begin{vmatrix} f_{11} & f_{12} & f_{13} \\ f_{12} & f_{22} & f_{23} \\ f_{13} & f_{23} & f_{33} \end{vmatrix}}{\begin{vmatrix} f_{11} & f_{12} \\ f_{12} & f_{22} \end{vmatrix}}dx_3{}^2 < 0 , \qquad \begin{array}{l}\text{if } f \text{ is to be a} \\ \textit{regular} \text{ maximum.}\end{array}$$

The reader can easily see that each of these coefficients will be negative if

---

[20] The reader may check this easily by expanding the bracketed terms on the right-hand side of (3) one at a time and isolating the terms of equation (2) in the following order

$$f_{11}dx_1{}^2 , \qquad 2f_{12}dx_1dx_2 , \qquad 2f_{13}dx_1dx_3 , \qquad f_{22}dx_2{}^2 , \qquad 2f_{23}dx_2dx_3 , \qquad f_{33}dx_3{}^2 .$$

(5) $\qquad f_{11} < 0 \, , \qquad \begin{vmatrix} f_{11} & f_{12} \\ f_{12} & f_{22} \end{vmatrix} > 0 \, , \qquad \begin{vmatrix} f_{11} & f_{12} & f_{13} \\ f_{12} & f_{22} & f_{23} \\ f_{13} & f_{23} & f_{33} \end{vmatrix} < 0 \, .$

These are sufficient conditions for d^2f to be negative definite. That is, if conditions (5) are true, then d^2f is negative definite. The last determinant shown is said to be the determinant of the quadratic form, d^2f.

That the conditions (5) on the determinants in d^2f are also necessary if d^2f is to be negative definite may easily be seen by considering alternative values of dx_1, dx_2, and dx_3 not all zero. If, for instance

$$dx_2 = dx_3 = 0 \, , \qquad dx_1 \neq 0$$

inequality (4) implies that

$$f_{11} < 0 \, .$$

To show that (4) also implies the rest of conditions (5) we simply show that there exist values for dx_1, dx_2, and dx_3 which are not all zero and for which various of the squared terms in (4) vanish. For example, if we can find a relationship between dx_1, dx_2, and dx_3 such that

$$dx_1 + \frac{f_{12}}{f_{11}} dx_2 + \frac{f_{13}}{f_{11}} dx_3 = 0 \qquad \text{and} \qquad dx_3 = 0 \, ,$$

then the first and last terms of (4) will vanish, and since

$$f_{11} < 0 \, ,$$

the second of conditions (5) will be implied. Clearly, if

$$dx_1 = -\frac{f_{12}}{f_{11}} dx_2 \qquad \text{and} \qquad dx_3 = 0$$

both the equations above will be satisfied without all dx_i $(i = 1, 2, 3)$ vanishing. Thus the condition that inequality (4) holds for all values of dx_1, dx_2, and dx_3 such that they do not all vanish implies that

$$\begin{vmatrix} f_{11} & f_{12} \\ f_{12} & f_{22} \end{vmatrix} > 0 \, .$$

The reader may solve the two equations

$$dx_1 + \frac{f_{12}}{f_{11}} dx_2 + \frac{f_{13}}{f_{11}} dx_3 = 0$$

$$dx_2 - \frac{f_{13}f_{12} - f_{11}f_{23}}{f_{11}f_{22} - f_{12}^2} dx_3 = 0$$

to find a relationship between dx_1, dx_2, and dx_3 which, with the conditions

$$f_{11} < 0 , \qquad \begin{vmatrix} f_{11} & f_{12} \\ f_{12} & f_{22} \end{vmatrix} > 0$$

and inequality (4) implies that

$$\begin{vmatrix} f_{11} & f_{12} & f_{13} \\ f_{12} & f_{22} & f_{23} \\ f_{13} & f_{23} & f_{33} \end{vmatrix} < 0 .$$

If d^2f is negative definite, then conditions (5) hold. Conditions (5) are both necessary and sufficient to insure that the quadratic form (2) be negative definite.

The last determinant of conditions (5) is the determinant of the quadratic form (2) as may be seen if we rewrite[21] (2)

$$\begin{aligned} d^2f = \quad & f_{11}dx_1{}^2 && + f_{12}dx_1dx_2 && + f_{13}dx_1dx_3 \\ & + f_{12}dx_1dx_2 && + f_{22}dx_2{}^2 && + f_{23}dx_2dx_3 \\ & + f_{13}dx_1dx_3 && + f_{23}dx_2dx_3 && + f_{33}dx_3{}^2 . \end{aligned}$$

Notice that we might rearrange d^2f in many ways, for instance

$$\begin{aligned} d^2f = \quad & f_{22}dx_2{}^2 && + f_{23}dx_2dx_3 && + f_{12}dx_1dx_2 \\ & + f_{23}dx_2dx_3 && + f_{33}dx_3{}^2 && + f_{13}dx_1dx_3 \\ & + f_{12}dx_1dx_2 && + f_{13}dx_1dx_3 && + f_{11}dx_1{}^2 . \end{aligned}$$

By arguments identical with those above, the necessary and sufficient conditions for d^2f to be negative definite then are

$$f_{22} < 0 , \qquad \begin{vmatrix} f_{22} & f_{23} \\ f_{23} & f_{33} \end{vmatrix} > 0 , \qquad \begin{vmatrix} f_{22} & f_{23} & f_{12} \\ f_{23} & f_{33} & f_{13} \\ f_{12} & f_{13} & f_{11} \end{vmatrix} < 0 .$$

The last of these three determinants is (the reader may verify for himself) equal to the last determinant of conditions (5). Thus the only differences between these conditions and conditions (5) are to be found in the first two determinants of each set of conditions. Either conditions (5) or these conditions are necessary and sufficient for d^2f to be negative definite. By rearranging d^2f in other ways, we could get different necessary and sufficient conditions. These would all have a certain form. *Definition:* A principal minor of a determinant is any determinant formed by deleting certain rows and *like-numbered* columns. A determinant is said to be a principal minor of itself.

Thus in their most general form, the necessary and sufficient

---

[21] This is the determinant of the *Hessian* of $f(x_1, x_2, x_3)$. The Hessian of a function is the matrix of all its second partial derivatives ordered as in the last determinant of conditions (5).

conditions for d^2f to be negative definite are that the determinant

$$\begin{vmatrix} f_{11} & f_{12} & f_{13} \\ f_{12} & f_{22} & f_{23} \\ f_{13} & f_{23} & f_{33} \end{vmatrix}$$

be negative, all its principal minors of order 2 be positive, and all its principal minors of order 1 be negative.

In general, a function of n variables will have a *regular* maximum at an extreme value if the quadratic form corresponding to equation (2) for that function of n variables is negative definite at that extremum. If the function in question is

$$f(x_1, \ldots, x_n)$$

then necessary and sufficient conditions for the quadratic form corresponding to equation (2) to be negative definite are

$$f_{11} < 0, \quad \begin{vmatrix} f_{11} & f_{12} \\ f_{12} & f_{22} \end{vmatrix} > 0, \quad \begin{vmatrix} f_{11} & f_{12} & f_{13} \\ f_{12} & f_{22} & f_{23} \\ f_{13} & f_{23} & f_{33} \end{vmatrix} < 0, \ldots, \quad \begin{vmatrix} f_{11} & f_{12} & \ldots & f_{1n} \\ f_{12} & f_{22} & \ldots & f_{2n} \\ \multicolumn{4}{c}{\dotfill} \\ f_{1n} & f_{2n} & \ldots & f_{nn} \end{vmatrix} \begin{array}{l} < 0 \text{ if } n \\ \text{is odd,} \\ \\ > 0 \text{ if } n \\ \text{is even.} \end{array}$$

If d^2f is negative definite all principal minors of like order to those listed here will have like signs.

If we wanted to find the minimum value for $f(x_1, x_2, x_3)$ our second-order conditions would be that d^2f be positive definite. The reader should have no difficulty in seeing that necessary and sufficient conditions for d^2f to be positive definite are

$$f_{11} > 0, \quad \begin{vmatrix} f_{11} & f_{12} \\ f_{12} & f_{22} \end{vmatrix} > 0, \quad \begin{vmatrix} f_{11} & f_{12} & f_{13} \\ f_{12} & f_{22} & f_{23} \\ f_{13} & f_{23} & f_{33} \end{vmatrix} > 0.$$

Similarly, the second-order conditions for

$$f(x_1, \ldots, x_n)$$

to be a *regular* minimum at a given extremum are

$$f_{11} > 0, \quad \begin{vmatrix} f_{11} & f_{12} \\ f_{12} & f_{22} \end{vmatrix} > 0, \quad \begin{vmatrix} f_{11} & f_{12} & f_{13} \\ f_{12} & f_{22} & f_{23} \\ f_{13} & f_{23} & f_{33} \end{vmatrix} > 0, \ldots, \quad \begin{vmatrix} f_{11} & f_{12} & \ldots & f_{1n} \\ f_{12} & f_{22} & \ldots & f_{2n} \\ \multicolumn{4}{c}{\dotfill} \\ f_{1n} & f_{2n} & \ldots & f_{nn} \end{vmatrix} > 0.$$

As above, if d^2f is positive definite all principal minors of like order to those shown above will have like sign. All will be positive.

Constrained Maxima, the Method of Lagrange

Suppose that the only values of the variables x_1, x_2, and x_3 that were of interest to us were those such that some equation,

(1) $$\Phi(x_1, x_2, x_3) = 0,$$

was satisfied, and that from the values of x_1, x_2, and x_3, satisfying (1) we wanted to choose those values such that the function

$$(2) \qquad\qquad f = f(x_1, x_2, x_3)$$

was at a *regular* maximum. That is, we want to find that set of values for the x_i ($i = 1, 2, 3$) such that (2) takes its largest value consistent with (1) being true.

Perhaps the most obvious way to attack such a problem would be to attempt to solve equation (1) for one of the variables x_1, x_2, x_3 in terms of the other two and then to substitute the result into equation (2), thus reducing the problem to a simple maximization of a function of two variables. This method has the disadvantage that it treats the variables asymmetrically. A more convenient method for dealing with such problems, and one which has the advantage that it treats all variables symmetrically, is *Lagrange's Method of undetermined multipliers*. We will simply state this method, making no attempt to convince the reader of its validity.[22]

To maximize

$$f = f(x_1, x_2, x_3)$$

subject to the constraint

$$\Phi(x_1, x_2, x_3) = 0$$

maximize the Lagrangian function,

$$(3) \qquad\qquad H = f(x_1, x_2, x_3) + \lambda\Phi(x_1, x_2, x_3)$$

treating the new variable, λ, as an independent variable. The variable, λ, is called *Lagrange's Multiplier*. We could equally well replace the plus sign in (3) with a minus sign. By Lagrange's method the first-order conditions for

$$f = f(x_1, x_2, x_3)$$

to be an extremum subject to the constraint

$$\Phi(x_1, x_2, x_3) = 0$$

are

$$\frac{\partial H}{\partial x_1} = f_1 + \lambda\Phi_1 = 0$$

$$\frac{\partial H}{\partial x_2} = f_2 + \lambda\Phi_2 = 0$$

$$\frac{\partial H}{\partial x_3} = f_3 + \lambda\Phi_3 = 0$$

$$\frac{\partial H}{\partial \lambda} = \Phi(x_1, x_2, x_3) = 0 \, .$$

---

[22] A more complete discussion of Lagrange's method may be found in Volume II of *Differential and Integral Calculus* by R. Courant (London: Blackie, 1934), pp. 188–99.

These four equations may then be solved to find values for the four variables x_1, x_2, x_3, and λ such that (2) is an extrema subject to the side condition (1).

In general, to maximize

$$f = f(x_1, \ldots, x_n)$$

subject to the $M \; (< n)$ side conditions

$$\Phi^i(x_1, x_2, \ldots, x_n) = 0 , \qquad i = 1, \ldots, M$$

we maximize

$$H = f(x_1, \ldots, x_n) + \sum_{i=1}^{M} \lambda_i \Phi^i(x_1, \ldots, x_n) .$$

The first-order conditions for an extrema of H are then

$$\frac{\partial H}{\partial x_1} = f_1 + \lambda_1 \Phi_1{}^1 + \lambda_2 \Phi_1{}^2 + \ldots + \lambda_M \Phi_1{}^M = 0$$

$$\cdots\cdots\cdots\cdots\cdots\cdots\cdots\cdots\cdots\cdots\cdots\cdots\cdots\cdots\cdots\cdots$$

$$\frac{\partial H}{\partial x_n} = f_n + \lambda_1 \Phi_n{}^1 + \lambda_2 \Phi_n{}^2 + \ldots + \lambda_M \Phi_n{}^M = 0$$

$$\frac{\partial H}{\partial \lambda_1} = \Phi^1(x_1, \ldots, x_n) = 0$$

$$\cdots\cdots\cdots\cdots\cdots\cdots\cdots\cdots\cdots\cdots\cdots\cdots\cdots\cdots\cdots\cdots$$

$$\frac{\partial H}{\partial \lambda_M} = \Phi^M(x_1, \ldots, x_n) = 0 .$$

Now consider the second-order conditions for maxima and minima of functions of several variables subject to side conditions. Suppose that we are interested in a maximum of

$$f(x_1, x_2, x_3)$$

subject to the constraint

$$\Phi(x_1, x_2, x_3) = 0 .$$

The first-order conditions for this extremum being established as above, we seek conditions that insure that the extremum is a maximum. If we form the Lagrangian

$$H = f(x_1, x_2, x_3) + \lambda \Phi(x_1, x_2, x_3) ,$$

a given extremum will be a maximum if, at that point,

$$d^2H < 0$$

for all dx_1, dx_2, dx_3 not all zero such that

$$\Phi_1 dx_1 + \Phi_2 dx_2 + \Phi_3 dx_3 = 0 .$$

This last condition is introduced in order to confine our attention to movements along the constraint. The Lagrangian is after all defined for points not in keeping with the constraint, and we do not wish to consider them.

Now

$$d^2H = H_{11}dx_1{}^2 + 2H_{12}dx_1dx_2 + 2H_{13}dx_1dx_3 \\ + H_{22}dx_2{}^2 + 2H_{23}dx_2dx_3 \\ + H_{33}dx_3{}^2 \, .$$

We rewrite the constraint on dx_1, dx_2, and dx_3,

$$dx_1 = -\frac{1}{\Phi_1}(\Phi_2 dx_2 + \Phi_3 dx_3) \, .$$

Substituting this value for dx_1 wherever that term appears in d^2H and collecting terms yields

$$d^2H = \left[H_{11}\left(\frac{\Phi_2}{\Phi_1}\right)^2 - 2H_{12}\frac{\Phi_2}{\Phi_1} + H_{22} \right] dx_2{}^2 \\ + 2\left[H_{11}\frac{\Phi_2\Phi_3}{\Phi_1{}^2} - H_{12}\frac{\Phi_3}{\Phi_1} - H_{13}\frac{\Phi_2}{\Phi_1} + H_{23} \right] dx_2 dx_3 \\ + \left[H_{11}\left(\frac{\Phi_3}{\Phi_1}\right)^2 - 2H_{13}\frac{\Phi_3}{\Phi_1} + H_{33} \right] dx_3{}^2 \, .$$

This is a quadratic form in two variables, dx_2 and dx_3. To insure a maximum this must be negative definite. We may write this condition

$$d^2H = A dx_2{}^2 + 2C dx_2 dx_3 + B dx_3{}^2 < 0$$

for dx_2 and dx_3 not both zero, where

$$A = \frac{1}{\Phi_1{}^2}[H_{11}\Phi_2{}^2 - 2H_{12}\Phi_1\Phi_2 + H_{22}\Phi_1{}^2] \, ,$$

$$B = \frac{1}{\Phi_1{}^2}[H_{11}\Phi_3{}^2 - 2H_{13}\Phi_1\Phi_3 + H_{33}\Phi_1{}^2] \, ,$$

and

$$C = \frac{1}{\Phi_1{}^2}[H_{11}\Phi_2\Phi_3 - H_{12}\Phi_1\Phi_3 - H_{13}\Phi_1\Phi_2 + H_{23}\Phi_1{}^2] \, .$$

This form, unburdened with side conditions, is of the type discussed above in connection with unconstrained maxima and, as was shown there, it will be negative definite if and only if

$$A < 0, \quad \begin{vmatrix} A & C \\ C & B \end{vmatrix} > 0 \, .$$

These conditions may be written in more appropriate form:

$$A = \frac{1}{\Phi_1{}^2}[H_{11}\Phi_2{}^2 - 2H_{12}\Phi_1\Phi_2 + H_{22}\Phi_1{}^2] = -\frac{1}{\Phi_1{}^2}\begin{vmatrix} 0 & \Phi_1 & \Phi_2 \\ \Phi_1 & H_{11} & H_{12} \\ \Phi_2 & H_{21} & H_{22} \end{vmatrix} \, .$$

Since $\frac{1}{\Phi_1{}^2}$ is a perfect square number it is positive. Thus a necessary and sufficient condition for A to be negative is

$$\begin{vmatrix} 0 & \Phi_1 & \Phi_2 \\ \Phi_1 & H_{11} & H_{12} \\ \Phi_2 & H_{21} & H_{22} \end{vmatrix} > 0 .$$

It is far too cumbersome to show here, however, it is true that

$$\begin{vmatrix} A & C \\ C & B \end{vmatrix} = -\frac{1}{\Phi_1{}^2} \begin{vmatrix} 0 & \Phi_1 & \Phi_2 & \Phi_3 \\ \Phi_1 & H_{11} & H_{12} & H_{13} \\ \Phi_2 & H_{21} & H_{22} & H_{23} \\ \Phi_3 & H_{31} & H_{32} & H_{33} \end{vmatrix} .$$

The left-hand side of this expression will be positive if and only if

$$\begin{vmatrix} 0 & \Phi_1 & \Phi_2 & \Phi_3 \\ \Phi_1 & H_{11} & H_{12} & H_{13} \\ \Phi_2 & H_{21} & H_{22} & H_{23} \\ \Phi_3 & H_{31} & H_{32} & H_{33} \end{vmatrix} < 0 .$$

From the definition of the Lagrangian $H_{ij} = f_{ij} + \lambda \Phi_{ij}$ so that the second-order conditions for

$$f(x_1, x_2, x_3)$$

to be a maximum subject to

$$\Phi(x_1, x_2, x_3) = 0$$

are

$$\begin{vmatrix} 0 & \Phi_1 & \Phi_2 \\ \Phi_1 & f_{11} + \lambda\Phi_{11} & f_{12} + \lambda\Phi_{12} \\ \Phi_2 & f_{21} + \lambda\Phi_{21} & f_{22} + \lambda\Phi_{22} \end{vmatrix} > 0 ,$$

$$\begin{vmatrix} 0 & \Phi_1 & \Phi_2 & \Phi_3 \\ \Phi_1 & f_{11} + \lambda\Phi_{11} & f_{12} + \lambda\Phi_{12} & f_{13} + \lambda\Phi_{13} \\ \Phi_2 & f_{21} + \lambda\Phi_{21} & f_{22} + \lambda\Phi_{22} & f_{23} + \lambda\Phi_{23} \\ \Phi_3 & f_{31} + \lambda\Phi_{31} & f_{32} + \lambda\Phi_{32} & f_{33} + \lambda\Phi_{33} \end{vmatrix} < 0 .$$

If d^2H is negative definite subject to

$$\Phi_1 dx_1 + \Phi_2 dx_2 + \Phi_3 dx_3 = 0$$

both border preserving[23] principal minors of order three of the last determinant above will be positive (that is $B < 0$). Typically the constraints which arise in traditional microeconomic theory are linear so that their second partials (Φ_{ij} in the example) are zero.

---

[23] Those which are not formed by deleting the first row and column.

The second-order conditions for a function of n variables

$$f = f(x_1, \ldots, x_n)$$

to be a maximum subject to the constraint,

$$\Phi(x_1, \ldots, x_n) = 0 \,,$$

are

$$\begin{vmatrix} 0 & \Phi_1 & \Phi_2 \\ \Phi_1 & f_{11} + \lambda\Phi_{11} & f_{12} + \lambda\Phi_{12} \\ \Phi_2 & f_{21} + \lambda\Phi_{21} & f_{22} + \lambda\Phi_{22} \end{vmatrix} > 0 \,,$$

$$\begin{vmatrix} 0 & \Phi_1 & \Phi_2 & \Phi_3 \\ \Phi_1 & f_{11} + \lambda\Phi_{11} & f_{12} + \lambda\Phi_{12} & f_{13} + \lambda\Phi_{13} \\ \Phi_2 & f_{21} + \lambda\Phi_{21} & f_{22} + \lambda\Phi_{22} & f_{23} + \lambda\Phi_{23} \\ \Phi_3 & f_{31} + \lambda\Phi_{31} & f_{32} + \lambda\Phi_{32} & f_{33} + \lambda\Phi_{33} \end{vmatrix} < 0 \,, \ldots,$$

$$\begin{vmatrix} 0 & \Phi_1 & \cdots & \Phi_n \\ \Phi_1 & f_{11} + \lambda\Phi_{11} & \cdots & f_{1n} + \lambda\Phi_{1n} \\ \cdots & \cdots & \cdots & \cdots \\ \Phi_n & f_{n1} + \lambda\Phi_{n1} & \cdots & f_{nn} + \lambda\Phi_{nn} \end{vmatrix} \begin{array}{l} > 0 \text{ if } n \text{ is even}, \\[4pt] < 0 \text{ if } n \text{ is odd}. \end{array}$$

Once again if f is a *regular* maximum subject to Φ, then all the border preserving principal minors of appropriate order will alternate in sign as do those shown.

The second-order conditions for a function of n variables

$$f = f(x_1, \ldots, x_n)$$

to be a *minimum* subject to the constraint

$$\Phi(x_1, \ldots, x_n) = 0$$

are that the second differential of the Lagrangian

$$H = f(x_1, \ldots, x_n) + \lambda\Phi(x_1, \ldots, x_n) \,,$$

$$d^2H = \sum_{i=1}^{n} \sum_{j=1}^{n} H_{ij}dx_i dx_j \,,$$

be *positive definite* for all dx_i, $i = 1, \ldots, n$ not all zero, such that

$$\sum_{i=1}^{n} \Phi_i dx_i = 0 \,.$$

This would be true if and only if the border preserving principal minors mentioned in the preceding paragraphs are all negative in sign. Similarly, *all* border preserving principal minors of order three or more of

$$\begin{vmatrix} 0 & \Phi_1 & \cdots & \Phi_n \\ \Phi_1 & f_{11} + \lambda\Phi_{11} & \cdots & f_{1n} + \lambda\Phi_{1n} \\ \cdots\cdots\cdots\cdots\cdots\cdots\cdots\cdots\cdots\cdots\cdots \\ \Phi_n & f_{n1} + \lambda\Phi_{n1} & \cdots & f_{nn} + \lambda\Phi_{nn} \end{vmatrix}$$

would be negative.[24]

Cramer's Rule

Given a system of simultaneous equations

$$a_1 X + b_1 Y + c_1 Z + d_1 W = k_1$$
$$a_2 X + b_2 Y + c_2 Z + d_2 W = k_2$$
$$a_3 X + b_3 Y + c_3 Z + d_3 W = k_3$$
$$a_4 X + b_4 Y + c_4 Z + d_4 W = k_4 .$$

We call

$$\begin{vmatrix} a_1 & b_1 & c_1 & d_1 \\ a_2 & b_2 & c_2 & d_2 \\ a_3 & b_3 & c_3 & d_3 \\ a_4 & b_4 & c_4 & d_4 \end{vmatrix} = D ,$$

the determinant of the system of equations. Then Cramer's Rule tells us that if $D \neq 0$,

$$X = \frac{\begin{vmatrix} k_1 & b_1 & c_1 & d_1 \\ k_2 & b_2 & c_2 & d_2 \\ k_3 & b_3 & c_3 & d_3 \\ k_4 & b_4 & c_4 & d_4 \end{vmatrix}}{D} \qquad Y = \frac{\begin{vmatrix} a_1 & k_1 & c_1 & d_1 \\ a_2 & k_2 & c_2 & d_2 \\ a_3 & k_3 & c_3 & d_3 \\ a_4 & k_4 & c_4 & d_4 \end{vmatrix}}{D}$$

$$Z = \frac{\begin{vmatrix} a_1 & b_1 & k_1 & d_1 \\ a_2 & b_2 & k_2 & d_2 \\ a_3 & b_3 & k_3 & d_3 \\ a_4 & b_4 & k_4 & d_4 \end{vmatrix}}{D} , \quad \text{and} \quad W = \frac{\begin{vmatrix} a_1 & b_1 & c_1 & k_1 \\ a_2 & b_2 & c_2 & k_2 \\ a_3 & b_3 & c_3 & k_3 \\ a_4 & b_4 & c_4 & k_4 \end{vmatrix}}{D}$$

In general in a system of n linear equations in n unknowns, with all constant terms collected on the right-hand sides of the equal signs as in the example above, the solution value of the jth variable may be found by evaluating the determinant formed by replacing the

---

[24] The most general case, in which $f = f(x_2, \ldots, x_n)$ is to be a maximum or minimum subject to the m ($< n$) side conditions

$$\Phi^i(x_1, \ldots, x_n) = 0 , \qquad (i = 1, \ldots, m)$$

will not arise in our discussion. Accordingly we will forgo a statement of the second-order conditions for this case. The interested reader is referred to Chapter 10 of *The Differential Calculus* by T. Chaundy (Oxford: The Clarendon Press, 1935).

coefficients of the jth variable in the determinant of the system by the column of constant terms, and dividing the value of the determinant so formed by the value of the determinant of the system.

Elasticity

We conclude our list of special mathematical topics with a very brief discussion of a concept which we will not frequently employ. For some purposes it is convenient to use a dimension-free notion of the rate of change of one variable with respect to another. To this end the concept of elasticity has been introduced. An elasticity is a ratio of percentage changes in variables, as

$$\frac{\frac{\Delta y}{y}}{\frac{\Delta x}{x}}.$$

Introducing differentials this may be written

$$\frac{\frac{\Delta y}{y}}{\frac{dx}{x}},$$

where $y = f(x)$ and Δy and dx are as defined above. In the limit as dx approaches zero this may be written

$$\frac{\frac{dy}{y}}{\frac{dx}{x}}.$$

Definition: *If $y = f(x)$ the x elasticity of y is given by* $\dfrac{dy}{dx} \cdot \dfrac{x}{y}$.

Section 2: The Mathematical Theory of Consumer Equilibrium

In this section, we will extend the analysis of Chapter 1 to cover cases in which more than two commodities exist. We will also establish additional comparative-statics results. In order to do these things, we will change our approach slightly. In particular, we will make use of the consumer's utility function.

The Utility Function

In Figure 1–16 we draw a curve (called the indexer) having positive finite slope throughout and passing from the origin, a point inferior, by Assumption 1, Chapter 1, to any other point in the commodity space. Given any point in the commodity space we may

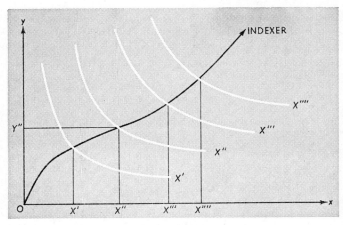

FIGURE 1–16

reach a point preferred to it by extending the indexer sufficiently far. By Assumption 2 above the indexer if sufficiently extended will pass through points indifferent to any point in the commodity space. Thus it must cut any indifference curve in the commodities space. Since the indexer is positively sloped, no two points on it may be indifferent; hence, it may cut any indifference curve only once. Thus the indexer will cut each indifference curve once and only once.

To construct a utility function for a given individual, we draw a positively sloped indexer into a commodity space in which his indifference curves are defined. The indexer will cut each indifference curve once and only once, and each point on the indexer will lie on exactly one indifference curve. Further, each point on the indexer corresponds to exactly one value for the variable X, and each value of X determines precisely one point on the indexer. Thus, in Figure 1–16 the point (X'', Y'') corresponds to X'' of X and no other point on the indexer corresponds to X'' of X. Consider the point at which a given indifference curve, say the lowest indifference curve in Figure 1–16, cuts the indexer. This point will correspond to exactly one value of X, in this case to X'. Associate with *each point on this indifference curve* a utility value X'. Associate with each indifference curve a utility value (index) equal to the X value of the point of intersection of the indifference curve and the chosen indexer. By this process, or one similar to it, we construct our utility function.

Since every point in the space has precisely one indifference curve passing through it, and since the above process gives a definite utility index to each indifference curve, the process assigns a definite utility value to each point in the commodity space. The reader should not get the impression that because we have assigned our utility index according to X values alone, utility is a function of X only. The indifference curve given the utility value X' may be typified by the equation

$$U(X, Y) = X'$$

which is a function of both X and Y. Note that $U(X', Y)$ will be greater than, less than, or equal to X' depending upon the particular value that Y takes. The above process attaches to each point in the commodity space a particular utility index or value. It defines utility as a function of X and Y. What is more, under our assumptions, it may be shown that the utility function $U = U(X, Y)$ is continuous. We only point this out; we will not attempt to prove it.

We are now in a position to determine some of the properties of our utility index. Consider two commodity bundles (X_1, Y_1) and (X_2, Y_2) such that (X_2, Y_2) is preferred to (X_1, Y_1). Thus (X_2, Y_2) is in the region preferred to (X_1, Y_1). The indexer must then cut the indifference curve through (X_2, Y_2) in the region preferred to the point at which it cuts the indifference curve through (X_1, Y_1). If it did not, the two indifference curves would have to cross. Since the indexer is everywhere positively sloped, the X value of points on the indexer increases as the indexer passes to more preferred points, i.e., to higher indifference curves. Thus the X value of the point (X_2, Y_2) will be greater than the X value of the point (X_1, Y_1). Thus if (X_2, Y_2) is preferred to (X_1, Y_1), then

$$U(X_2, Y_2) > U(X_1, Y_1) \, ,$$

that is (X_2, Y_2) has a higher utility value than has (X_1, Y_1). The reader should establish the truth of the converse statement: if $U(X_2 Y_2) > U(X_1, Y_1)$, then $(X_2, Y_2) \, P(X_1, Y_1)$. Consider the behavior of the utility index as X increases, Y being held constant. This is shown in Figure 1–17. The line parallel to the X axis must,

FIGURE 1–17

by Assumption 1 above, cut higher and higher indifference curves as X increases. Since our utility index increases as we pass to higher and higher indifference curves, the utility index must increase as we move to the right along the line $\overline{Y}$. Thus, where the utility function has a defined slope in the direction of the X axis, that slope will be positive. By similar reasoning, where the utility function has a defined slope in the direction of the Y axis, that slope is positive. *Thus, where the partial derivative of the utility function with respect to either X or Y exists, it will be positive.*

As we said above, our assumption about consumer's preferences insure that the utility function that we have constructed will be continuous. They do not, however, insure that it will be everywhere differentiable.

> **Assumption 5:** *The consumer's preferences are such that the utility function, $U(X, Y)$, defined above has continuous first and second partial derivatives with respect to all its variables.*

Thus, from the above discussion,

$$U_x > 0$$

and

$$U_y > 0 .$$

What is more, Assumption 4 implies

$$U_{xy} = U_{yx} .$$

We noted above that if (X_2, Y_2) is preferred to (X_1, Y_1) then

$$U(X_2, Y_2) > U(X_1, Y_1) .$$

We have assumed that the consumer chooses that bundle that he prefers among those that he can afford. Since the above relationship is true this is equivalent to choosing that bundle with the highest utility value among those bundles that he can afford. This, in turn, is equivalent to maximizing his utility function subject to his budget restraint. We may restate behavioral Assumption 1 as follows: *The consumer chooses that bundle of commodities which maximizes his utility function subject to his budget restraint.*

The reader's attention is drawn to the fact that the utility function is entirely an artifact of our invention. There is nothing in our analysis that implies that the consumer gains any "utiles," or some such, from the consumption of commodities. We assume only that he behaves according to a set of preferences having the properties assumed in Chapter 1. On the basis of this assumption, *we are able to construct* a utility function on the consumer's preferences having the property that a position of consumer equilibrium will be a position such that the utility function is maximized subject to the consumer's budget restraint. Notice that this utility function is an ordinary real-valued function. The preference ordering is *ordinal*. We may say that A is preferred to B but it would make no sense at all to say, for example, that A is "twice as preferred" as B. The preference ordering is an ordering not a measure. It tells us that one point is preferred to another, but not by how much. The utility function, on the other hand, is *cardinal*. If some point has a utility of 2 and another has a utility of 4 then the second point has, indeed, twice the utility value of the first. Of course *we gave it* twice the utility value, it would still make no sense to assert that it was "twice as preferred."

The utility function is an *arbitrary* order preserving continuous function. For example, we could employ any number of indexers each of which would give us a different utility function. Having employed an indexer, however, and constructed an order preserving real-valued utility function on the consumer's ordinal preference ordering, we may apply the tools of differential calculus to this function. We emphasize this point because it is fairly common for economists to confuse the utility function (which is arbitrary and cardinal) with the preference ordering (which is given and ordinal) and claim that the utility function is ordinal. If the utility function were ordinal, nonzero values of its partial derivatives would make no sense, only their signs would. One cannot evaluate the rate of change of something when only the direction of change is defined.

While we are on the subject of the partial derivatives of the utility function we may as well make one further point. The rate of change of utility with respect to a change in X, U_x, is called the *marginal utility* of X. Earlier economists made use of an assumption of *diminishing marginal utility*. They assumed that

$$U_{xx} < 0 .$$

We have not made this assumption, but it is sometimes supposed that our assumption—that of the diminishing marginal rate of substitution—implies diminishing marginal utility. This is not true. Assumption 4 implies that along an indifference curve the rate of change of Y with respect to X increases (since this rate of change is negative if it increases the curve becomes flatter) as X increases. Along an indifference curve

$$U(X, Y) = \bar{U} ,$$

a constant. Thus, along an indifference curve

$$d\bar{U} = 0 = U_x dX + U_y dY \,,$$

so that

$$U_x dX = - U_y dY \,,$$

and

$$\frac{dY}{dX} = - \frac{U_x}{U_y}.$$

Suppose that we are at a point such that $U_x = 12$ and $U_y = 2$. Then

$$\frac{dY}{dX} = - 6 \,.$$

Let $U_{xy} = U_{yx} = \overset{\circ}{0}$, $U_{xx} > 0$, and $U_{yy} < 0$ so that X exhibits *increasing* marginal utility. Consider a movement along the indifference curve that increases X and decreases Y. According to our statement about the second partials both U_x and U_y will increase. Suppose that U_x increases to 15 and U_y increases to 5, then

$$\frac{dY}{dX} = - 3 \,.$$

Assumption 4 holds, but diminishing marginal utility does not. The former does not imply the latter.

The n Commodity Case

It is possible to generalize our analysis of consumer preferences to cover n dimensional commodity spaces. Under assumptions exactly similar to those in Chapter 1, we may derive a continuous utility function of n variables having the properties that we established above for $U(X, Y)$. Generalizing Assumption 5 above, we then have a utility function,

$$U = U(X_1, X_2, \ldots, X_n) \,,$$

having continuous first and second partials with respect to all its variables, such that

$$U_i = \frac{\partial U}{\partial X_i} > 0 \,, \qquad i = 1, \ldots, n \,,$$
$$U_{ij} = U_{ji} \,, \qquad i, j = 1, \ldots, n \,.$$

Here, of course, $X_i, i = 1, \ldots, n$, is the consumption of commodity i. Finally, according to Behavioral Assumption 1 as restated, the consumer's equilibrium consumption bundle will be a set of values of $X_1, X_2, \ldots, X_n$ such that

$$U(X_1, X_2, \ldots, X_n)$$

is a maximum subject to the budget restraint

$$\sum_{i=1}^{n} X_i P_i = Y ,$$

where P_i is the price of X_i and Y is the consumer's income. To specify our model a bit more completely we suppose that the consumer receives, each period, a certain income, Y. He is faced with a set of prices, $P_1, P_2, \ldots, P_n$, and wishes to choose those quantities of commodities $X_1, X_2, \ldots, X_n$ which he will most prefer to consume during the period among all the bundles that he can afford. In exactly the same way that we specified $U(X, Y)$ in the two commodity case above, we can then specify a utility function

$$U = U(X_1, X_2, \ldots, X_n) ,$$

such that the most preferred bundle of commodities that the consumer can afford for each set of prices and each income will be the bundle such that

$$U(X_1, X_2, \ldots, X_n)$$

is maximized subject to

$$\sum_{i=1}^{n} X_i P_i = Y .$$

The Derivation of Demand Functions
Maximize

(1) $$U = U(X_1, \ldots, X_n)$$

subject to

(2) $$\sum_{i=1}^{n} X_i P_i = Y$$

where X_i is the consumption per period of the ith commodity, P_i is the price of the ith commodity, and Y is the individual's income. Following the method of Lagrange outlined above we maximize[25]

$$G = U(X_1, \ldots, X_n) + \lambda \left[\sum_{i=1}^{n} X_i P_i - Y \right],$$

treating the Lagrange multiplier, λ, as a variable. The first-order conditions for (1) to be a maximum subject to (2) are given by

---

[25] Note that in applying Lagrange's method we always write the restraint in such a way as to make it equal to zero. The reader is also warned that we are implicitly assuming here that some of each commodity is brought in equilibrium.

$$(3) \begin{cases} \dfrac{\partial G}{\partial \lambda} = \displaystyle\sum_{i=1}^{n} X_i P_i - Y = 0 \\[2mm] \dfrac{\partial G}{\partial X_1} = \lambda P_1 + U_1(X_1, \ldots, X_n) = 0 \\[2mm] \dfrac{\partial G}{\partial X_2} = \lambda P_2 + U_2(X_1, \ldots, X_n) = 0 \\[2mm] \cdots\cdots\cdots\cdots\cdots\cdots\cdots\cdots\cdots\cdots \\[2mm] \dfrac{\partial G}{\partial X_n} = \lambda P_n + U_n(X_1, \ldots, X_n) = 0 \end{cases}$$

where we have rearranged some terms for convenience.

These first-order conditions are $n + 1$ in number. They form $n + 1$ equations which may be solved for the values of the $n + 1$ variables $X_1, X_2, \ldots, X_n$, and λ such that (1) is an extremum subject to (2). Under our Assumption 4 which insures that indifference curves are everywhere convex to the origin, this extremum will be a maximum. Thus the values of $X_1, X_2, \ldots, X_n$ determined by conditions (3) above will be the equilibrium consumption levels of commodities 1 through n for the given set of prices, $P_1, P_2, \ldots, P_n$, and income, Y. If we consider the values of $X_1, \ldots, X_n$ satisfying conditions (3) as the parameters, $P_1, \ldots, P_n$ and Y vary, we get a set of equations

$$(4) \begin{cases} X_1 = X_1(P_1, P_2, \ldots, P_n, Y) \\ X_2 = X_2(P_1, P_2, \ldots, P_n, Y) \\ \cdots\cdots\cdots\cdots\cdots\cdots\cdots\cdots \\ X_n = X_n(P_1, P_2, \ldots, P_n, Y) \end{cases}$$

showing the equilibrium levels of consumption of n commodities as functions of prices and income. These, of course, are the consumer's demand functions. Equations (4) are not very useful unless we can say something about their form. Comparative-statics analysis of consumer behavior (which we discussed in Chapter 1) has as its goal the derivation of conditions which these demand functions must satisfy; accordingly, we will now turn to the deduction of some of these conditions.

Consider the consumer's budget restraint,

$$\sum_{i=1}^{n} X_i P_i = Y .$$

Should all prices and the consumer's income be multiplied by $\alpha > 0$ the budget restraint would be unchanged. Neither prices nor income enter the consumer's utility function. Thus nothing affecting the consumer's choice of commodities is changed. Accordingly the quantities that the consumer will purchase of the various commodities will remain fixed. A function having this property is said to be *homogeneous of degree zero.*[26] Each of demand functions (4) is homogeneous of degree zero.

In deducing remaining implications of traditional demand theory, we will utilize the second-order conditions for (1) to be a maximum subject to (2). In accordance with our discussion of the second-order conditions for a constrained maximum these are

(5)
$$\begin{cases} \begin{vmatrix} 0 & P_1 & P_2 \\ P_1 & U_{11} & U_{12} \\ P_2 & U_{12} & U_{22} \end{vmatrix} > 0, \quad \begin{vmatrix} 0 & P_1 & P_2 & P_3 \\ P_1 & U_{11} & U_{12} & U_{13} \\ P_2 & U_{12} & U_{22} & U_{23} \\ P_3 & U_{13} & U_{23} & U_{33} \end{vmatrix} < 0, \dots, \\ \\ \begin{vmatrix} 0 & P_1 & \dots & P_n \\ P_1 & U_{11} & \dots & U_{1n} \\ \dots & \dots & \dots & \dots \\ P_n & U_{1n} & \dots & U_{nn} \end{vmatrix} \begin{array}{l} > 0 \text{ if } n \text{ is even,} \\ \\ < 0 \text{ if } n \text{ is odd.} \end{array} \end{cases}$$

If (1) is a *regular* maximum subject to (2), then all the border preserving principle minors of the last determinant here alternate in sign as their order diminishes down to order three. Moreover, the last determinant will not equal zero.

The Comparative Statics of Consumer Equilibrium

In this section we will work out the implications of traditional demand theory regarding the form of equations (4). The values of $X_1, \dots, X_n$ determined by equations (4) must always satisfy equations (3). Thus anything that we can establish about the rates of change of the values of $X_1, \dots, X_n$ that satisfy equations (3), with respect to the parameter $P_1, \dots, P_n$ and Y, must be true of the partial derivatives of the demand functions, equations (4). Comparative-statics analysis being the study of the changes in the equilibrium values of the variables under consideration with respect to changes in parameters, it is the partial derivatives of equations (4) that we are interested in. What is of far greater practical importance, our theory tells us things about these partial derivatives, and these partials can be estimated empirically.

The Effect on Demand of a Change in Income (the Income Effect)

Differentiating conditions (3) partially[27] with respect to Y, we have

---

[26] For a definition of homogeneity of degree K see Chapter 3, p. 115.

[27] And thus holding the other arguments of equations (4), $P_1, \dots, P_n$, constant.

$$(6) \begin{cases} P_1 \dfrac{\partial X_1}{\partial Y} + P_2 \dfrac{\partial X_2}{\partial Y} + \ldots + P_n \dfrac{\partial X_n}{\partial Y} = 1 \\[2mm] P_1 \dfrac{\partial \lambda}{\partial Y} + U_{11} \dfrac{\partial X_1}{\partial Y} + U_{12} \dfrac{\partial X_2}{\partial Y} + \ldots + U_{1n} \dfrac{\partial X_n}{\partial Y} = 0 \\[2mm] P_2 \dfrac{\partial \lambda}{\partial Y} + U_{21} \dfrac{\partial X_1}{\partial Y} + U_{22} \dfrac{\partial X_2}{\partial Y} + \ldots + U_{2n} \dfrac{\partial X_n}{\partial Y} = 0 \\[1mm] \cdots\cdots\cdots\cdots\cdots\cdots\cdots\cdots\cdots\cdots\cdots\cdots \\[1mm] P_n \dfrac{\partial \lambda}{\partial Y} + U_{n1} \dfrac{\partial X_1}{\partial Y} + U_{n2} \dfrac{\partial X_2}{\partial Y} + \ldots + U_{nn} \dfrac{\partial X_n}{\partial Y} = 0 \,. \end{cases}$$

This is a set of $n + 1$ equations in the $n + 1$ variables $\dfrac{\partial X_1}{\partial Y}, \ldots, \dfrac{\partial X_n}{\partial Y}$,

and $\dfrac{\partial \lambda}{\partial Y}$. The determinant of this system of equations is

$$\begin{vmatrix} 0 & P_1 & \cdots & P_n \\ P_1 & U_{11} & \cdots & U_{1n} \\ P_2 & U_{21} & \cdots & U_{2n} \\ \multicolumn{4}{c}{\cdots\cdots\cdots\cdots} \\ P_n & U_{n1} & \cdots & U_{nn} \end{vmatrix} = A\,.$$

This is the largest determinant listed in conditions (5), the second-order conditions for (1) to be a maximum subject to (2). One of the properties that we have assumed our utility function to possess is

$$U_{ij} = U_{ji}, \qquad i, j = 1, \ldots, n\,.$$

From this property it follows that the determinant A is symmetrical, that is, the ith row of A is exactly the same as the ith column of A. Since A is symmetrical, there is no ambiguity in defining the cofactor of P_i as A_i. (There is no ambiguity since the cofactor of P_i in the first column is equal to the cofactor of P_i in the first row.) Similarly, we define the cofactor of U_{ij} $(i, j = 1, \ldots, n)$ in A as A_{ij} (since A is symmetrical, the reader should note that $A_{ij} = A_{ji}$). Applying Cramer's rule we may solve equations (6) for $\partial X_s / \partial Y$, $s = 1, \ldots, n$, to get

$$\frac{\partial X_s}{\partial Y} = \frac{\begin{vmatrix} 0 & P_1 & \cdots & P_{s-1} & 1 & P_{s+1} & \cdots & P_n \\ P_1 & U_{11} & \cdots & U_{1s-1} & 0 & U_{1s+1} & \cdots & U_{1n} \\ \multicolumn{8}{c}{\cdots\cdots\cdots\cdots\cdots\cdots\cdots\cdots\cdots\cdots} \\ P_n & U_{n1} & \cdots & U_{ns-1} & 0 & U_{ns+1} & \cdots & U_{nn} \end{vmatrix}}{A}$$

The $s + 1^{st}$ column of the numerator of the right-hand side of this equation contains only 1 nonzero element. Expanding this numerator by cofactors of its $s + 1^{st}$ column thus yields

$$(7) \qquad\qquad \frac{\partial X_s}{\partial Y} = \frac{A_s}{A}\,.$$

If the right-hand side of equation (7) is to be defined

$$A \neq 0,$$

the equilibrium point must be a *regular* maximum.[28] Equation (7) is called the *income effect;* it is the rate of change of consumption of commodity s with respect to income. It is analogous to a movement along the income consumption curve. Our theory does not tell us anything about the sign or size of the income effect taken alone. On the other hand, it is possible to observe the change in a consumer's purchases of any particular commodity that results when his income changes; thus by careful empirical work it would be possible to estimate the size of the income effect.

The Effect on Demand of a Change in a Price

Differentiating equations (3) partially with respect to a given price, P_r,[29] we get

$$(8) \quad \begin{cases} P_1 \dfrac{\partial X_1}{\partial P_r} + P_2 \dfrac{\partial X_2}{\partial P_r} + \ldots + P_n \dfrac{\partial X_n}{\partial P_r} = -X_r \\[2mm] P_j \dfrac{\partial \lambda}{\partial P_r} + U_{j1} \dfrac{\partial X_1}{\partial P_r} + U_{j2} \dfrac{\partial X_2}{\partial P_r} + \ldots + U_{jn} \dfrac{\partial X_n}{\partial P_r} = 0, \\[2mm] \hspace{6cm} j = 1, \ldots, n \neq r \\[2mm] P_r \dfrac{\partial \lambda}{\partial P_r} + U_{r1} \dfrac{\partial X_1}{\partial P_r} + U_{r2} \dfrac{\partial X_2}{\partial P_r} + \ldots + U_{rn} \dfrac{\partial X_n}{\partial P_r} = -\lambda. \end{cases}$$

Solving these equations by Cramer's rule yields

$$\frac{\partial X_s}{\partial P_r} = \frac{\begin{vmatrix} 0 & P_1 & \ldots & P_{s-1} & -X_r & P_{s+1} & \ldots & P_n \\ P_1 & U_{11} & \ldots & U_{1s-1} & 0 & U_{1s+1} & \ldots & U_{1n} \\ \cdots & & & & & & & \\ P_r & U_{r1} & \ldots & U_{rs-1} & -\lambda & U_{rs+1} & \ldots & U_{rn} \\ \cdots & & & & & & & \\ P_n & U_{n1} & \ldots & U_{ns-1} & 0 & U_{ns+1} & \ldots & U_{nn} \end{vmatrix}}{A}$$

Expanding the numerator by the cofactors of its $s + 1^{st}$ column we have

---

[28] As conditions (5) and our discussion of the second-order conditions for a constrained maximum of a function of n variables indicate, A is the determinant of a quadratic form. Call this form d^2G. If the maximum is *regular*, d^2G is negative definite, $d^2G < 0$. If it is not *regular*, $d^2G \leq 0$, so that d^2G is said to be *negative semidefinite*. If a quadratic form is symmetric; negative semidefinite and if $d^2G = 0$ for some nonzero $dX_1, \ldots, dX_n$, then it can be shown that the determinant of the form is equal to zero. Accordingly for (7) to make sense the consumer equilibrium point must be a *regular* maximum.

[29] So that all other prices and income are held constant.

$$\frac{\partial X_s}{\partial P_r} = -X_r \frac{A_s}{A} - \lambda \frac{A_{rs}}{A}.$$

Substituting from equation (7), we may write this,

(9) $$\frac{\partial X_s}{\partial P_r} = -X_r \frac{\partial X_s}{\partial Y} - \lambda \frac{A_{rs}}{A}.$$

This is called the *price effect*, the rate of change of consumption of commodity s with respect to the price of commodity r. It shows that the price effect is comprised of an income effect and an additional term, $-\lambda \dfrac{A_{rs}}{A}$, called the *substitution effect*. Once again, our theory implies nothing about the price effect taken alone. It is, however, possible to observe the change in a consumer's purchases of a given commodity which follows from a change in a given price. Thus the price effect like the income effect may be estimated empirically.

Observable Implications of Traditional Demand Theory

Transferring the income effect across the equal sign of equation (9), we have

(10) $$\frac{\partial X_s}{\partial P_r} + X_r \frac{\partial X_s}{\partial Y} = -\lambda \frac{A_{rs}}{A}.$$

The substitution effect is equal to a sum of terms, each one of which can be observed (estimated). Thus anything that our theory says about substitution effects is a statement about this observable sum and may be tested.

The Symmetry of Substitution Effects

We noted above that since the determinant A is symmetrical,

$$A_{ij} = A_{ji},$$

so that

$$-\lambda \frac{A_{rs}}{A} = -\lambda \frac{A_{sr}}{A}$$

and

(11) $$\frac{\partial X_s}{\partial P_r} + X_r \frac{\partial X_s}{\partial Y} = \frac{\partial X_r}{\partial P_s} + X_s \frac{\partial X_r}{\partial Y}.$$

Traditional demand theory implies that for any two commodities r and s, the above relationship must be true. That is, the price effect on commodity s with respect to the price of commodity r plus the rate of consumption of commodity r times the income effect on commodity s must be equal to the price effect on commodity r with respect to the price of commodity s plus the rate of consumption of commodity s times the income effect on commodity r. If this equality is observed not to hold, then traditional demand theory is refuted.

The Negativity of the Own Substitution Effect

A is of order $n + 1$. By our second-order conditions (5), any border preserving principal minor of A of order n must be opposite in sign to A. Also, by the definition of a cofactor, the sign of the cofactor of an element of the principal diagonal of a determinant is equal to the sign of the minor of that element. Thus

$$\frac{A_{rr}}{A} < 0 , \qquad\qquad r = 1, \ldots, n .$$

Since

$$U_i(X_1, \ldots, X_n) > 0 , \qquad i = 1, \ldots, n$$

and

$$P_i > 0 , \qquad\qquad i = 1, \ldots, n$$

by our assumptions of Chapter 1, conditions (3) imply

$$\lambda < 0 .$$

Thus

$$-\lambda \frac{A_{rr}}{A} < 0$$

and

$$(12) \qquad \frac{\partial X_r}{\partial P_r} + X_r \frac{\partial X_r}{\partial Y} = -\lambda \frac{A_{rr}}{A} < 0$$

for all r. That is, the rate of change of consumption of any commodity with respect to its own price plus the rate of consumption of the commodity times the rate of change of consumption of the commodity with respect to income must be negative.

If, for example, we observe that the equilibrium consumption of commodity r increases with income, our theory implies that if P_r increases, equilibrium consumption of commodity r will fall. That is, if

$$X_r \frac{\partial X_r}{\partial Y} > 0 \qquad \text{then}$$

$$\frac{\partial X_r}{\partial P_r} < 0 .$$

We mention this example because empirical work indicates that in most cases the former inequality holds. Thus in most cases our theory would indicate

$$\frac{\partial X_r}{\partial P_r} < 0 \, .$$

Notice that this latter inequality follows from traditional theory only in those cases in which it is observed that

$$X_r \frac{\partial X_r}{\partial Y} > 0 \, .$$

In general, economic theory implies nothing whatever about either the price effect or the income effect taken alone.[30]

$\partial X_r / \partial P_r$ is the rate of change of the consumption of commodity r with respect to the price of commodity r. Thus it is the slope of the traditional demand curve for commodity r. The classical "Law of Demand" says that this slope must be negative. This is not true. Economic theory does not imply that demand curves slope downward from left to right. It implies only that the sum in result (12) will be negative. In general all that one can say about the slope of the demand curve is

(13) $$\frac{\partial X_r}{\partial P_r} < -X_r \frac{\partial X_r}{\partial Y} \, .$$

Thus the demand curve must be negatively sloped only if the right-hand side of inequality (13) is negative (i.e., if X_r is a noninferior good so that $\frac{\partial X_r}{\partial Y} > 0$). In *all* cases of course, inequality (13) must be satisfied or traditional theory is wrong, but (13) does not, in general, say that $\frac{\partial X_r}{\partial P_r} < 0$.

It is sometimes argued that if a particular commodity comprises a relatively small portion of the consumer's total budget, then the income effect will be quite small so that we can (vaguely) ignore it. Examination of equation (9) reveals the reasoning behind this argument. For any value of $\partial X_s / \partial Y$ a small enough value of X_s will make the income term of the price effect as small as one may like. It is interesting to turn this argument around. As noted above $\partial X_s / \partial Y$ may have any value at all. We are unable to say anything about it. Thus, for any value of X_s, no matter how small, it is

---

[30] If $\frac{\partial X_r}{\partial Y} < 0$, then X_r is said to be an *inferior good*. If $\frac{\partial X_r}{\partial P_r} > 0$, then X_r is said to be a *Giffen good*.

possible for $\partial X_s/\partial Y$ to take on a value large enough to make $X_s \frac{\partial X_s}{\partial Y}$, the income term of equation (9), as *large* as one might like. One may ignore the income effect of a price effect if he likes; but he does so at his peril.

Expansions by Alien Cofactors

Two obvious expansions of A by alien cofactors are

$$\sum_{i=1}^{n} P_i A_{ij} = 0$$

and

$$\sum_{i=1}^{n} P_i A_{ji} = 0 .$$

From the first of these, we get

$$-\frac{\lambda}{A} \sum_{i=1}^{n} P_i A_{ij} = \sum_{i=1}^{n} P_i \left(-\lambda \frac{A_{ij}}{A} \right) = 0 ,$$

so that

(14)
$$\sum_{i=1}^{n} P_i \left(\frac{\partial X_j}{\partial P_i} + X_i \frac{\partial X_j}{\partial Y} \right) = 0 .$$

From the second

$$-\frac{\lambda}{A} \sum_{i=1}^{n} P_i A_{ji} = \sum_{i=1}^{n} P_i \left(-\lambda \frac{A_{ji}}{A} \right) = 0 ,$$

so that

(15)
$$\sum_{i=1}^{n} P_i \left(\frac{\partial X_i}{\partial P_j} + X_j \frac{\partial X_i}{\partial Y} \right) = 0 .$$

Both equations (14) and (15) are sums of observable terms, and are thus testable, in principle at least. As a practical matter it would be extremely difficult to test (14). It would require observation of changes in all prices. Result (15) on the other hand requires only that we observe all the consumer's reactions to a single price change which is more likely to be feasible.

Substitutes and Complements

Roughly speaking, two commodities are said to be *complements* if they are used together, if increased consumption of one of them increases the usefulness of the other. Prime examples are bread and butter, ham and eggs, or pretzels and beer. Two commodities are, roughly speaking, *substitutes* if one of them might be used to replace the other. Examples that spring to mind are butter and margarine, Fords and Chevrolets, etc. More precisely, we say that for a particular consumer the commodities X_s and X_r are *substitutes* if $-\lambda \dfrac{A_{rs}}{A} > 0$ and *complements* if $-\lambda \dfrac{A_{rs}}{A} < 0$. From the symmetry property above, it is clear that if X_r is a substitute for X_s then X_s is a substitute for X_r, etc. If we ignore the income effect of a price effect, the relationship between our two definitions of complementary goods and of substitute goods is clear. Thus if P_r increases and X_r and X_s are complementary, we would expect that the consumer would buy less of X_s. If we ignore the income effect of this price change, our precise definition of complementary commodities says exactly that in this case less of X_s would be bought. A similar example illustrates the appropriateness of our precise definition of substitute goods. From equation (10) we see that commodities X_r and X_s are complements if

$$\frac{\partial X_s}{\partial P_r} + X_r \frac{\partial X_s}{\partial Y} < 0$$

and substitutes if this inequality is reversed.

In connection with result (12), p. 72, we noted

$$-\lambda \frac{A_{rr}}{A} < 0 \, .$$

In connection with results (14) and (15), we noted

$$\sum_{i=1}^{n} P_i \left(-\lambda \frac{A_{ij}}{A} \right) = 0 \, .$$

Combining these two equations, we have

$$\sum_{\substack{i=1 \\ i \neq j}}^{n} P_i \left(-\lambda \frac{A_{ij}}{A} \right) > 0 \, .$$

The direct implication of this is, no matter how many goods exist they cannot all be complementary to each other. Thus in the two commodities case the goods *must* be substitutes. One cannot draw a diagram of the indifference curves between two goods which are complementary according to our precise definition of complements.

Reciprocal Determinants Results

According to the theorem on reciprocal determinants stated earlier in this appendix,

$$a) \qquad A^{k-1}(A_{11,22,33,\ldots,\,kk}) = \begin{vmatrix} A_{11} & A_{12} & \ldots & A_{1k} \\ A_{21} & A_{22} & \ldots & A_{2k} \\ \ldots\ldots\ldots\ldots\ldots\ldots \\ A_{k1} & A_{k2} & \ldots & A_{kk} \end{vmatrix},$$

where A_{11} is the cofactor of U_{11} in A, $A_{11,22}$ is the cofactor of U_{22} in A_{11}, etc.[31] The second-order conditions for utility to be a maximum subject to the consumer's budget restraint imply

$$b) \qquad \frac{A_{11}}{A} < 0, \qquad \frac{A_{11,22}}{A} > 0, \qquad \frac{A_{11,22,33}}{A} < 0, \ldots, \text{etc.}$$

From (a)

$$\frac{A_{11,22,\ldots,\,kk}}{A} = \frac{A^{k-1}(A_{11,22,\ldots,\,kk})}{A^k}$$

$$= \frac{1}{A^k} \begin{vmatrix} A_{11} & \ldots & A_{1k} \\ \ldots\ldots\ldots\ldots\ldots \\ \ldots\ldots\ldots\ldots\ldots \\ A_{k1} & \ldots & A_{kk} \end{vmatrix} = \begin{vmatrix} \dfrac{A_{11}}{A} & \cdots & \dfrac{A_{1k}}{A} \\ \ldots\ldots\ldots\ldots\ldots \\ \ldots\ldots\ldots\ldots\ldots \\ \dfrac{A_{k1}}{A} & \cdots & \dfrac{A_{kk}}{A} \end{vmatrix}, \qquad k = 1, \ldots, m < n.$$

For convenience write

$$-\lambda \frac{A_{ij}}{A} \equiv X_{ij}.$$

Allowing k in the above equations to equal 1 then 2, etc., we have, since $-\lambda$ is positive,

$$X_{11} < 0, \qquad \begin{vmatrix} X_{11} & X_{12} \\ X_{21} & X_{22} \end{vmatrix} > 0, \qquad \begin{vmatrix} X_{11} & X_{12} & X_{13} \\ X_{21} & X_{22} & X_{23} \\ X_{31} & X_{32} & X_{33} \end{vmatrix} < 0, \ldots, \text{etc.}$$

These conditions are necessary and sufficient for the substitution terms, X_{ij}, to be the elements of a negative definite quadratic form,

$$(16) \qquad -\lambda \sum_{r=1}^{m} \sum_{s=1}^{m} \alpha_r \alpha_s \frac{A_{rs}}{A} < 0, \qquad m < n.$$

---

[31] Note that $A_{11,22,33,\ldots,\,nn} = 0$.

Expression (16) implies

$$X_{ii} < 0, \quad \begin{vmatrix} X_{ii} & X_{ij} \\ X_{ji} & X_{jj} \end{vmatrix} > 0, \quad \begin{vmatrix} X_{ii} & X_{ij} & X_{ik} \\ X_{ji} & X_{jj} & X_{jk} \\ X_{ki} & X_{kj} & X_{kk} \end{vmatrix} < 0, \dots, \text{etc.,}$$

where $i, j, k = 1, \dots, n$. From the first of these inequalities result (12) follows. From the second we have

$$(17) \quad \left(\frac{\partial X_i}{\partial P_i} + X_i \frac{\partial X_i}{\partial Y} \right) \left(\frac{\partial X_j}{\partial P_j} + X_j \frac{\partial X_j}{\partial Y} \right) - \left(\frac{\partial X_i}{\partial P_j} + X_j \frac{\partial X_i}{\partial Y} \right)^2 > 0,$$

where $i \neq j$. One may derive virtually as many testable results from traditional demand theory as he likes simply by writing out in full further of the determinantal conditions implied by the negative definiteness of (16).

Market Demand Functions

All the results established thus far refer to the demand functions of individual consumers. In order to test them we must observe variations in consumption by individuals as parameters change. It would be far handier to observe variations in market purchases as these parameters change. It is unfortunate that our theory may not enable us to gain much advantage in this way.

Consider the market demand function for commodity i, a commodity sold exclusively to consumers. Let X_i^j denote consumer j's demand for i and let D_i denote the market demand for commodity i. Suppose that there are L consumers. Then

$$(18) \qquad D_i = \sum_{j=1}^{L} X_i^j (P_1, \dots, P_n, Y_j)$$

where individual j's demand function is as derived above and Y_j is his income. Equation (18) yields market demand functions

$$(19) \qquad D_i = D_i(P_1, \dots, P_n, Y_1, \dots, Y_L), \qquad i = 1, \dots, n.$$

The first thing to notice is that community income does not enter the market demand function. It is not difficult to find in the literature (even in recent journal articles on demand theory) the assertion that the appropriate income variable for market (or community) demand functions is aggregate community income. Such an assertion is without foundation in demand theory. It matters who receives the income, and since the market demand function is obtained by adding up individual demand functions, every individual's income variable enters the market demand function, not just as an element in a sum but as a separate variable.

Moreover Y_j affects D_i only through its effect on X_i^j so that

(20)
$$\frac{\partial D_i}{\partial Y_j} = \frac{\partial X_i^j}{\partial Y_j}.$$

Aggregation of equation (9) above over all consumers yields

(21)
$$\frac{\partial D_s}{\partial P_r} = \sum_{j=1}^{L} \frac{\partial X_s^j}{\partial P_r} = \sum_{j=1}^{L} \left[-X_r^j \frac{\partial X_s^j}{\partial Y_j} - \lambda^j \frac{A_{rs}^j}{A_j} \right]$$

where λ^j is individual j's Lagrange multiplier and A_{rs}^j and A^j are as defined above but for individual j. Rearranging (21) and substituting from (20) we get

(22)
$$\frac{\partial D_s}{\partial P_r} + \sum_{j=1}^{L} X_r^j \frac{\partial D_s}{\partial Y_j} = - \sum_{j=1}^{L} \lambda^j \frac{A_{rs}^j}{A^j}.$$

The right-hand side of (22) is an aggregation of substitution terms and satisfies all the results established for individual substitution terms above. In particular it should be fairly easy for the reader to satisfy himself that

(23)
$$- \sum_{j=1}^{L} \lambda^j \frac{A_{rr}^j}{A^j} < 0,$$

(24)
$$- \sum_{j=1}^{L} \lambda^j \frac{A_{rs}^j}{A^j} = - \sum_{j=1}^{L} \lambda^j \frac{A_{sr}^j}{A^j},$$

(25)
$$\sum_{j=1}^{L} \sum_{i=1}^{n} P_i A_{ir}^j = 0, \qquad \text{etc.}$$

The terms on the left-hand side of (22) are all observable so that implications (23), (24), (25), etc., can be tested. Notice, however, that in utilizing (22) we gain little convenience for, even though it is market demand that concerns us, because individual incomes, not aggregate income, are the arguments of (19), we would have to observe individual consumption changes and levels of consumption in order to employ (22) to test (23), (24), (25), etc. What is more, to utilize (22) and thus gain the advantages of aggregation in the first term of that expression we would have to observe the consumption levels and income adjustments of *every* individual in the market. Testing consumer equilibrium theory by observing the reactions of each and every member of a smaller group of people to variations in prices and in income might well be much easier.

SELECTED BIBLIOGRAPHY

ALLEN, R. G. D. "A Reconsideration of the Theory of Value II," *Economica,* N.S.1 (1934), pp. 196–219.

BUSHAW, D. W., AND CLOWER, R. W. *Introduction to Mathematical Economics.* Homewood, Ill.: Richard D. Irwin, Inc., 1957.

HENDERSON, J. M., AND QUANDT, R. E. *Microeconomic Theory.* New York: McGraw-Hill, Inc., 1958.

HICKS, J. R. *Value and Capital.* 2d ed. Oxford: Clarendon Press, 1946.

———. *A Revision of Demand Theory.* Oxford: Clarendon Press, 1956.

———. "A Reconsideration of the Theory of Value I," *Economica,* N.S.1 (1934), pp. 52–76.

SAMUELSON, P. A. *Foundations of Economic Analysis.* Cambridge, Mass.: Harvard University Press, 1948.

SLUTSKY, E. E. "On the Theory of the Budget of the Consumer." Reprinted in *Readings in Price Theory* (eds. G. STIGLER AND K. BOULDING). Homewood, Ill.: Richard D. Irwin, Inc., 1952.

MATHEMATICS BOOKS

AITKEN, A. C. *Determinants and Matrices.* 9th ed. Edinburgh: Oliver & Boyd, Ltd., 1956.

APOSTOL, T. M. *Mathematical Analysis.* Reading, Mass.: Addison-Wesley Publishing Co., Inc., 1957.

COURANT, R. *Differential and Integral Calculus.* London: Blackie, 1934.

HANCOCK, H. *Theory of Maxima and Minima.* New York: Dover Publications, 1960.

Chapter 2 | THE THEORY OF EXCHANGE AND PARETO OPTIMALITY

Believe it or not
You won't find it so hot
If you ain't got the Do-Re-Mi.
—*"The Do-Re-Mi Song"**

To this point we have been discussing how the consumer, given the prices of all commodities, his income, and preferences satisfying certain assumptions, chooses the set of commodities that he most prefers from those that he can afford. Thus, taking prices and incomes as given, we have determined the equilibrium quantities purchased. In this chapter we will turn the problem around and discuss how, given the equilibrium quantities demanded *at each set of prices,* a set of prices is determined at which the quantity demanded of each good is exactly equal to the quantity of that good available. The independent economic variables of the previous discussion have been incomes and prices, and the problem has been to derive demand *functions* relating quantities demanded to income and prices. In the following pages we will take the *demand functions* and quantities supplied as given and determine prices such that the demand functions will yield quantities demanded equal to certain fixed quantities supplied.

In order to deal with the theory of exchange in its simplest form we will abstract from problems of production altogether. We will assume that each week each consumer receives a bundle of commodities on his doorstep. The consumers also hold money savings. After receiving their commodities the consumers exchange them with each other, each trying to attain the most preferred position that his money holdings and his grant of commodities will afford him. Finally, we assume that individuals like to hold money so that if we construct utility functions for the individuals, their final money holdings enter these functions in the same way that other commodities do.[1]

In a given week each consumer will have a certain amount of purchasing power at his disposal. This purchasing power will be the value of his income in commodities and money for the given week plus his money holdings from previous weeks. He will use this purchasing power to buy his preferred bundle of goods and money. As defined in the last chapter we then have for each consumer a demand function of the form

$$X_i = X_i\left(P_1, \ldots, P_n, \sum_{t=1}^{n} \overline{X}_t P_t\right) \qquad (i = 1, \ldots, n),$$

for each commodity, where X_i is the given individual's equilibrium consumption of commodity i, P_i is the price of commodity i, $\overline{X}_t$ is his initial endowment of commodity t $(t = 1, \ldots, n - 1)$, and $\overline{X}_n$ is the sum of his money income and his savings from previous periods (i.e., his initial endowment of money). Note that there is one such equation for each commodity, including money. If there are k individuals and X_i^r is individual r's demand for commodity i, then

$$X_i^r = X_i^r\left(P_1, \ldots, P_n, \sum_{t=1}^{n} \overline{X}_t^r P_t\right),$$

where r superscripts identify variables, the values of which are particular to the rth individual. Total market demand for commodity i is then given by

$$\sum_{r=1}^{k} X_i^r\left(P_1, \ldots, P_n, \sum_{t=1}^{n} \overline{X}_t^r P_t\right)$$

$$= d_i\left(P_1, \ldots, P_n, \sum_{t=1}^{n} \overline{X}_t^1 P_t, \ldots, \sum_{t=1}^{n} \overline{X}_t^k P_t\right).$$

Once again there is a market demand function for each of the n commodities including money. Throughout what follows we will suppose that all consumers' initial endowments of commodities and money are fixed. Accordingly we will not write them out, but will consider our demand functions as being defined for a given set of

---

[1] Note, it is nominal money, dollars, that enters the consumer's utility function, not purchasing power or "real balances." Utility is not a function of prices. If we also assume that it is only this week's consumption of the various goods and final holdings of money that enter the utility function, then the results of the mathematical appendix to Chapter 1 remain valid for the demand functions of this chapter.

initial endowments. Thus we may express market demand as a function of prices only,

$$D_i = D_i(P_1, \ldots, P_n), \qquad i = 1, \ldots, n.$$

Suppose that for the week in question the fixed total market supplies of the n commodities are $S_1, S_2, \ldots, S_n$ (i.e., $S_1 = \sum_{r=1}^{k} \bar{X}_1^r$). Consider values of $P_1, \ldots, P_n$, such that the set of equations,

(1)
$$\begin{cases} D_1(P_1, \ldots, P_n) = S_1 \\ D_2(P_1, \ldots, P_n) = S_2 \\ D_3(P_1, \ldots, P_n) = S_3 \\ \ldots\ldots\ldots\ldots\ldots\ldots \\ D_n(P_1, \ldots, P_n) = S_n, \end{cases}$$

is satisfied. At this set of prices the quantity of each commodity demanded by all the consumers taken together will exactly equal the total quantity of that commodity supplied.[2] Thus if one can find a set of P's such that equations (1) are simultaneously satisfied, the consumers, choosing their most preferred consumption bundles at that set of P's and their given purchasing powers, will choose to purchase, between them, precisely that set of commodities that is available.

The question is, under what conditions can we find such a set of prices. The reader is probably familiar with the solution of

---

[2] We might alternatively write equations (1) in the following form:

$$D_1(P_1, \ldots, P_n) - S_1 = 0$$
$$D_2(P_1, \ldots, P_n) - S_2 = 0$$
$$\ldots\ldots\ldots\ldots\ldots\ldots\ldots\ldots$$
$$D_n(P_1, \ldots, P_n) - S_n = 0.$$

These are *excess demand functions*. In general the excess demand function for commodity i is given by

$$E_d = D_i - S_i.$$

The *excess supply function* for commodity i is

$$E_s = -E_d = S_i - D_i.$$

In the context of this chapter the consumer begins trading with some commodity which he will trade as he sees fit for other commodities. If $\bar{X}_i^r$ is person r's initial endowment of commodity i and X_i^r is his equilibrium demand for i, then his excess demand for i is

$$X_i^r - \bar{X}_i^r,$$

while his excess supply is

$$\bar{X}_i^r - X_i^r.$$

simultaneous equations from algebra. He will recall that he was not usually called upon to solve one equation for two unknowns, nor to solve three equations for two unknowns. Consider the equation

$$5X + 4Y = 31 \,.$$

Given any value for Y we may use this equation to find the appropriate value for X. Similarly given any X we can find the resultant Y. We cannot, however, find *unique* values of both X and Y which satisfy this equation, because no such unique values exist. Now consider the three equations

$$5X + 4Y = 31 \,,$$
$$3X + 8Y = 41 \,,$$
$$X + Y = 5\tfrac{1}{3} \,.$$

If the first two equations are both true, $X = 3$ and $Y = 4$ and the last equation is not satisfied. If the last two equations are both true, $Y = 5$ and $X = 1/3$ and the first equation is not satisfied. Similarly if the first and last equations are satisfied, then the second cannot be. The three cannot be simultaneously true. We cannot solve these three equations for values of the two variables X and Y such that all three equations are true. Using any two of the three equations alone, however, we are able to find unique values for X and Y which satisfy both of them at once. Considerations of this sort led early economists to make a convention of the following *untheorem:*

> In a system of simultaneous equations, if there are exactly as many equations as there are unknowns, a unique set of values for the unknowns exists which will satisfy the equations. If there are more unknowns than equations then an infinity of solution values for the equations exist. If there are less unknowns than equations then no solution values exist.

In fact, equality of the number of equations and the number of unknowns is neither a necessary nor a sufficient condition for the existence of a unique set of values for the unknowns satisfying the system of equations. That it is not necessary can be seen by considering the equation

$$3X^2 + 4Y^2 + 5Z^2 = 0$$

which has a unique real[3] solution, $X = 0$, $Y = 0$, and $Z = 0$. That the equality of the number of equations and the number of

---

[3] Imaginary solutions to economic problems are frequently said to be unrealistic.

unknowns is not a sufficient condition can be seen by considering the two equations

$$2X + 3Y = 15 \quad \text{and}$$
$$5X + 7\tfrac{1}{2}Y = 17$$

which cannot be simultaneously true. Having shown that this convention is unwarranted we will now proceed to employ it wherever we must do so in order to explain traditional economic theory. We shall leave it to the reader to apply his own grains of salt when they are called for.

From the point of view of our equation counting convention, equations (1) look good. There seem to be n demand equations in n unknown prices so that we would (by untheorem) expect a unique set of prices to exist such that the quantities demanded at that set of prices just equal the fixed supplies. Things are not that nice however. What, after all, is a set of prices? It is a set of ratios of exchange between commodities traded one for another. Thus the price of a given good is the number of units of some other good which must be given up in exchange for a unit of the given good. For simplicity we usually state all prices in terms of units of some particular good (called the *numéraire*). Then if one thing costs 10 units and another costs 20 we know that the latter is twice as valuable as the former. The difficulty is this: whatever the *numéraire* might be, it takes exactly one unit of it to buy a unit of itself. The *numéraire* price of the *numéraire* is necessarily 1. There are not n unknown P's to be selected, but $n - 1$ because whatever our *numéraire* is, its price will be 1.

To make our language simpler we will choose money as the *numéraire*. Thus P_i will be the money price of commodity i. With money the nth commodity, $P_n = 1$, a dollar is worth a dollar.[4] This is rather difficult. Equations (1) are n in number, and there are only $n - 1$ unknowns. By our convention, no solution exists for such a problem.

Walras' Law

It is often noted that one cannot get something for nothing. If one is to purchase something he must give a thing of equal value in exchange for it. More particularly, in the model we are discussing, if the consumer is to demand some quantity, X_i, of commodity i he must offer money or other commodities of value $P_i X_i$ in exchange. This is the reason for the consumer's budget restraint. Since $\bar{X}_i^r$ denotes individual r's initial holding of commodity i, that is, what i

---

[4] Whatever our grandfathers might say to the contrary.

he receives as income, and, in the case of money (where $i = n$), the sum of both his money income and his holdings from previous periods, we may write the consumer's budget restraint,

$$\sum_{i=1}^{n} P_i X_i^r = \sum_{i=1}^{n} P_i \bar{X}_i^r .$$

This equation must hold for every set of prices. Suppose that there are K persons. Then summing all budget restraints yields

(2) $$\sum_{r=1}^{K} \sum_{i=1}^{n} P_i X_i^r = \sum_{r=1}^{K} \sum_{i=1}^{n} P_i \bar{X}_i^r .$$

Whatever commodities exist in the economy are owned by someone. Thus

$$\sum_{r=1}^{K} \bar{X}_i^r = S_i .$$

Similarly, by the definition of market demand given above

$$\sum_{r=1}^{K} X_i^r = D_i .$$

We may rewrite equation (2)

$$\sum_{i=1}^{n} P_i \sum_{r=1}^{K} X_i^r = \sum_{i=1}^{n} P_i \sum_{r=1}^{K} \bar{X}_i^r$$

or

(3) $$\sum_{i=1}^{n} P_i D_i = \sum_{i=1}^{n} P_i S_i ,$$

the total value of everything demanded must equal the total value of everything supplied.

The reader should notice that (3) is an *identity*. No matter what set of prices we might introduce to the system, the total value of all offers to sell at those prices must equal the total value of all offers to buy. Accordingly we will write (3) below with an identity sign rather than with an equal sign. Rearranging terms then we may rewrite (3)

(4) $$\sum_{\substack{i=1 \\ i \neq j}}^{i=n} (D_i - S_i) P_i \equiv (S_j - D_j) P_j .$$

In an n good economy, the value of the sum of the excess demands of any $n - 1$ goods is identically equal to (i.e., equal at any set of prices to) the value of the excess supply of the other good. This is helpful because it means that if we take any $n - 1$ equations from equations (1) and find values of $P_1, \ldots, P_{n-1}$ (P_n being 1) such that they are satisfied, then the other equation of equations (1) must be satisfied. This is true because summing the $n - 1$ satisfied equations as in the left-hand side of identity (4), we get zero. Then, by identity (4), the value of the excess supply of the other commodity must be zero. Since prices are positive this excess supply must be zero.

Identity (4) is called *Walras' Law*. So that the reader might more fully understand how Walras' Law has been used here, we will offer the following illustration. We saw above that we were unable to solve the three independent equations

$$5X + 4Y = 31 ,$$
$$3X + 8Y = 41 , \quad \text{and}$$
$$X + Y = 5\tfrac{1}{3}$$

simultaneously for X and Y. Walras' Law says that equations (1) are not like these three equations. Equations (1) are *dependent*, each of them is equal to an appropriately weighted sum of the others. A proper illustration of equations (1) would be

$$5X + 4Y = 31 ,$$
$$3X + 8Y = 41 ,$$
$$27X + 44Y = 257 .$$

Solving any two of these equations one gets $X = 3$ and $Y = 4$, values which can then be seen to satisfy the third.

Equations (1) are n in number, and they are functions of only $n - 1$ variables; however, by Walras' Law, the equilibrium values of these $n - 1$ variables may be found by simultaneously solving any $n - 1$ of the equations. The problem of finding a set of prices such that the demand for each commodity will equal the fixed supply then comes down to one of solving $n - 1$ equations in $n - 1$ unknowns. By our untheorem a unique set of P's satisfying these equations will exist. This set of P's will be the market clearing, or equilibrium, set of money prices.

General Equilibrium and Partial Equilibrium

In the above discussion of equilibrium price determination, the supplies and demands of all markets were considered simultaneously. There was no question of any particular price being determined by any single pair of supply and demand curves. There was not even any question of determining any particular price. Rather the problem was to find a *set* of prices satisfying a *set* of supply and demand equations. A change in any one of the equations would usually change the *entire set* of prices. All prices depend upon all supply and demand relationships, or, in the more popular but less accurate statement, "everything depends upon everything else."[5]

The reader might justifiably wonder about the relationship between the general equilibrium system that we are discussing in which the equilibrium levels of all prices are determined simultaneously and the partial equilibrium approach in which the equilibrium level of a single price is determined by the equality of a single demand function with a single supply function. The partial equilibrium approach is meant to be a simplified approximation to the general equilibrium solution. It concentrates attention on what is supposed to be the most important single pair of supply and demand equations in the determination of the given equilibrium price. Thus to determine the price of commodity i we solve

$$D_i(P_1, \ldots, P_n) = S_i .$$

In order that this may be done it is assumed that all P's except P_i are fixed.[6] (This is the famous *Ceteris Paribus* Assumption.) Thus

---

[5] One peculiarity of general equilibrium analysis of the sort that we have been discussing is that a great many different things go by the name of P. One hears discussion of absolute prices, relative prices, the absolute price level, and sometimes even the price of money. As we pointed out above, prices are ratios of exchange between commodities. For convenience we usually state all prices in terms of some particular commodity (*numéraire*). If, for instance, the *numéraire* is a pound of wheat and the price of a given fountain pen is six, then six pounds of wheat will buy the fountain pen. When the *numéraire* is some commodity other than money, the *numéraire* prices are called *relative prices* because they are relative to the nonmoney *numéraire*. When the *numéraire* is money, the *numéraire* prices are called *absolute prices*. Thus absolute prices are money prices. The *absolute price level* is a price index, a weighted sum of money prices. Finally, the price of money depends upon what *numéraire* is chosen. The absolute (money) price of money is necessarily one. In general the relative price of money is (obviously) the reciprocal of the money price of the *numéraire*. These would be the prices one would pay if he chose to *buy* some money. If he chose only to borrow or to rent the money, he would pay much less. He would pay the rate of interest, the yearly rental rate on money, for so long as he rented it; one can include interest rates in our analysis quite easily. One of the commodities traded can be individuals' promises to pay one dollar a year in perpetuity. In this case, the money price of this commodity would be the reciprocal of the rate of interest. At a rate of interest of 4 percent, a promise to pay $1.00 per year in perpetuity should be good for a permanent loan of $25.00. One could sell such a promise for $25.00 and $25 = 1/.04$.

[6] In general a variation in P_i will lead to variation in peoples' purchasing power both because some consumers will be sellers of commodity i and because some people (in a production economy) will possess firms that profit from the sale of commodity i (see Chapter 9).

it is a matter of choosing that value of P_i such that this equality holds, all other P's constant.

Under what conditions will the value of P_i so determined be equal to the value of P_i determined by equations (1)? To best illustrate the answer to this question reconsider the equations

$$5X + 4Y = 31,$$
$$3X + 8Y = 41,$$
$$27X + 44Y = 257,$$

which will all be true if $X = 3$ and $Y = 4$. Let $X = P_1$ and $Y = P_2$. We will use these equations to determine values of P_1, given a value of P_2. If $P_2 = 2$ then the first equation yields $P_1 = 4\frac{3}{5}$, the second equation yields $P_1 = 8\frac{1}{3}$, and the third yields $P_1 = 7$. All three of the equations taken together (or any two of them) yield equilibrium values $P_1 = 3$, $P_2 = 4$. Because we gave P_2 a value different from its equilibrium value we do not get the equilibrium value of P_1 by solving any of our equations. In exactly the same way, if, in partial equilibrium analysis, the price of any commodity is fixed at a value other than its equilibrium level, then the value of P_i that is attained by solving

$$D_i(P_1, \ldots, P_n) = S_i$$

will be different from the value of P_i determined by equations (1).

Now suppose we take $P_2 = 4$. Then the first equation above would yield $P_1 = 3$, as would the second and the third. This, of course, is the equilibrium value of P_1, and it can be obtained from any of our equations if P_2 is given *its* equilibrium value. Similarly, in partial equilibrium analysis, if all prices except P_i are taken as given at their equilibrium values then not only

$$D_i(P_1, \ldots, P_n) = S_i$$

can be solved to yield the equilibrium value of P_i, but any excess demand function at all may be solved to get the equilibrium value of P_i.

THE PARETO OPTIMALITY OF PURELY COMPETITIVE EXCHANGE EQUILIBRIUM

Edgeworth's Box

One hears a great deal about the benefits of the competitive system. The basis for such claims is that the equilibrium state of a *purely competitive* economy can be shown to be *Pareto optimal*. An economy is said to be *purely competitive* if every economic unit in it (in our pure exchange system that means every consumer) takes prices as given. Since the only economic units in a pure exchange economy are consumers, the system that we have been describing *is* purely competitive. An economic situation is said to be *Pareto optimal* if no consumer can be made better off without another consumer being made worse off. We will show that in equilibrium in the model that we are describing, no consumer can move to a position that he prefers to the equilibrium position without forcing some other consumer to move to a position he thinks inferior to the equilibrium position.

Consider an economy in which there are only two consumers

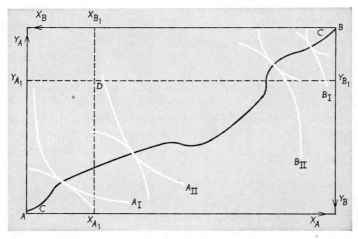

FIGURE 2–1

and two commodities. The conditions for exchange equilibrium in such an economy may be shown in a simple diagram, Figure 2–1. In this diagram we plot the indifference curves of two individuals, call them Mr. *A* and Mr. *B*. Take point *A* as the origin of the commodity space in which we show Mr. *A*'s consumption of commodities *X* and *Y*. Thus along the *Y* axis from point *A* we plot Y_A, individual *A*'s consumption of *Y*. Along the *X* axis from *A* we plot X_A, *A*'s consumption of *X*. Curves A_I, A_{II}, etc., are indifference curves reflecting Mr. *A*'s preferences. Similarly, we take point *B* as the origin for Mr. *B*'s commodity consumption space and plot X_B, Mr. *B*'s consumption of commodity *X*, along the horizontal axis through *B*. Mr. *B*'s consumption of *X* increases from right to left. Along the vertical axis through *B* we plot Mr. *B*'s consumption of commodity *Y*, Y_B. *B*'s consumption of commodity *Y* increases as one moves down along Y_B away from point B. Curves B_I, B_{II}, etc., are indifference curves reflecting Mr. B's preferences.

It is easy to see that we construct this diagram in part by pivoting B's commodity space around the origin so that the positive quadrant is swung into the position formerly occupied by the negative quadrant (the quadrant in which both X_A and Y_A would take on negative values). This determines the *directions* of the four axes in Figure 2–1. The positions of the axes are determined in the following way. If individual A were given the total (fixed) quantity of commodity X in existence, this would correspond to a particular point, $X_A{}^1$, on axis X_A. If he were given the total (fixed) quantity of commodity Y in existence, it would determine a particular point, $Y_A{}^1$, on axis Y_A. We place point B so that the X_B axis cuts the Y_A axis at $Y_A{}^1$ and the Y_B axis cuts the X_A axis at $X_A{}^1$. Then (i) every single point either enclosed between the four axes or lying on any of the four axes is a possible distribution of the fixed quantities of commodities X and Y between Mr. A and Mr. B. Moreover (ii) any possible distribution of the fixed quantities of commodities X and Y between Mr. A and Mr. B will correspond to a single point either between the four axes or on one of them. Any point in the box will have an X_A value, a Y_A value, an X_B value, and a Y_B value. What is more, for all such points

$$X_A + X_B = X_A{}^1 \quad \text{and}$$
$$Y_A + Y_B = Y_A{}^1$$

so that statement (i) above is true. Any possible distribution of the fixed quantities will have to be one such that the total fixed quantities are distributed between the two individuals so that for any distribution

$$X_A + X_B = X_A{}^1 \quad \text{and}$$
$$Y_A + Y_B = Y_A{}^1 .$$

Neither individual may be given a negative quantity of either good so that

$$X_A \geq 0 ,$$
$$X_B \geq 0 ,$$
$$Y_A \geq 0 , \quad \text{and}$$
$$Y_B \geq 0 .$$

Since all points such that these conditions are true are either between or on the axes of Figure 2–1, statement (ii) above is true. Some example of how a single point determines both individuals' quantities of both commodities may be seen by considering the origin A at which individual B has all of both commodities, origin B at which individual A

has all of both commodities, and point D at which individual A has X_{A_1} of X and Y_{A_1} of Y while individual B has X_{B_1} of X and Y_{B_1} of Y. Since it must be true by construction that

$$X_{A_1} + X_{B_1} = X_A{}^1 \quad \text{and}$$
$$Y_{A_1} + Y_{B_1} = Y_A{}^1$$

there can be no more of either commodity to distribute, and all of both commodities must be distributed.

Figure 2–1 is called *Edgeworth's* box diagram, and all the points either between the four axes or on any of them may be referred to as points in the box.

Price Determination, the Tâtonnement Process

Suppose that trading was organized along the following lines. Each individual brings his endowment of commodities and money to the marketplace. An auctioneer calls out a set of ratios of exchange between the commodities (i.e., a set of prices in terms of some *numéraire*). The individuals offer to exchange commodities in such a way as to get on the highest of their indifference curves attainable for the called out set of prices and their given endowments of commodities (the endowments of commodities are their purchasing power). In so doing the individuals offer to supply quantities of some commodities and demand quantities of others. If these offers are such that the total demand for *each* commodity is equal to the total supply of it, then the set of prices called out will be the equilibrium set. The individuals then would be allowed to make good their offers to demand and supply commodities. All markets would be cleared, and the process would stop. If the offers are such that the total demands for some commodities do not equal the total supplies of them, then the called out set of prices is not an equilibrium set, no trading is permitted, and a new set of prices is called out, etc. This process is continued until an equilibrium set of prices is found, and then and only then does trading take place. Such a process is called a *tâtonnement process*.

For simplicity we will assume here that prices are determined via a *tâtonnement* process. If the initial endowment of commodities is point D in Figure 2–2, then A will start trading with X_{A_1} of X and Y_{A_1} of Y while B will start with X_{B_1} and Y_{B_1}. Since the point D is in both men's commodity space, each will have an indifference curve passing through it. Call A's indifference curve through D, A_1, and B's, B_1. It is easily seen that D is not a position of market equilibrium. There is no set of prices such that both consumers would be happy to remain at D. Mr. A would be pleased to stay at D only if the price set were represented by the budget line P_A,[7] but at these prices B would want to be on indifference curve B_2 supplying $Y_{B_1} - Y_{B_2}$ of Y in exchange for $X_{B_2} - X_{B_1}$ of X. At this price set there would be an excess supply (equal to $Y_{B_1} - Y_{B_2}$) of Y and an excess demand (equal to $X_{B_2} - X_{B_1}$) for X. Under the *tâtonnement* arrangements no trading could take place since the market would not be cleared. Indeed, with Mr. A willing to "stand pat" at D, Mr. B would be hard put to find anyone to trade with. Mr. B would be content to remain at D if prices were as represented by budget line P_B. At this set of prices, however, A would maximize his utility by moving to indifference curve A_2. He would offer to supply $X_{A_1} - X_{A_2}$ of X in exchange for $Y_{A_2} - Y_{A_1}$ of Y. There would be an excess supply of X and an excess demand for Y. Once again, markets would not be cleared and a new price set would be called for.

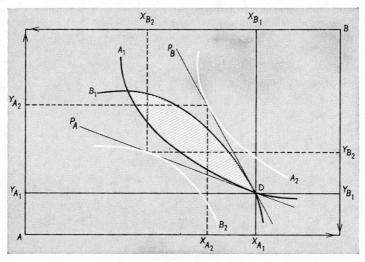

FIGURE 2–2

Mr. A is already on indifference curve A_1. He will not be willing to move to any indifference curve below A_1. Similarly Mr. B is already on indifference curve B_1 and will be unwilling to move to a lower indifference curve. The only price sets that qualify as possible equilibrium price sets will be those that enable both A and

---

[7] Since the initial endowments of both men are at point D, any budget line for either man must pass through D. The budget line will then (as usual) be the outer limit of the set of bundles that they could trade their initial endowments for at the given price set. Since they could obviously exactly afford to keep their initial endowments intact at any price set, all budget lines must pass through D. Furthermore, there can only be one set of prices called out at a time so that A's and B's budget lines must have the same slope. Since A's budget line and B's budget line must have the same slope and must both pass through point D, they must be the same line.

B to move to higher indifference curves. The only region in the box in which *both* A and B are on higher indifference curves is the shaded area enclosed between A_1 and B_1 (this area is said to be *Pareto superior* to D). Thus the equilibrium budget line must lie between P_A, the flattest budget line consistent with Mr. A's being in the shaded area, and P_B, the steepest budget line consistent with Mr. B's being in the shaded area.

Just as the initial distribution of commodities between A and B must be given by a single point in the Edgeworth box, so must the exchange equilibrium distribution be given by a single point. More than one point would represent more than one distribution. The exchange equilibrium point must be a point such that *both Mr. A and Mr. B are maximizing their utility at the given price set*. In Figure 2–3, $\overline{D}$ is such a point of exchange equilibrium. At the given prices Mr. A maximizes his utility by offering to exchange $X_{A_1} - X_{\overline{A}}$ of X for $Y_{\overline{A}} - Y_{A_1}$ of Y. Mr. B maximizes his utility by offering to exchange $Y_{B_1} - Y_{\overline{B}} = Y_{\overline{A}} - Y_{A_1}$ of Y for $X_{\overline{B}} - X_{B_1} = X_{A_1} - X_{\overline{A}}$ of X. A's supply of X is equal to B's demand for X, and B's supply of Y is equal to A's demand for Y. At the prices shown by budget line $\overline{P}$ all markets are cleared.

Since both men are maximizing their utility at the point of exchange equilibrium, and since there is only one set of prices, their indifference curves must have the same slope at point $\overline{D}$. Thus the indifference curve of Mr. A through point $\overline{D}, \overline{A}$ must be just tangent to Mr. B's indifference curve, $\overline{B}$, through the same point. $\overline{B}$ is the highest of Mr. B's indifference curves that $\overline{A}$ touches.

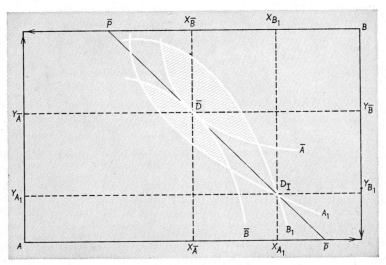

FIGURE 2–3

Thus if Mr. B is to reach a point preferred to $\overline{D}$, Mr. A must move to an indifference curve lower than $\overline{A}$. Similarly $\overline{A}$ is the highest of Mr. A's indifference curves consistent with Mr. B's being on indifference curve $\overline{B}$. Neither man can be made better off (moved to a position preferred to $\overline{D}$) unless the other is made worse off (moved to a position inferior to $\overline{D}$). By the definition above, the point of purely competitive exchange equilibrium, $\overline{D}$, is Pareto optimal. *All competitive exchange equilibria are Pareto optimal.* They are Pareto optimal because, in effect, each man's utility is maximized subject to the constraint that the other man's utility be fixed at the equilibrium level. Since we took the initial distribution, D_1, of commodities as given, we arrived at point $\overline{D}$. In general, by varying the initial distribution of commodities between the two consumers we could vary the final point of Pareto optimal equilibrium. All possible points of Pareto optimal equilibrium have a single characteristic: they are points such that each person's indifference curve touches the highest indifference curve that it reaches of the other person. The locus of all such points, the line CC in Figure 2–1, is called the *contract curve*. This curve is the locus of all points such that neither individual can be made better off without the other being made worse off. Thus, it is the locus of all Pareto optimal points.

The contract curve is the locus of all Pareto optimal points. Consider any point on the contract curve. If the point is in the interior of the Edgeworth box, then an indifference curve of Mr. A will be tangent to one of Mr. B at the point. Thus the two curves will have the same slope. Pass a budget line having this slope through the point. We then have something like Figure 2–3, with $\overline{D}$ the original point on the contract curve and $\overline{P}\overline{P}$ the budget line that we have constructed. For any initial endowment point along this budget line, the point that we began with on the contract curve will be a position of competitive exchange equilibrium, just as $\overline{D}$ is a point of competitive equilibrium for any initial endowment point along $\overline{P}\overline{P}$ in Figure 2–3. Now consider a point on the contract curve where that curve coincides with a boundary of the Edgeworth box. Such a point is shown by D in Figure 2–4. At this point Mr. B's indifference curve B_1 touches the highest of Mr. A's indifference curves that it reaches, A_1. Thus Mr. B could not be made better off without making Mr. A worse off and vice versa. Point D is Pareto optimal and is thus on the contract curve, CC, which coincides with the Y_A axis for much of its length. Should Mr. A and Mr. B mutually possess budget line $P_A D$, then D would be an equilibrium point. Should they possess the budget line $P_B D$, point D would again be an equilibrium point. In fact, should the initial endowment lie on

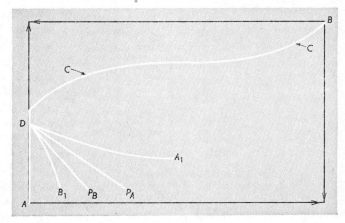

FIGURE 2–4

or between P_AD and P_BD, then point D would be a position of purely competitive equilibrium. All points of Pareto optimality are on the contract curve. All points on the contract curve are either interior to the Edgeworth box or coincide with a boundry of the box. In either case the points on the contract curve are positions of competitive equilibrium. *All Pareto optima are potentially positions of competitive equilibrium.* Of course such points could be achieved by other means, for example, accident.

Competitive equilibria are Pareto optimal for two reasons. All of the commodities produced are distributed, and at each given price set each individual does the best he can possibly do (maximizes his utility) given the purchasing power that he has. Thus to make a given person better off one would have to give him more purchasing power, but since all commodities are distributed one would have to take this purchasing power away from someone else. The result of this would be to lower the other person's purchasing power and make him *worse off*. In a purely competitive exchange system, any set of prices consistent with all participants doing what they like (maximizing utility) will be Pareto optimal; however, as we saw in examining Figures 2–2 and 2–3, the only price set consistent with all individuals maximizing their utility simultaneously will be an equilibrium set. Hence the Pareto optimality of purely competitive equilibrium. The reader will perhaps have noticed that we have said nothing *here* to limit the number of persons or commodities to two.

In purely competitive exchange equilibrium each individual maximizes his utility subject to his budget restraint. As we saw in the mathematical appendix to Chapter 1, the first-order conditions for this to be true can be written,[8]

$$\frac{MU_i}{MU_j} = \frac{P_i}{P_j},$$

where MU_i is the first derivative of the utility function with respect to commodity i, the marginal utility of commodity i, MU_j is the marginal utility of commodity j, P_i is the price of commodity i, and P_j is the price of commodity j. Every consumer maximizes his utility subject to his budget restraint. Accordingly, for every consumer the equality above holds between every two commodities i and j. Since only one set of prices rules in the marketplace at a given time, this means that where MU_i^r denotes individual r's marginal utility from commodity i and there are k individuals,

$$\frac{MU_i^1}{MU_j^1} = \frac{MU_i^2}{MU_j^2} = \frac{MU_i^3}{MU_j^3} = \cdots = \frac{MU_i^k}{MU_j^k} \qquad i, j = 1, \ldots, n.$$

In a purely competitive exchange equilibrium the ratio of the marginal utilities of any two commodities will be the same for all consumers, because each individual maximizes his utility subject to the same price set. All commodities being distributed, and on our assumptions regarding the shapes of consumer's indifference curves, these equalities are sufficient to insure that a competitive pure exchange equilibrium is Pareto optimal (see Chapter 9).

A great many people have been most impressed with the fact that competitive equilibria are Pareto optimal and vice versa. Indeed it is a most impressive fact. Consider origin B of Figure 2–4. Notice that the contract curve CC passes through B. Thus origin B is Pareto optimal. In particular it is the competitive equilibrium point when Mr. A is endowed with all of both commodities. One would imagine that even if Mr. B were an educated man, fully aware of the Pareto optimality of his hunger, he might justifiably be less than impressed with the efficiency of the competitive system.

The competitive system is possessed of a certain deftness in the distribution (and as we will see in Chapter 9 in the production and distribution) of commodities. Even from a completely theoretical point of view, however, one can see problems. All economic systems have their faults, and that of the competitive system is that it admits poverty amidst plenty, albeit Pareto optimal poverty.

---

[8] In our discussion of this topic in Section 2 of the mathematical appendix to Chapter 1, we used a utility function with only two independent variables. The reader may examine the argument there to see that the ratio we mention here will hold true for a function of any number of variables greater than or equal to 2.

Summary

In this chapter we have discussed the determination of equilibrium prices in a market in which goods are exchanged but not produced. Taking the demand functions determined from the theory of consumer equilibrium as given, we determined a set of prices such that the quantities demanded would be equal to the externally given fixed supplies of commodities. Using the untheorem that equality of the number of equations to be solved with the number of variables to be solved for implies the existence of a unique set of values for the variables such that the equations will be simultaneously true, we established the existence of a market clearing set of prices. In doing this we made use of a linear dependence which must exist between the excess demand equations of an economy of the type that we described. This dependence was called "Walras' Law." Finally we have shown that in market equilibrium in the purely competitive economy we have been describing, no individual can be made better off without another individual's being made worse off. Such a situation we have called Pareto optimal.

SELECTED BIBLIOGRAPHY

BATOR, F. M. "The Simple Analytics of Welfare Maximization," *American Economic Review,* Vol. XLVII, No. 1 (March, 1957).

CASSEL, G. *Theory of Social Economy.* New York: Harcourt, Brace & World, 1924.

HICKS, J. R. *Value and Capital.* 2d ed. Oxford: Clarendon Press, 1946.

KUENNE, R. E. *The Theory of General Economic Equilibrium.* Princeton, N.J.: Princeton University Press, 1963.

PATINKIN, D. *Money Interest and Prices.* New York: Harper & Row, 1965.

WALRAS, L. *Elements of Pure Economics.* Translated by W. Jaffé. Homewood, Ill.: Richard D. Irwin, Inc., 1954.

PART II

The Theory of Production and Costs

THE THEORY OF
LEAST COST PRODUCTION

Last week a premature blast went off
And a mile in the air went big Jim Goff.
. . . .
When the next payday came around
Jim Goff a dollar short was found
When he asked, "What for" came this reply
"You're docked for the time you was up in the sky."
—"Drill Ye Tarriers Drill"*

Introduction

It will be the purpose of this section to discuss how the firm, taking the conditions under which it can purchase inputs, and the technical conditions under which it can convert inputs into outputs, as given, determines the cost of producing each level of output and decides what inputs it will use in producing each level of output. Our discussion of this topic will take two chapters. In the first (this chapter) we will discuss how, on the basis of technical production conditions and the supply conditions of inputs, the firm decides what inputs to use in producing each possible level of output. Using this information we are able to derive cost functions which we will discuss at some length in Chapter 4. These tell us various things about the cost to the firm of producing each level of output.

Behavioral Assumption 2: *The fundamental assumption of the theory of the firm: The firm attempts to produce that output for which its profit will be a maximum.*

Definition: *The firm's profit from any level of output is the difference between its costs of producing and marketing the output and its revenue from selling the output.*

From Behavioral Assumption 2 and the definition of profits we see that the firm attempts to maximize the function:

$$\pi(Z) = R(Z) - C(Z),$$

---

* "Drill Ye Tarriers Drill," composed by Thomas F. Casey. To the best of my knowledge, this song is in the public domain.

where Z is output, $\pi(Z)$ is the profit from output, $R(Z)$ is the revenue from sales of the output, and $C(Z)$ is the cost associated with producing and distributing the output. Now there may be many ways of producing a given output, and, in general, each of these ways will have a different cost associated with it. In order that our profit function be defined, we must decide how each level of output will be produced. For any given demand situation (revenue function) the lower the cost for each level of output the higher the profits. Thus the firm in attempting to maximize profits will attempt to minimize the cost of producing *each level of output*. The reader's attention is drawn to the fact that this does not mean that the firm will attempt to minimize the cost function $C(Z)$. The problem is one of *defining* the cost function, not minimizing it. We do not wish to find that output for which $C(Z)$ is a minimum, rather do we wish to find the least cost at which the firm may produce every individual output level. Thus we will not discuss the theory of cost minimization which is sometimes misleadingly referred to, but rather the theory of least cost production. To this end we will first discuss the technical considerations governing the conversion of inputs into outputs.

Production Information Available to the Firm

Suppose that the firm has definite information available to it regarding what it can produce using varying amounts of inputs. This information is embodied in the firm's production function which shows how much output can be produced with each possible combination of inputs. Suppose that the firm produces a commodity, Z, and uses two commodities, X and Y, as inputs, the production function may then be written

$$Z = Z(X, Y).$$

This function associates with each possible bundle of inputs (X and Y) a given level of output, Z. The set of all points (X^0, Y^0) such that X^0 is not negative and Y^0 is not negative constitutes the nonnegative quadrant of a commodities space which we shall here refer to as the inputs space. We will assume (1) that the production function attaches a unique level of output to each point in the inputs space, (2) that the production function is continuous and has continuous first and second partial derivatives, and (3) that the level of output increases as more of any input is used in the production process.[1]

---

[1] That is $\frac{\partial Z}{\partial X} > 0$ and $\frac{\partial Z}{\partial Y} > 0$; all inputs are productive.

Definition: *An isoquant is the locus of all points in the inputs space which yield a given output.*

Thus an isoquant is the locus of all combinations (X, Y) such that

$$Z(X, Y) = \bar{Z},$$

a constant. It is a contour line of the production function. Consider Figure 3–1 depicting a two-dimensional inputs space. On the basis of our three assumptions regarding the production function we may work out most of the properties of isoquants. Since the production function attaches a unique level of output to each point in the inputs space, every point in Figure 3–1 must have an isoquant passing through it. Since the level of output attached to any point is unique, no point may have two isoquants passing

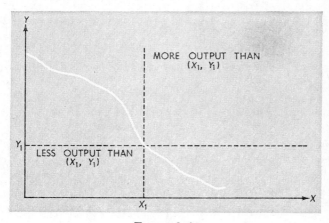

FIGURE 3–1

through it, so that isoquants may not cross. Consider the unique isoquant through the point (X_1, Y_1). Since more inputs lead to more output, the region to the north, northeast, or east of (X_1, Y_1) must represent combinations of inputs which lead to more output than does (X_1, Y_1). Since an isoquant is the locus of points yielding a given output, no point in this region may be on the isoquant through (X_1, Y_1). Similarly points to the south, west, and southwest of (X_1, Y_1) must be associated with smaller outputs than is (X_1, Y_1). Thus the isoquant must be negatively sloped from the northwest of (X_1, Y_1) to the southeast, as shown.

Since the production function is continuous, each isoquant must be continuous. If some isoquant were not continuous, then there would be a discontinuity in $Z(X, Y)$ somewhere along

$$Z(X, Y) = \bar{Z}$$

where $\bar{Z}$ is the level of output associated with the given isoquant, but $Z(X, Y)$ is continuous, so that no such discontinuity may exist. If the isoquant were to end at some point other than at the X or Y axis, then a discontinuity would exist at the end point. Thus an isoquant may not end (except of course at an axis). The isoquant is a continuous negatively sloped line that separates the inputs space into two regions. Taking any point in either of these regions one could extend a straight line from the origin through the point. If the line reached the point before it reached the isoquant (i.e., at lower values of X or Y or both), then the point would be associated with an output less than that associated with the isoquant because output increases as inputs increase. If the line from the origin reached the isoquant before it reached the point, then the production function would associate a larger output with the point than with the isoquant for the same reason. Thus every input combination on one side of the isoquant (below it) will be associated with a lesser output than is the isoquant, and every input combination on the other side of the isoquant (above it) will be associated with a larger output than is the isoquant. These two regions are themselves densely packed with isoquants. We will refer to isoquants associated with a lesser output than a given isoquant as being *lower* than the given isoquant and those associated with a greater output as being *higher* than the given isoquant.

Assume finally that isoquants are convex from below. This is sometimes called the assumption of the *diminishing marginal rate of factor substitution,* and it may be stated in the following way:

Along a given isoquant, the decrease in Y so as to just maintain production when a single unit of X is added to the production process decreases continuously as X increases.

Thus the inputs space is completely covered with convex, continuous isoquants. Each given one of these isoquants divides the inputs space into two regions every point in one of which is associated with a greater output than is associated with the given isoquant and every point in the other of which is associated with a lesser output. Such a set of isoquants is depicted in Figure 3–2. The number associated with each isoquant is the level of output associated with the isoquant by the production function.

The reader will presumably have noticed the similarity between isoquants and indifference curves. Aside from the obvious differences that one represents bundles of commodities such that the consumer does not prefer one to another and the other represents bundles of commodities that, when employed as inputs, will yield the same level of output, there seems to be little to distinguish between the two. There is, however, a significant difference. In the case of indifference curves the curves themselves represent the basic ordering on which we construct an arbitrary utility function. We had to worry about the transitivity of the ordering, the uniqueness of the ordering, etc. Isoquants are *derived from* a function which is already supposed to exist. What is more, the dependent variable of the function, output, is something we may simply define units for and count in terms of the real numbers. The transitivity and uniqueness of the ordering of the level of production is insured by the transitivity and uniqueness of the real number system. We may rest assured that if three bushels of wheat is more than two bushels of wheat which is more than one bushel of wheat, then three bushels of wheat is more than one bushel of

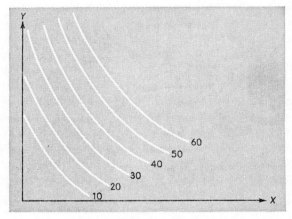

FIGURE 3–2

wheat. That, in part, is what the numbers mean. Similarly, three bushels of wheat being more than one bushel we needn't concern ourselves that it is also *less* than one bushel. The real number system is handy that way. For all these differences between indifference curves and isoquants, however, it is their similarity which is most important. As will become clearer as we proceed, in traditional microeconomics we do a couple of things only. We find extrema of functions subject to constraints (this involves things like isoquants and indifference curves) and we solve systems of simultaneous equations. To be sure interesting complications arise, but not enough so that the cynic would be prohibited from referring to traditional microeconomic theory as variations on a theme by Lagrange. This is a good thing because it represents the essential unity of economic theory, and it makes our job easier.

Factor Supply Conditions

If it is to discover the lowest possible cost at which it can produce each level of output, the firm must know under what conditions it may purchase the inputs it uses in production. In particular the firm must know what quantities of inputs will be available to it at what prices.

Definition: *The firm's expenditure function associates with each possible bundle of inputs that unique level of expenditure that the firm would have to undertake in order to purchase the bundle of inputs.*[2]

Since this function attaches a unique level of expenditure to each possible bundle of inputs, it is unique and exhaustive. We also assume that the expenditure function is continuous and has continuous first and second partial derivatives with respect to all inputs. Finally we assume that the function is monotonically increasing; that is, it always costs the firm money to purchase more of any input. If input prices vary as the quantities of inputs used vary, they always remain positive. The firm's expenditure function embodies all the information that the firm needs regarding the conditions under which factors of production (inputs) are supplied to the firm. In order to show how the firm may use the information contained in the expenditure function to advantage, we define the contour lines of the expenditure function.

Definition: *An isoexpenditure function (curve) is the locus of all bundles in the inputs space that the firm could just purchase for a given amount of expenditure.*

Since the expenditure function is monotonically increasing, we could show in the same way that we did for isoquants and indifference curves that the isoexpenditure curve must be negatively sloped. If the formula for the expenditure function is written

$$E = E(X, Y)$$

in the two inputs case, then the formula for a particular isoexpenditure curve would be

$$E(X, Y) = \bar{E},$$

---

[2] We differentiate between this expenditure function and the firm's cost function which associates a level of costs with each possible level of *output*. The cost function is derived, in part, from knowledge of the expenditure function as we will show below.

where $\overline{E}$ is a constant level of expenditure. Thus if there were a discontinuity in any isoexpenditure curve, it would be a discontinuity in

$$E(X, Y) = \overline{E}$$

for some $\overline{E}$. This, however, is simply a particular segment of the expenditure function, and since the expenditure function is continuous, all such segments of it must be continuous. The reader will recall that each isoquant must separate the inputs space into two regions every point in one of which is associated with a larger output than is the isoquant and every point in the other of which is associated with a smaller output than is the isoquant. Similarly, isoexpenditure curve must separate the inputs space into two regions every point in one of which would be associated (by the expenditure function) with a greater expenditure than would the isoexpenditure curve, and every point in the other of which would be associated with a lesser expenditure than would the isoexpenditure curve. Thus isoexpenditure curves are continuous negatively sloped curves completely covering the inputs space in such a way that each curve separates the space into two disjoint regions.

In order to complete our specification of the firm's expenditure function, we will assume that the firm purchases all its inputs in purely competitive markets. That is, we assume that the prices of inputs are given constants which *do not* vary as the quantities that the firm buys vary. In a later chapter we will discuss cases in which this assumption does not hold. In view of this restriction we may write our expenditure function

$$E(X, Y) = P_x X + P_y Y .$$

Thus the equation for a given isoexpenditure curve becomes

$$P_x X + P_y Y = \overline{E} .$$

This is the equation of a straight line; moreover, it should be familiar to the reader since its form is identical with that of the consumer's budget restraint where M, the symbol for consumer's income, is replaced by $\overline{E}$, the symbol for the firm's expenditure.

Since the form of any given isoexpenditure curve is the same as that of the consumer's budget restraint, we may show, as we did in Chapter 1 for the consumer's budget line, the slope of the isoexpenditure curve. Rewriting the above equation we have

$$Y = \frac{\overline{E}}{P_y} - \frac{P_x}{P_y} X,$$

so that when X changes by 1 unit Y will change by $-P_x/P_y$ units. Thus the slope of an isoexpenditure curve is given by the ratio of the prices of inputs. The Y intercept of the isoexpenditure curve is $\overline{E}/P_y$ where $\overline{E}$ denotes the level of expenditure on factors associated with the given isoexpenditure curve. For a given set of prices, by allowing the level of expenditure to vary, we may generate the entire set of isoexpenditure curves associated with a particular expenditure function. In Figure 3–3 we have drawn a group of isoexpenditure curves. The numbers associated with the curves show the levels of expenditure that the curves represent. Thus the Y intercept of the first curve is $10/P_y$, etc.

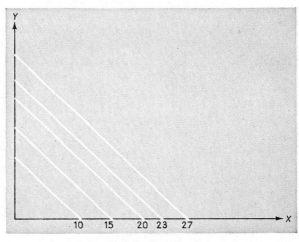

FIGURE 3–3

Each isoexpenditure curve shows the set of input bundles that the firm could just purchase with a given expenditure. The firm, as we see below, will vary its level of expenditure as it varies its level of output. It is not constrained to remain on or below any particular isoexpenditure curve and will freely select whatever level of expenditure it finds to be associated with maximum profit production. Thus, their similarity not withstanding, isoexpenditure curves are in no way budget restraints. They simply embody a mass of information regarding the availability of inputs to the firm. Under our assumptions about the expenditure function, each individual isoexpenditure curve looks very much like a budget line, but appearances can be deceiving. Since the expenditure function is represented by an entire set of isoexpenditure curves, each having a different level of expenditure associated with it but all having the same slope, and since this slope is determined by the set of input prices, isoexpenditure curves are sometimes referred to as price lines.

Least Cost Production

The technical information contained in the firm's production function is summarized in the firm's isoquant map (Figure 3–2). The factor supply information from the firm's expenditure function is summarized in the firm's isoexpenditure map (Figure 3–3). Using this information we wish to define the firm's cost function by finding the least expenditure at which each possible level of output can be produced. To this end we construct Figure 3–4. On this two-dimensional inputs space we draw some of the firm's isoquants and

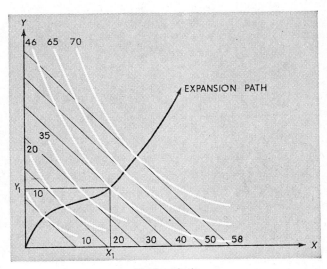

Figure 3–4

some of its isoexpenditure curves. The numbers near the X axis are the levels of expenditures associated with the isoexpenditure curves shown. The isoquants are similarly labeled with numbers showing the level of output associated with each of them. Consider the ways in which the firm could produce 46 units of output. Since the isoquant associated with 46 units of output crosses the isoexpenditure curve associated with an expenditure of 58, one could produce 46 units at a cost of 58. However, every input bundle inside isoexpenditure curve 58 could be purchased for a lesser expenditure. Since isoquant 46 *cuts* isoexpenditure curve 58, it reaches bundles costing less than 58. Isoquant 46 continues to cut isoexpenditure curves until it touches but does not cross isoexpenditure curve 40. Since isoquant 46 touches isoexpenditure curve 40, the firm could produce 46 units of output at a cost of 40. Since the isoquant does not cut isoexpenditure curve 40, the firm could not produce 46 units of output at a lesser expenditure. Thus the least possible expenditure associated with an output of 46 units is 40. This is the lowest expenditure associated with 46 units of output because 40 is the lowest isoexpenditure curve touching isoquant 46, and 40 is the lowest isoexpenditure curve touching isoquant 46 because the two curves are tangent.

The firm wanting to produce 46 units of output should do so using X_1 of X and Y_1 of Y at a cost of 40. For each possible level of output there is an isoquant showing the set of bundles of inputs which could be used to produce that output. Each such isoquant will touch some isoexpenditure curve which is lower than any other isoexpenditure curve it touches. What is more, under our assumptions regarding the firm's production function and expenditures function the isoquant will touch this lowest isoexpenditure curve at a single point. The coordinates of this point will be the inputs that the firm will use to produce the given output at the least possible expenditure. For a fixed set of prices the locus of all these least expenditure production points as output varies is called the *expansion path*. This is shown in Figure 3–4. So long as both factors of production are used in the production process, the expansion path is the locus of all points such that the isoquants have the same slope as the isoexpenditure curves or price lines, i.e., it is the locus of all points of tangency between the two sets of curves. The expansion path, as the name implies, shows for a given set of input prices how the firm will vary its use of inputs as it expands (contracts) its output.

Just as the isoexpenditure curve is very similar in form to a budget restraint, so the expansion path is very similar to the income consumption curve. The difference between the two is quite simple. The consumer has a given budget and so may be on or below a given point on his income consumption curve. As his income varies the consumer will move along his income consumption curve. The firm on the other hand is free to choose any point on its expansion path with no limit on what it might cost to get there. The income consumption curve shows how the consumer will vary his purchases if we allow him to do so by varying his income. The expansion path is simply a collection of information that the firm can use, as it wishes, in its attempt to maximize profits.

We should once again emphasize the senses in which we are and are not concerned with minimizing costs. In Figure 3–4 the point (X_1, Y_1) is the least expenditure combination consistent with producing 46 units of output, thus 40 is the minimum expenditure at which 46 units of output could be produced. Notice, however, that this is decidedly not a point at which expenditures are minimum. every point below isoexpenditure curve 40 is associated with an expenditure less than 40. The significant thing about (X_1, Y_1) is that this combination of factors will produce an output of 46 units, and no other input bundle costing the firm 40 or less will do so. Expenditures are minimal provided that one produces 46 units of outputs. They are not minimal in any other sense.

The Firm's Total Cost Function

Definition: *The firm's total cost function (curve) associates with each level of output the minimum total expenditure at which the output can be produced and distributed, given factor prices.*

Suppose that there are n inputs, the quantities of which are denoted $X_1, \ldots, X_n$. These may be combined to produce an output, the quantity of which is denoted Φ, according to the production function,

$$\Phi = \Phi(X_1, \ldots, X_n) .$$

The firm's total cost function may then be written

$$C = f(\Phi, P_1, \ldots, P_n)$$

where C is cost, Φ is the level of output, and P_i is the price of the ith input. Since we will frequently want to work with a given set of input prices, we usually write the cost function in the form,

$$C = C(\Phi) ,$$

for simplicity.

The total cost function, as its definition implies, is derived from the analysis of least cost production embodied in Figure 3–4. Observe Figure 3–4 again. Notice that it associates with each of the levels of output shown a definite minimum expenditure at which the output can be produced. Thus 10 units of output may be produced at a cost of 10, 20 units at a cost of 20, 35 units at a cost of 30, 46 at a cost of 40, etc. This is exactly the information that the total cost function is to embody. In Figure 3–5 we have constructed the total cost curve that follows from the information in Figure 3–4. Constructing this curve is simply a matter of constructing a space the points in which represent quantities of output and of dollars. We then record the dollar expenditure associated with each quan-

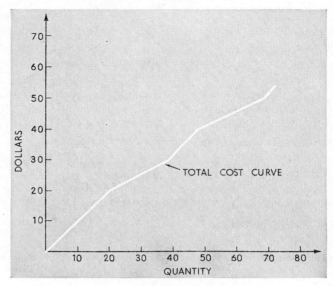

FIGURE 3–5

tity of output in Figure 3–4 and connect all these points. The resultant curve is the total cost curve.[3]

An interesting thing about traditional microeconomic theory, to which we have already alluded, is the formal similarity between the theory of consumer equilibrium and the theory of least cost production. We are now in a position to make use of this similarity to show that the total cost curve of the firm must be positively sloped. To this end let us reconsider the firm's cost and production information as it is given in Figure 3–4. We have gone to some pain to make it clear that the firm does not operate under a budget restraint. Thus the firm is *not* in a position in which it must decide what is the maximum output associated with a given level of expenditure. This does not prohibit *our* doing so however. Consider the maximum output the firm can produce with an expenditure of 40 dollars. Isoexpenditure curve 40 in Figure 3–4 cuts isoquant 35. Since the isoquant separates the inputs space in the manner discussed above, the fact that isoexpenditure 40 cuts isoquant 35 means that for a cost of 40 dollars the firm can produce more than 35 units. Since the space is covered with isoquants, isoexpenditure 40 continues to cross isoquants until it touches but does not cross isoquant 46. Thus 46 is the maximum output associated with an expenditure of 40 dollars, just as 40 dollars is the minimum

---

[3] If all factors of production are variable this curve represents what we will call in Chapter 4 a *long-run* total cost curve.

expenditure associated with production of 46 units of output. Examination of Figure 3–4 makes it fairly clear that in general if *A* is the minimum expenditure at which an output of *B* can be produced then *B* is the maximum output which can be produced at a cost of *A*. Thus the total cost curve in Figure 3–5 may be viewed in two ways. We may say that it shows the minimum total expenditure at which each level of output may be produced or we may say that it shows the maximum output forthcoming at each possible level of expenditure. Thus, given any point on the total cost curve, if we wish to *increase* output we must increase expenditure. *The total cost curve must be positively sloped.*

Our assumptions about the firm's production function and expenditure function do not imply more than that the total cost curve is everywhere positively sloped. Consider a firm possessed of a physical plant designed to produce some specific level of output. One might suppose that as the firm built up to this level of output, the rate of increase of cost with respect to output might diminish since the fixed plant was being employed more and more nearly at the level for which it was designed. On the other hand, as the firm pushed its output beyond the level for which its plant was designed, its costs would presumably rise faster and faster with output. This would lead to a total cost curve having the elongated S shape shown in Figure 3–6. It is conventional in microeconomic theory to draw total cost curves with this shape.

Notice that our justification of the shape of the total cost curve in Figure 3–6 depends upon the existence of some fixed factor, the quantity of which was appropriate to a particular level of output. The argument is based on fairly convincing (I think) intuitive

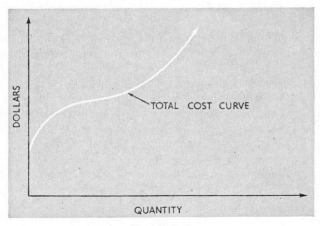

FIGURE 3–6

notions about the sort of returns in output that will accrue as increasing quantities of variable factors are combined with some fixed factor. I know of no such convincing justification for this shape of the total cost curve if *all* factors of production are variable. Such arguments as I am aware of come down either to the notion that really, even when all factors are variable some are fixed, which is gibberish, or to the assertion that production functions are of a form that yields total cost curves as shown. This latter assertion may be true, but if it is and production functions are simply known to be "like that" then we know more about them than our assumptions (1), (2), and (3) indicate. It would be far better if we included this additional information in our assumptions. It is not universally essential that our total cost curves possess the elongated S shape.[4] However, having stated our misgivings about this convention we will continue, for the most part, to employ the elongated S shape for total cost curves even when all factors are variable.

We have drawn the curve in Figure 3–6 so that it does not pass through the origin. In general the total cost curve need not pass through the origin. If, for some reason, the firm has expenses which it cannot avoid even by ceasing to produce, then a positive cost will be associated with a zero output.[5]

Scale Phenomenon

To this point we have been concerned with how a firm interested in producing each level of output at the least expenditure possible for that output will choose what factors it should employ and what the cost of each level of output will be. A property of production functions which *may be* relevant to this choice is *scale phenomenon*. This has to do with the change in output that results if the firm increases its use of all factors in the same proportion. If, when the firm increases its use of all factors by a given proportion, output increases by a lesser proportion, then the firm is said to produce under *decreasing returns to scale*. If output increases by the same proportion as the use of factors, then the firm is said to produce under *constant returns to scale*. Finally if an increase in the employment of all factors by a given proportion leads to an increase in output of an even greater proportion, then the firm produces under *increasing returns to scale*.

---

[4] It is essential to the theory of competitive markets that we will develop below (Chapter 5) that the total cost curve ultimately "turns up" as in Figure 3–6.

[5] See the distinction between the long run and the short run in Chapter 4.

Under our assumptions, since the firm maximizes profits, when it varies its output it will change its employment of factors in such a way as to keep its expenditures as low as possible for each level of output that it produces (i.e., given input prices it will move along its expansion path). Thus in general the firm will not necessarily vary its output by changing all its inputs in the same proportion because, in general, the expansion path need not be a straight line from the origin. A special case in which the expansion path of the firm *is* a straight line (ray) from the origin is of particular interest.

Definition: *A function $f(X_1, \ldots, X_n)$ is said to be homogeneous of degree K if*

$$f(\lambda X_1, \ldots, \lambda X_n) = \lambda^K f(X_1, \ldots, X_n) .$$

Thus if each of the independent variables is multiplied by λ, the value of the function is increased by λ^K. This must be true no matter what values of the independent variables $X_1, \ldots, X_n$ we start with.

If $\Phi(X_1, \ldots, X_n)$ is a production function, as defined above, and if it is homogeneous of order K, then an equiproportional change in the amount of all factors used in the production process will lead to a change in output of the same proportion raised to the power K. This statement must be true no matter what the level of operation at which the changes occur. This clearly is a statement about scale phenomenon. In particular, a firm with a production function which is homogeneous of order K will have the same sort of returns to scale at every level of output (i.e., while a firm with a nonhomogeneous production function may face decreasing returns to scale over some range of the production function, increasing returns over another, etc., a firm with a homogeneous production function will face the same returns to scale everywhere). Moreover if $K > 1$ the firm will face increasing returns to scale for all levels of output. If $K = 1$ the firm will face constant returns to scale at all levels of output, and if $K < 1$ the firm will always produce under decreasing returns to scale.

We now wish to show that this information is relevant to the firm's behavior, i.e., that a firm having a homogeneous production function and producing each level of output at the least possible cost will (under constant factor prices) vary its output by changing its use of all factors in the same proportion. Since the expansion path is the locus of all least cost levels of production for a given set of factor prices, and since to change all inputs in the same proportion is to move out along a ray from the origin into the inputs space (call such a ray a *scale path*), it will be sufficient for us to show that if the firm has a homogeneous production function then its expansion path is a scale path. To this end consider Figure 3–7. We construct two scale paths, R_1 and R_2, from the origin into the inputs space (X, Y). We next choose on each scale path a point associated with an output of a. These points are a_1 and a_2. Since they are associated with the same output, a_1 and a_2 are on the same isoquant. Next we construct point b_1, a point with double the amount of each input associated with a_1. Similarly we construct b_2 with double the amount of each input associated with a_2. Since the production function is homogeneous of order K, the output associated with b_1 must equal 2^K times the output associated with a_1.

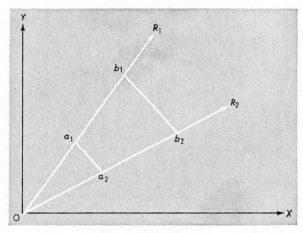

FIGURE 3–7

Also the output associated with b_2 is equal to 2^K times the output associated with a_2. Because a_1 and a_2 are associated with the same output, a, b_1, and b_2 must be associated with the same output. Call it b. The line a_1a_2 is a chord connecting the two points on the isoquant a. Similarly the line b_1b_2 is a chord connecting the two points on the isoquant b. The line Ob_1 is twice as long as the line Oa_1 and the line Ob_2 is twice as long as the line Oa_2, hence the triangle b_1Ob_2 is similar to the triangle a_1Oa_2. Two sides being common to both triangles, the third sides, a_1a_2 and b_1b_2, are parallel. Suppose that we were to collapse R_1 toward R_2, causing the angle between them to approach zero as a limit. As we do this, the point of intersection between R_1 and isoquant a will move along R_1, as will the point of intersection between R_1 and isoquant b, i.e., the points a_1 and b_1 will move along R_1. Since the production function is homogeneous, Ob_1 will continue to be twice as long as Oa_1 so that a_1a_2 will continue to be parallel with b_1b_2. These two lines are chords of isoquants a and b respectively so that the slope of isoquant a at a_2 will equal the limit of the slope of a_1a_2 as R_1 goes to R_2 (as the angle between R_1 and R_2 approaches zero), and the slope of isoquant b at point b_2 will equal the limit of the slope of b_1b_2 as R_1 goes to R_2. However, as R_1 goes to R_2, a_1a_2 remains parallel to b_1b_2 so that in the limit as well, they have the same slope. Thus the slope of isoquant a at a_2 is equal to the slope of isoquant b at b_2. The isoquants being parallel along R_2, R_2 is an expansion path. By a similar argument we could show that any other scale path is an expansion path for some prices. Since an isoquant has any given slope at most only at one point (by the diminishing marginal rate of factor substitution assumption) and since any scale path is an expansion path, it could also be established that any expansion path must be a scale path (the reader should attempt to prove this proposition). If the production function is homogeneous, the expansion path is a scale path.

The main reason for the interest in homogeneous production functions stems from a particular bit of "common sense." It "stands to reason" that if a firm can produce a given amount of output using a particular bundle of factors, then if it uses precisely twice as much of each factor, it will be able to produce exactly twice as much output. It stands to reason, that is, that if you double all inputs you will double output, that the production function is homogeneous of degree one (this is also called linear homogeneity). Under these conditions production of X units of output will obviously cost precisely half as much as production of $2X$ units of output. The firm's total cost curve will be a straight line like Figure 3–8 (a). This is the case when the firm produces under constant returns to scale, i.e., has a linear homogeneous production function, one homogeneous of degree $K = 1$. If the firm's production function is homogeneous of degree $K < 1$, then the firm, producing under

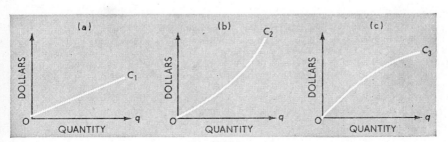

FIGURE 3–8

decreasing returns to scale, will vary its production (with constant prices) by changing its use of all factors in the same proportion, and an equiproportionate increase in the amount of all factors employed will lead to a less than proportionate increase in output. Thus, as output increases, costs will increase by a greater proportion as shown by C_2 in Figure 3–8 (b). Finally, if $K > 1$ the firm will produce under increasing returns to scale and costs will increase less than proportionately as output increases. This is shown by C_3 in Figure 3–8 (c).

MATHEMATICAL APPENDIX TO CHAPTER 3

Under our assumptions the expenditure function may be written

$$(1) \qquad E = A + \sum_{i=1}^{n} X_i P_i \,,$$

where X_i is the quantity of input i used in the production process, P_i is the price of input i to the firm, E is the level of expenditure, and A is the "sunk" cost that the firm is unable to avoid paying even if it were to cease production altogether. Of course A may equal zero. Suppose that the firm's production function is given by

$$(2) \qquad \Phi = \Phi(X_1, \ldots, X_n) \,,$$

where Φ is the level of output and X_i is as above. We know of $\Phi(X_1, \ldots, X_n)$ the following:

$$\Phi_i > 0 \,, \qquad i = 1, \ldots, n \,,$$
$$\Phi_{ij} = \Phi_{ji} \,, \qquad j, i = 1, \ldots, n \,,$$

where Φ_i is the partial derivative of Φ with respect to i and Φ_{ij} is the second partial derivative of Φ first with respect to j and then with respect to i. These follow respectively from our assumptions that Φ is monotonically increasing (more inputs mean more output) and that the first and second partial derivatives of Φ are continuous. Our assumption about the behavior of firms implies that the firm will attempt to find the minimum possible cost at which it can produce each level of output. This may be formulated in a very familiar way. To find the least cost associated with a particular level of output, the firm need only consider values of $X_1, \ldots, X_n$ for which that output is forthcoming. It wishes to find the cheapest bundle of X's among all those that will lead to the given output, i.e., to find the minimum value of (1) among all those values $X_1, \ldots, X_n$ such that (2) has a given value.

Minimize the value of E subject to

$$(3) \qquad \bar{\Phi} = \Phi(X_1, \ldots, X_n) \,,$$

where $\bar{\Phi}$ is a particular level of output. Following the method of Lagrange, outlined in the mathematical appendix to Chapter 1, we minimize

$$(4) \qquad G = A + \sum_{i=1}^{n} X_i P_i - \lambda[\Phi(X_1, \ldots, X_n) - \bar{\Phi}] \,.$$

The first-order conditions for (4) to be a minimum (or maximum) are

(5)
$$P_i - \lambda\Phi_i(X_1, \ldots, X_n) = 0, i = 1, \ldots, n,$$
$$\bar{\Phi} - \Phi(X_1, \ldots, X_n) = 0.$$

From the first n equations we have, for all $i = 1, \ldots, n$,

$$\frac{P_i}{\Phi_i} = \lambda,$$

so that[6]

$$\frac{\Phi_i}{\Phi_j} = \frac{P_i}{P_j}, \qquad i, j = 1, \ldots, n.$$

Our theory implies that in equilibrium the firm will employ the factors of production in such a way that the marginal productivities of factors (the rate of change of output with respect to a unit increase in the use of the factor) are in the same proportions as the prices of the factors. The last dollar's worth of each input must produce the same amount of output.

We may solve equations (5) to find what set of inputs, $X_1, \ldots X_n$, the firm will use to produce the output $\bar{\Phi}$ at prices $P_1, \ldots, P_n$. As prices and output vary, the set of inputs used will vary. To see how inputs will vary, we solve equations (5) to obtain "reduced-form equations" showing the levels of inputs which will be used as functions of prices and output,

(6)
$$X_i = X_i(\Phi, P_1, \ldots, P_n), \quad i = 1, \ldots, n.$$

These are the firm's demand functions for factors of production. We will attempt to ascertain some of the properties of equations (6). Since we have not specified how the firm determines what output it will produce, we are not in a position to discuss how output will change when the price of a given input changes. Accordingly, we will discuss the properties of equations (6) *for a given level of output*. Equations (6) show the equilibrium quantity of inputs purchased as functions of the set of input prices and the level of output. These equations are derived from equations (5), the first-order conditions for (1) to be a minimum subject to (3). Thus, whatever values of $X_1, \ldots, X_n$ satisfy equations (5) must also satisfy equations (6). Accordingly, to discover the form of equations (6), we may examine equations (5). In the same way that we derived comparative-statics results regarding the consumer's demand for commodities we may derive the comparative-statics implications of the theory of least cost production.

In determining the properties of equations (6) we will make

---

[6] A notational reminder, $\Phi_i = \Phi_i(X_1, \ldots, X_n) = \dfrac{\partial}{\partial X_i} \Phi(X_1, \ldots, X_n).$

use of the second-order conditions for (1) to be a minimum subject to (3). The second-order conditions for a minimum of a function of n variables subject to a constraint were discussed in the mathematical appendix to Chapter 1. They are that a bordered determinant and all its border preserving principal minors be negative. These are necessary and sufficient conditions for the quadratic form d^2G to be positive definite for all dX_i such that

$$\sum_{i=1}^{n} \Phi_i dX_i = d\bar{\Phi} = 0 .$$

In our discussion of consumer equilibrium we made profitable use of the necessary and sufficient conditions for a quadratic form to be *negative* definite subject to a constraint. Since we are now familiar with these conditions it would be convenient to be able to continue to work with them. For that reason it is opportune that we may show that the second-order conditions for costs to be a minimum imply that a certain quadratic form must be negative definite subject to a side condition. The second-order conditions for (1) to be a minimum subject to (3) are that

(7) $$d^2G = - \lambda d^2\Phi = - \lambda \sum_{i=1}^{n} \sum_{j=1}^{n} \Phi_{ij} dX_i dX_j > 0$$

for all dX_i such that

(8) $$\sum_{i=1}^{n} \Phi_i dX_i = 0 .$$

Consider the first-order conditions (5). These imply $\lambda > 0$. Thus we may divide both sides of inequality (7) by $-\lambda$ thereby changing the direction of the inequality to get

$$\sum_{i=1}^{n} \sum_{j=1}^{n} \Phi_{ij} dX_i dX_j < 0 .$$

Similarly, conditions (5) imply that

$$\frac{1}{\lambda} P_i = \Phi_i$$

so that (8) may be written

$$\frac{1}{\lambda} \sum_{i=1}^{n} P_i dX_i = 0 .$$

Since the first-order conditions for a minimum are necessary conditions, they must be true at all minima. Thus our use of these relationships in rewriting the second-order conditions is valid.

Accordingly, the second-order conditions for E to be a minimum subject to the constraint

$$\Phi(X_1, \ldots, X_n) = \bar{\Phi},$$

may be written

$$(9) \qquad \sum_{i=1}^{n} \sum_{j=1}^{n} \Phi_{ij} dX_i dX_j < 0$$

for all dX_i such that

$$(10) \qquad \sum_{i=1}^{n} P_i dX_i = 0.$$

This will be true if and only if

$$\begin{vmatrix} 0 & P_1 & P_2 \\ P_1 & \Phi_{11} & \Phi_{12} \\ P_2 & \Phi_{21} & \Phi_{22} \end{vmatrix} > 0, \quad \begin{vmatrix} 0 & P_1 & P_2 & P_3 \\ P_1 & \Phi_{11} & \Phi_{12} & \Phi_{13} \\ P_2 & \Phi_{21} & \Phi_{22} & \Phi_{23} \\ P_3 & \Phi_{31} & \Phi_{32} & \Phi_{33} \end{vmatrix} < 0, \ldots, \quad \begin{vmatrix} 0 & P_1 & \ldots & P_n \\ P_1 & \Phi_{11} & \ldots & \Phi_{1n} \\ \ldots & \ldots & \ldots & \ldots \\ P_n & \Phi_{n1} & \ldots & \Phi_{nn} \end{vmatrix} \begin{array}{l} > 0 \text{ if } n \\ \text{ is even,} \\ \\ < 0 \text{ if } n \\ \text{ is odd,} \end{array}$$

that is, if and only if the border preserving principal minors of the last determinant, call it B, alternate in sign beginning with any third-order principal minor. If E is to be a *regular* minimum subject to $\Phi(X_1, \ldots, X_n) = \bar{\Phi}$, then all border preserving principal minors of order three must be positive, all of order four negative, etc., and $B \neq 0$.

We are now in a position to derive the comparative-statics properties of equations (6). To this end, we shall examine the rates of change of the equilibrium values of $X_1, \ldots, X_n$ (those satisfying equations (5), the first-order conditions for (1) to be a minimum subject to (3), i.e., the equations from which equations (6) are derived) with respect to changes in prices. Once again we remind the reader that we are not yet in a position to consider changes in output; thus our results in this section are valid only for a fixed level of output.[7] Following the technique employed in the mathematical appendix to Chapter 1 we would now differentiate conditions (5) with respect to P_r. An alternative method is to work with the total differential of conditions (5). The methods yield exactly the same results, but the reader may as well become conversant with both. Accordingly we employ the latter method here. The total differentials of conditions (5) are

---

[7] We will see below that similar results may be obtained when output is allowed to change so as to maintain maximum profits.

$$dP_i - d\lambda\Phi_i - \lambda \sum_{j=1}^{n} \Phi_{ij}dX_j = 0 , \quad i = 1, \ldots, n ,$$

$$- \sum_{j=1}^{n} \Phi_j dX_j = -d\overline{\Phi} = 0 ;$$

in more manageable form these may be written

$$\frac{1}{\lambda} \Phi_i d\lambda + \sum_{j=1}^{n} \Phi_{ij}dX_j = \frac{1}{\lambda} dP_i , \quad i = 1, \ldots, n ,$$

$$\sum_{j=1}^{n} \Phi_j dX_j = d\overline{\Phi} = 0 ,$$

or better still, substituting P_i/λ for Φ_i as conditions (5) indicate

(11)
$$\frac{1}{\lambda^2} P_i d\lambda + \sum_{j=1}^{n} \Phi_{ij}dX_j = \frac{1}{\lambda} dP_i , \quad i = 1, \ldots, n$$

$$\sum_{j=1}^{n} P_j dX_j = \lambda d\overline{\Phi} = 0 .$$

Equations (11) are $n + 1$ in number and contain $n + 1$ variables, $dX_1, \ldots, dX_n$ and $d\lambda$. We may solve them, using Cramer's rule and simplifying to get

(12)
$$dX_j = \frac{1}{\lambda} \sum_{i=1}^{n} dP_i \frac{B_{ij}}{B} + \lambda d\overline{\Phi} \frac{B_j}{B}$$

where B_{ij} is the cofactor of Φ_{ij} in B, and

(13)
$$d\lambda = \lambda \frac{\sum_{i=1}^{n} dP_i B_i}{B} + \lambda^3 d\overline{\Phi} \frac{B_0}{B}$$

where B_i is the cofactor of P_i in B, and B_0 is the cofactor of the term $_0$ in B.

Empirical Implications of the Theory of Least Cost Production

1. *Own Price Changes.* In order to find the partial derivative of the equilibrium rate of use of input X_r with respect to P_s, we simply examine (12) with $d\overline{\Phi} = 0$ and $dP_i = 0$, for $i = 1, \ldots,$ $n \neq s$. This yields

$$dX_r = \frac{1}{\lambda} dP_s \frac{B_{sr}}{B} ,$$

so that

(14)
$$\frac{\partial X_r}{\partial P_s} = \frac{1}{\lambda} \frac{B_{sr}}{B}.$$

Similarly (13) yields

(15)
$$\frac{\partial \lambda}{\partial P_s} = \lambda \frac{B_s}{B}.$$

Taking $r = s$, equation (14) becomes

(16)
$$\frac{\partial X_r}{\partial P_r} = \frac{1}{\lambda} \frac{B_{rr}}{B} < 0.$$

Since conditions (5) imply that λ must be positive, the negativity of this term follows from the second-order conditions for a minimum. B_{rr} is a border preserving principal minor of B, and is of order n. B is also a border preserving principal minor and is of order $n + 1$. Hence the sign of B_{rr}, whatever it is, is opposite to the sign of B. Result (16) says that if the price of an input rises, and if the firm continues to produce the same level of output in equilibrium after the factor price change as before it, then the amount of the input used in equilibrium will fall.

2. *The Symmetry Property.* Our assumptions about the firm's production function include

$$\Phi_{ij} = \Phi_{ji} \text{ for } i, j = 1, \ldots, n.$$

Clearly, $P_i = P_i$ so that determinant B is symmetrical. Thus

$$B_{ij} = B_{ji}.$$

This, together with results (14) yields

(17)
$$\frac{\partial X_s}{\partial P_r} = \frac{\partial X_r}{\partial P_s}.$$

For any situations in which a change in the price of an input does not lead to a change in the equilibrium level of output, the rate of change of the use of input r with respect to a change in the price of input s is equal to the rate of change of the use of input s with respect to a change in the price of input r.

3. *Expansions by Alien Cofactors.* The determinant B is bordered by $P_1, \ldots, P_n$ and 0. Thus we may expand B by cofactors alien to its $j + 1^{st}$ column to get

$$\sum_{i=1}^{n} P_i B_{ij} = 0,$$

and by its $j + 1^{st}$ row to get

$$\sum_{i=1}^{n} P_i B_{ji} = 0.$$

Thus

$$\frac{1}{\lambda} \sum_{i=1}^{n} P_i \frac{B_{ij}}{B} = \frac{1}{\lambda} \sum_{i=1}^{n} P_i \frac{B_{ji}}{B} = 0 .$$

This together with result (14) yields the following

(18)
$$\sum_{i=1}^{n} P_i \frac{\partial X_i}{\partial P_j} = 0 ,$$

and

(19)
$$\sum_{i=1}^{n} P_i \frac{\partial X_j}{\partial P_i} = 0 .$$

The meaning of these results should be fairly clear to the reader. The partial derivatives in (18) and (19) refer to situations in which the equilibrium level of output does not change when input prices change. The sum is taken in result (18) over all inputs when one price changes. This result could be tested with a single instance of an input price change for which equilibrium output remains constant. Result (19) is of much more doubtful usefulness. The sum is taken over all price changes. My intuition leads me, at least, to doubt that we would often be able to find situations in which we could get observations of each of the n partials in (19) in order to form the sum shown.

4. *Reciprocal Determinants Results.* We have shown that the second-order conditions for the cost function to be a minimum subject to the output constraint can be written in a form identical with that of the second-order conditions for utility to be a maximum subject to the budget restraint. Exactly as in the mathematical appendix to Chapter 1, these conditions imply

$$\frac{1}{\lambda} \sum_{r=1}^{m} \sum_{s=1}^{m} \alpha_r \alpha_s \frac{B_{rs}}{B} < 0 , \qquad m < n .$$

The terms $\frac{1}{\lambda} \frac{B_{rs}}{B}$ are the elements of a negative definite quadratic form. From result (14) we may define

$$\frac{\partial X_s}{\partial P_r} = \frac{1}{\lambda} \frac{B_{rs}}{B} = X_{rs} .$$

Then from our discussion in the mathematical appendix to Chapter 1 of the necessary and sufficient conditions for a quadratic form to be negative definite, we have

$$X_{ii} < 0 , \qquad \begin{vmatrix} X_{ii} & X_{ij} \\ X_{ji} & X_{jj} \end{vmatrix} > 0 , \qquad \begin{vmatrix} X_{ii} & X_{ij} & X_{ik} \\ X_{ji} & X_{jj} & X_{jk} \\ X_{ki} & X_{kj} & X_{kk} \end{vmatrix} < 0 , \ldots$$

for all i, j, $k = 1, \ldots, n$, and for determinants up to order $n - 1$. The first of these results is simply a repeat of result (16). From the second determinant we have

$$(20) \qquad \frac{\partial X_r}{\partial P_r} \cdot \frac{\partial X_s}{\partial P_s} - \frac{\partial X_r^2}{\partial P_s} > 0$$

for all r and all s such that $r \neq s$. Similarly by expanding the third determinant we would get further inequalities which the rate of change of equilibrium factor employment with respect to factor prices would have to satisfy. Once again we remind the reader that in deriving these partial derivatives we have assumed output to be constant. Thus our results refer only to situations in which the input price changes do not result in changes in the firm's equilibrium output.

The reader's attention is drawn to the similarity between the results derived here and those derived in the mathematical appendix to Chapter 1. For every result that we were able to prove regarding the substitution effect, we were able to prove an exactly similar implication regarding $\partial X_r/\partial P_s$. The reason for this is simply that we have been able to write the first- and second-order conditions for costs to be a minimum subject to the output constraint in exactly the same form as the first- and second-order conditions for utility to be a maximum subject to the budget restraint. Thus the similarity of the results should not come as any particular surprise to the reader. In fact, the reader may be surprised that the results of this mathematical appendix are not *more* similar to those in the mathematical appendix to Chapter 1. The results that were established in the appendix to Chapter 1 referred to the substitution effect, that is, to the sum of an income effect and a price effect. The results that are established in this chapter refer to the effect of a price change, a price effect. What then of the income effect? Has it no counterpart in the theory of least cost production? The answer is no, it has not.[8]

Perhaps the easiest way to see that no income type effect enters the theory of least cost production is to examine the differences between the production constraint of the theory of least cost production and the budget restraint of the theory of consumer equilibrium. The budget restraint

---

[8] This does not mean that an income type effect could not arise anywhere in the theory of the firm. Should the firm decide for some reason to maximize output subject to an expenditure constraint, an income type effect would indeed arise. It is traditional to suppose that the firm has no budget or expenditure restraint, and in this context no income type effect can arise for the reasons given.

$$\sum_{i=1}^{n} X_i P_i = Y$$

is a function of the prices. A change in the price of any commodity will change the set of commodity bundles that the consumer is able to purchase. The restraint will shift. Thus, if a price changes, an income effect will arise. The production constraint is of the form

$$\overline{\Phi} = \Phi(X_1, \ldots, X_n) .$$

It is not a function of prices. If a price should change, the output that could be produced from any bundle of inputs would not be changed. Thus, no income type effect arises when a price changes in the theory of least cost production. The adjustments under consideration are movements along a constraint, and the constraint does not move when prices change.

Results of a Change in the Constraint

An interesting sort of result which we could have derived in connection with the theory of consumer equilibrium but did not is this. The rate of change of the function of which one seeks an extrema (utility in the appendix to Chapter 1, expenditure here) with respect to the constraint is equal to the Lagrangian multiplier. In the context of consumer equilibrium theory this fact yields no testable results. In the current context, however, it does yield such results. Reconsider equations (11) supposing that $dP_i = 0$, $i = 1, \ldots, n$, while Φ is no longer fixed at $\overline{\Phi}$ so that

$$d\Phi \neq 0 ,$$

i.e., consider a movement along an expansion path, a change in the output constraint. Then from (12)

$$dX_r = \lambda d\Phi \frac{B_r}{B}$$

so that

(21) $$\frac{\partial X_r}{\partial \Phi} = \lambda \frac{B_r}{B} .$$

The expenditure function is

$$E = A + \sum_{i=1}^{n} X_i P_i$$

so that

(22) $\quad \dfrac{\partial E}{\partial \Phi} = \sum_{i=1}^{n} P_i \dfrac{\partial X_i}{\partial \Phi} = \lambda \sum_{i=1}^{n} P_i \dfrac{B_i}{B} = \lambda \dfrac{B}{B} = \lambda , \qquad \dfrac{\partial E}{\partial \Phi} = \lambda .$

This, with conditions (5), the first-order conditions for costs to be a minimum, yields

$$P_i = \dfrac{\partial E}{\partial \Phi} \Phi_i , \qquad i = 1, \ldots , n ,$$

so that

$$\dfrac{P_1}{\Phi_1} = \dfrac{P_2}{\Phi_2} = \ldots = \dfrac{P_n}{\Phi_n} = \dfrac{\partial E}{\partial \Phi} = \text{marginal cost.}[9]$$

This result will be relevant to our discussion of marginal productivity theory in a later chapter.

Results (21) and (15) taken together yield

(23) $\qquad\qquad\qquad\qquad \dfrac{\partial X_r}{\partial \Phi} = \dfrac{\partial \lambda}{\partial P_r} .$

Since, by result (22), λ is equal to marginal cost, result (23) says that the change in the *equilibrium use* of commodity r which results from a unit change in output is equal to the change in equilibrium marginal cost that results from a unit change in the *price* of commodity r.

Homogeneous Production Function and the Firm's Expansion Path

Suppose that the firm's production function is homogeneous of degree k. Then

(24) $\qquad\qquad \Phi(\lambda X_1, \ldots , \lambda X_n) = \lambda^k \Phi(X_1, \ldots , X_n)$

differentiating with respect to X_i and X_j we have

$$\lambda \Phi_i(\lambda X_1, \ldots , \lambda X_n) = \lambda^k \Phi_i(X_1, \ldots , X_n)$$

and

$$\lambda \Phi_j(\lambda X_1, \ldots , \lambda X_n) = \lambda^k \Phi_j(X_1, \ldots , X_n) ,$$

thus

$$\dfrac{\lambda \Phi_i(\lambda X_1, \ldots , \lambda X_n)}{\lambda \Phi_j(\lambda X_1, \ldots , \lambda X_n)} = \dfrac{\lambda^k \Phi_i(X_1, \ldots , X_n)}{\lambda^k \Phi_j(X_1, \ldots , X_n)} .$$

So that,

---

[9] The *marginal cost* associated with a level of output is the change in expenditure (cost) associated with a unit change in output.

(25)
$$\frac{\Phi_i(\lambda X_1, \ldots, \lambda X_n)}{\Phi_j(\lambda X_1, \ldots, \lambda X_n)} = \frac{\Phi_i(X_1, \ldots, X_n)}{\Phi_j(X_1, \ldots, X_n)} \, .$$

Thus the ratio of the marginal product of input i to the marginal product of input j is the same at the input bundle $\lambda X_1, \ldots, \lambda X_n$ as it is at $X_1, \ldots, X_n$ for any λ. This means simply that the ratios of Φ_i to Φ_j for all i and all j are constant along any scale path.

The $\overline{\Phi}$ isoquant is

$$\Phi(X_1, \ldots, X_n) = \overline{\Phi} \, .$$

Consider the slope of the $\overline{\Phi}$ isoquant in the ji direction, i.e., the rate of change of X_j with respect to a change in X_i along the isoquant. From the equation for the isoquant $\overline{\Phi}$ we get

$$\sum_{i=1}^{n} \Phi_i dX_i = d\overline{\Phi} = 0 \, .$$

Suppose $dX_k = 0$, for all k from 1 to n except i and j. Then

$$\Phi_i dX_i + \Phi_j dX_j = 0$$

or

$$\frac{dX_j}{dX_i} = -\frac{\Phi_i}{\Phi_j} \, .$$

Result (25) then indicates that along a scale path the isoquants of a homogeneous production function have the same slope. Thus, as was shown diagrammatically above, if the production function is homogeneous then the expansion path is a scale path.

This result is of some empirical significance. Economists frequently attempt to discover whether or not a particular production function is homogeneous. If it is possible to observe the firm producing two different levels of output at (roughly) the same set of input prices, and if the observer has reason to believe that, at both levels of output, the firm is more or less fully adjusted to its surroundings (i.e., it is in long-run equilibrium), and if there has been no significant technological changes in the firm's production process in the period between which the two levels of output are produced, then unless all factors of production are used in (about) the same proportion at the two levels of output there is reason to believe that the firm's production function is not homogeneous.

SELECTED BIBLIOGRAPHY

CARLSON, S. *A Study on the Theory of Production*. New York: Kelly and Millman, 1956.

DOUGLAS, P. H. *The Theory of Wages*. New York: Macmillan Co., 1934.

HENDERSON, J. M., AND QUANDT, R. E. *Microeconomic Theory*. New York: McGraw-Hill, Inc., 1958.

HICKS, J. R. *Value and Capital*. 2d ed. Oxford: Clarendon Press, 1946.

SAMUELSON, P. A. *Foundations of Economic Analysis*. Cambridge, Mass.: Harvard University Press, 1948.

SMITH, V. L. *Investment and Production*. Cambridge, Mass.: Harvard University Press, 1961.

Chapter 4

COST CURVES AND
HOW THEY BEND

> *For the water bills are terribly high*
> *And meths is shockingly dear*
> *And there isn't the money there used to be*
> *In watering the workman's beer.*
> —*"The Man What Waters the Workman's Beer"**

Introduction

In the preceding chapter and the mathematical appendix thereof we have, among other things, derived the firm's total cost function (curve). For various purposes economists make use of various different cost functions. In this chapter we shall define these various cost functions and establish the relationships between them. Functions related to one and another in the same way that these cost functions are related to one and another are widely used in economics. Thus the relationships which we will describe between cost functions will be of considerable interest in themselves since they will arise several times in the chapters that follow. Accordingly we will go to some length to describe the general nature of these relationships when we introduce them in connection with cost functions in this chapter.

Concepts of Cost: Relationships between Totals, Averages, and Marginals

In the preceding chapter we defined a total cost function for the firm. This function associated with each possible level of output the lowest cost at which that output could be produced. The cost, so associated, is sufficient to pay all factors necessary to the production and distribution of the output. Since a firm, if it is to produce, must realize a normal return (normal means simply as much as the

---

* Edith Fowke and Joe Glazer (eds.), *Songs of Work and Freedom* (Chicago: Roosevelt University, Labor Education Division, 1960), pp. 158–59.

firm could expect to get elsewhere), the cost figure associated with a given output must include such a normal return to the firm. Having emphasized that the total cost associated with any output is the least such total cost, we shall, from now on, leave the fact securely imbedded in the reader's memory and simply refer to the total cost associated with a given level of output.

Definition: *The average cost associated with a given level of output is the per unit cost of producing that level of output.*

The average cost of producing a given output is thus the total cost of producing that output divided by the number of units produced.

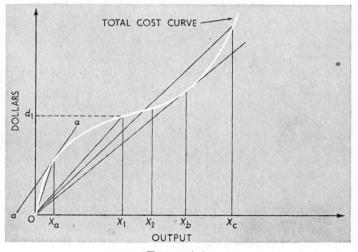

FIGURE 4–1

Definition: *The marginal cost associated with a given level of output is the additional cost which must be incurred in order to produce an additional unit of output at the given level of output. Marginal cost is the rate of change of cost with respect to a change in output.*

From the convention discussed in the previous chapter we draw the total cost curve as in Figure 4–1. On the basis of the shape of this curve and the definition of the average cost associated with a given level of output we are able to derive the average cost curve (function). Consider the average cost of producing the output X_1 in Figure 4–1. The total cost of this level of output is d_1. The average cost is the total cost divided by the level of output that is Od_1/OX_1. Notice that Od_1/OX_1 is the tangent of the angle between the output axis and the line from the origin to the point (X_1, d_1).

Put in another way, Od_1/OX_1 is the ratio of the change in costs from O to d to the change in output from O to X_1. It is equal to the increase in the dollars direction of the line from the origin to the point (X_1, d_1) that results from a unit increase in the output direction, equal, that is, to the slope of the line from the origin to the point (X_1, d_1). The average cost of producing a given output is equal to the total cost of producing the output divided by the level of output or, geometrically, it is equal to the slope of a line from the origin to the point on the total cost curve associated with the given output.

For a low level of output, given the shape of the total cost curve, a line from the origin to the total cost curve would be quite steep. For example, the average cost of producing an output of X_a would be relatively high. The slope of lines from the origin to points on the total cost curve will, as can be seen in Figure 4–1, fall as output increases from very low levels. Thus the average cost associated with an output of X_1 will be less than that associated with an output of X_a, etc. At the output X_b in Figure 4–1, a line from the origin is tangent to the total cost curve. Given the shape of the total cost curve this means that of all lines from the origin to points on the total cost curve, the one to the point associated with an output of X_b has the least slope. Thus the average cost associated with an output of X_b is the least average cost associated with any level of output. Average cost, starting relatively high, falls continuously to a minimum point at that output at which a line from the origin is tangent to the total cost curve. Thereafter average cost increases continuously. In Figure 4–2 we show a conventional total cost curve and the average cost curve associated with it.

Some objection may be made to the fact that in Figure 4–2 we apparently measure both total cost and average cost on the same axis. The former quantity is a number of dollars, the latter a number of dollars per unit. Thus average and total costs are measured in different units. The justification for our using a single axis in Figure 4–2 is that the two quantities *can be* measured in the same unit if one is careful. The total cost curve associates with each level of output the number of dollars that it costs to produce that output. The average cost curve associates with each level of output the number of dollars it costs on the average to produce each unit at that level of output. Since we may unambiguously state this as a number of dollars, we may plot the average cost curve like the total cost curve as a number of dollars associated with each level of output. We must label each curve clearly so that we may know what the numbers of dollars mean, but having so labeled the curves our conscience need not bother us for measuring both quantities along

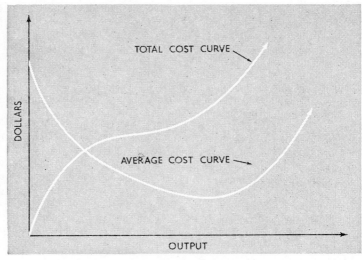

FIGURE 4–2

one axis. Similar considerations arise below when we plot both total and marginal costs against a single axis. Once again we will be without fault so long as we carefully label our curves.

We will have reason to define several functions or curves in the discussion that follows. Many of these will represent totals of some sort, just as the total cost curve represents a total. In connection with these total curves, we will frequently define average curves. In all cases in which we define a total (something)[1] curve and an average (something) curve in association with it, the average (something) will be equal to the total (something) divided by the independent variable. The height of the average (something) curve will be equal, at a particular value of the independent variable, to the slope of the line from the origin to the point on the total (something) curve corresponding to that value of the independent variable.

The marginal cost associated with a given level of output was defined above as the additional cost which must be incurred in order to produce an additional unit of output at the given level of output. This does not mean that it is the cost of the next unit of output, nor yet that of the previous unit of output, rather, the marginal cost associated with a given level of output is the rate of change of total cost with respect to a change in output, at that level of output. Thus

---

[1] The word "something" is to stand for all the various concepts of which we will deal with the totals, averages, and marginals. The reader may substitute words like revenue, cost, productivity, etc.

the marginal cost associated with a given level of output is the slope of the total cost curve at that level of output.[2]

Reconsider Figure 4–1. The slope of the total cost curve at the level of output X_a is the slope of the straight line aa tangent to the total cost curve at the point associated with the output X_a. In general, the slope of the total cost curve at any point will be equal to the slope of the straight line tangent to the total cost curve at that point. Now total costs rise as output increases; hence the slope of the total cost curve is always positive. It follows that marginal cost is always positive. Examination of Figure 4–1 indicates that the slope of the total cost curve falls monotonically from the origin to the point associated with an output of X_2, a point of inflection.

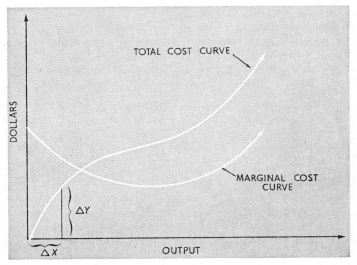

FIGURE 4–3

Thereafter the slope rises monotonically. Thus marginal costs that start at a fairly high level fall monotonically until an output equal to X_2 is reached. Thereafter (that is at higher levels of output) marginal costs increase monotonically. In Figure 4–3 we depict a conventional total cost curve and the marginal cost curve associated with it.

In all cases in which we define a total (something) curve and a marginal (something) curve associated with it, the marginal (something) associated with any particular value of the independ-

---

[2] The reader who does not see why this is the graphical representation of marginal cost as defined above may take this graphical representation as the definition of the marginal cost concept.

ent variable will be equal to the slope of the total (something) curve at that value of the independent variable. Moreover where the total (something) curve has a point of inflection, the marginal (something) curve will have an extremum.

Let us now consider the relationship between the marginal cost curve and the average cost curve. The marginal cost associated with a given level of output is equal to the slope of the total cost curve at the point associated with that level of output. The average cost associated with a given level of output is equal to the slope of a straight line from the origin to the point on the total cost curve associated with the given level of output. On the basis of these results, we will now establish certain relationships between the marginal cost curve and the average cost curve.

Given the shape that we have accepted for the total cost curve (i.e., that it pass through the origin), the marginal cost curve and the average cost curve must start at the same point, that is they must have the same dollars intercept; the marginal cost associated with an output of zero if it is to be defined at all must be equal to the average cost associated with an output of zero if that is to be defined. For a proof of this statement consider Figure 4–3. The average cost associated with a zero output would be equal to the limit of the ratio $\Delta Y/\Delta X$ as ΔX approaches zero. The reader familiar with elementary calculus will recognize this as the definition of marginal cost, the slope of the total cost curve at the origin (abstracting from difficulties associated with defining the slope of a line at its end point). If one is to define these concepts as we have done and wishes to apply that definition to the marginal cost and average cost of a zero output, then the average cost and marginal cost of a zero output will be equal. If the reader feels no compulsion to have these concepts defined for a zero output, then we may say simply that as output approaches zero, marginal cost approaches equality with average cost. This statement will serve our purposes nicely. In general, so long as the total (something) curve is continuous, smooth, and passes through the origin, the marginal (something) curve and the average (something) curve will approach equality as they approach the Y axis.

So long as average cost is falling, marginal cost must be less than average cost. The economic reason for this statement is quite clear. So long as the average cost of production is falling as output increases, it must be the case that each additional unit of output costs less to produce than does the average unit. Otherwise the average would not fall. This may be made clearer by consideration of the following discrete example. Suppose that it cost $10 to produce a single unit of output. Then the average cost (cost per unit) is $10. For the discrete case we shall call the additional cost of the last unit of output marginal cost. Hence in this example the marginal cost of one unit of output will also be $10. Suppose that it cost $19 to produce two units, then marginal cost will be $9. Since this is less than average (per unit) cost for a production of one unit, the average will fall to $9.50. If the marginal (additional) cost of the third unit were $8, then average cost would fall to $9 for the third unit, etc.[3] By an exactly similar argument, so long as average cost is rising, marginal cost must exceed average cost, causing it to rise.

The reader's attention is now directed to Figure 4–2. In this diagram and in the discussion connected with it, we showed that, given the shape of the total cost curve, the average cost curve must fall monotonically to a minimum value, and thereafter, rise monotonically. We have now shown that so long as the average cost curve is falling the marginal cost curve must be below it, while so long as the average cost is increasing the marginal cost curve must lie above it. Hence, at points to the left of the minimum point of the average cost curve the marginal cost curve lies below the average cost curve. At points to the right of the minimum point the marginal cost curve must lie above the average cost curve. Con-

---

[3] The reader may reasonably be disturbed by our discrete example in connection with a phenomenon defined (originally) in terms of the derivatives of continuous functions. Accordingly we offer the following proof for the continuous case. Let the total cost function be $C(X)$, then marginal cost is given by $C'(X)$ and average cost is given by $\dfrac{C(X)}{X}$.

Proposition: If $\dfrac{d}{dX}\left(\dfrac{C(X)}{X}\right) < 0$, then $C'(X) < \dfrac{C(X)}{X}$.

Proof:

$$\frac{d}{dX}\left(\frac{C(X)}{X}\right) = \frac{X \cdot C'(X) - C(X)}{X^2} < 0$$

hence

$$X \cdot C'(X) - C(X) < 0,$$
$$X \cdot C'(X) < C(X)$$
$$C'(X) < \frac{C(X)}{X}, \qquad \text{for } X > 0.$$

By reversing the inequality we get:

$$\text{If } \frac{d}{dX}\left(\frac{C(X)}{X}\right) > 0, \text{ then } C'(X) > \frac{C(X)}{X}.$$

If average cost is rising, marginal cost must exceed average cost. Notice that this does not depend upon $C(X)$ being a cost function but only upon the independent variable's being positive. So long as the average (something) curve is falling (rising), the marginal (something) curve must lie below (above) it causing it to fall (rise).

versely, if marginal cost is less than average cost, the latter must fall, while if marginal cost exceeds average cost, then the latter must rise. At the minimum point of the average cost curve, average cost is neither rising nor falling, hence marginal cost may neither exceed nor be exceeded by average cost. They must be equal at this point; that is, they must cross.

The relationship between the marginal cost curve and the average cost curve must be as shown in Figure 4–4. Starting at the same point on the dollars axis both curves fall, marginal cost being less than average cost. Marginal cost then reaches a minimum point and rises to intersect the average cost curve at its minimum point.

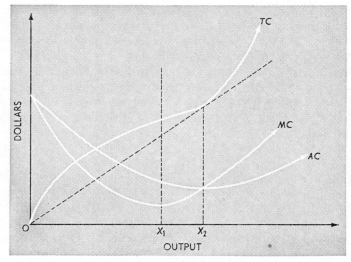

FIGURE 4–4

Thereafter both curves rise, the marginal cost curve being above the average cost curve.

In general, if the average (something) curve is falling, then the marginal (something) curve must be below it. Conversely, if the marginal (something) curve lies below the average (something) curve, then the average (something) curve must be falling. Similarly, if the average (something) curve is rising, then the marginal (something) curve must be above the average curve and conversely. Finally, wheresoever the average (something) curve is flat (has a zero slope), the marginal (something) must equal the average (something).

In Figure 4–4 we have summarized our discussion by placing all three cost curves on the same diagram. Three levels of output are of particular interest in the construction of Figure 4–4. At the origin (a zero level of output), marginal cost and average cost will be equal. At the point of inflection of the total cost curve (at an output of X_1), the marginal cost curve will be a minimum. At the output X_2 a straight line from the origin is just tangent to the total cost curve, hence the average cost curve reaches a minimum at this point. As we have shown above the marginal cost curve must equal (intersect) the average cost curve at this point. This may be seen directly by considering the definition of marginal cost and average cost in conjunction with diagram 4–4. The average cost associated with any level of output is equal to the slope of the straight line from the origin to the point on the total cost curve associated with that level of output. The marginal cost of any level of output is equal to the slope of the total cost curve at that level of output. At the point X_2 a straight line from the origin is just tangent to the total cost curve, so that, at this point, the total cost curve and the straight line from the origin to the total cost curve have the same slope. Thus, the average cost associated with this level of output must equal the marginal cost associated with it.

It should be clear to the reader by this time that each of our three cost curves contains much the same information as the other two. It is clear that when given the total cost curve (function), we can derive the average cost curve (function) simply by dividing the total cost function by the level of output. Similarly, anyone sufficiently learned to be able to differentiate the total cost function with respect to output could find the marginal cost curve (function). It is also clear that when given the average cost function, we could derive the other two curves, for by multiplying the average cost function by output we have the total cost function which we have just discussed. Problems would arise only if we were to try to derive the total and average cost functions from a given marginal cost function. The marginal cost function is equal to the *slope* of the total cost function. If we knew the marginal cost function we could tell what the *slope* of the total cost curve was at each level of output, but we would have no way of ascertaining the *height* of the total cost curve at *any* level of output. Suppose we knew that the marginal cost function was identical with that shown in Figure 4–4. We would then know that the total cost curve must be one of the infinity of possible curves parallel, at each level of output, to the total cost curve of Figure 4–4, but each having a different dollars intercept. In order to pinpoint one of these curves we would need to know the height of the total cost curve at some point, i.e., the total cost of producing some fixed level of output. From the family of total cost curves associated with the given marginal cost curve we would then choose the one associating the known total cost with the fixed level of output. For example, if we were given the marginal cost curve of Figure 4–4 and the additional information that in producing no output the firm incurred no costs at all, then we would know that the total cost curve through the origin of Figure 4–4 was the correct one for the firm.[4] At the end of Chapter 3 we drew total cost curves for firms facing increasing returns to scale, constant returns to scale, and decreasing returns to scale. As an exercise the reader should derive the average cost curves and marginal cost curves appropriate to these total cost curves.

Long-Run Analysis and Short-Run Analysis

Definition: *Long-run analysis is analysis of situations in which the quantities of all inputs purchased by the firm may be varied.*

Definition: *Short-run analysis is analysis of situations in which the quantity of at least one input purchased by the firm is fixed.*

We shall refer to any situation in which the quantities of all inputs used in the production process are variable as the long run. Any situation in which the quantity of at least one input used in the production process is fixed we shall call the short run. In Chapter 3, where we derived the total cost curve, we held no factors of production in fixed supply. Accordingly, in Chapter 3, we were engaged in long-run analysis. The total cost curve that we derived there may then be called the long-run total cost curve. Since the average and marginal cost curves which we have derived above in this chapter were based on the long-run total cost curve, they too are long-run cost curves. We will call them, respectively, the long-run average cost curve and the long-run marginal cost curve.

In the short run the firm has a fixed quantity of some factor of production. There is no way in which the firm can vary the quantity of this factor that it purchases. Since we have assumed that all factors of production have positive prices, this means that the firm has certain costs that it is not able to avoid paying, not even by ceasing to produce altogether. Such costs are called fixed costs, and we will discuss them at greater length below. An example of the

---

[4] Thus, if marginal cost is given by $C'(X)$, total cost must be

$$\int C'(X)dX = C(X) + K,$$

but lacking knowledge of the value of K we would be unable to plot the total cost curve.

sort of factor of production that the firm might easily find itself unable to vary its quantity of very rapidly would be some sort of specialized heavy capital input, buildings, large machinery, etc. Such things are commonly referred to as "plant." Thus the firm may be forced to use capitalized methods in order to produce. It may be forced, that is, to purchase a plant appropriate to the level of output that it intends to offer for sale. Associated with this plant will be certain costs, the fixed costs mentioned above.

Short-Run and Long-Run Total Cost Curves

In Figure 4–5 we will examine the way in which a firm minimizes cost when its use of some factor is fixed. Suppose that the firm has X_1 of commodity X. What are the lowest levels of cost at which it may produce the various levels of output, 10, 20, 30, 40, etc.? Notice, to begin with that when given the isoexpenditure curves shown, the fixed quantity, X_1 of X will, in itself, cost the firm $32. Notice also that the isoquants associate an output of 7 with an input of X_1 of X and none of Y while any output less than 7 may be produced with no more than X_1 of X and no Y. Since the firm is unable to purchase less than X_1 of X, the cheapest way for it to produce any given output is for it to combine this X_1 of X with whatever is the least quantity of Y consistent with the production of the given output. The firm may produce 7 or less units of output

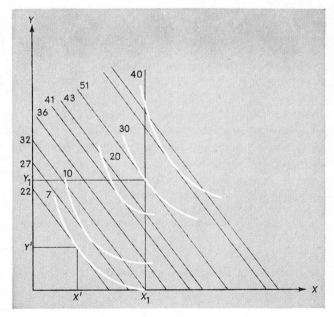

FIGURE 4–5

without purchasing any of commodity Y at all, employing input X only. Thus, for an output of 7 or less the short-run total cost will be $32.

If the firm were able to vary its purchases of factor X it could produce 7 units of output at a cost of $22 by employing X' units of X in conjunction with Y' units of Y. Since the (long-run) total cost curve (the curve derived in Chapter 3) is always positively sloped, if all factors were variable, the firm could produce outputs less than 7 at costs below $22. Thus, in the short run (with X fixed at X_1) the total cost for producing 7 or less units of output is greater than it would be in the long run (with all factors variable). Consider now an output of 10 units. If all factors were variable the firm could produce 10 units of output for $27. Given that the firm must purchase X_1 of X, however, the cheapest way to produce 10 units of output would be to combine this given quantity of X with the least possible quantity of Y such that 10 units can be produced. This will be the combination of X and Y associated with the point at which the line perpendicular to the X axis at the point X_1, cuts the isoquant associated with an output of 10 units. As can be seen from Figure 4–5, this combination of inputs will cost the firm $36. Once again the cost of producing in the short run is greater than the cost in the long run. Similarly, in the long run 20 units of output could be produced at a cost of $41 while, in the short run, it would cost $43.

If all factors were variable and the firm wanted to produce 30 units of output, it would employ X_1 units of X. In the short run, with X fixed at X_1, the firm would also employ X_1 units to produce 30 units of output. In either case the firm would produce an output of 30 units by employing X_1 of X and Y_1 of Y. Thus in the short run (with X fixed at X_1) the total cost of producing 30 units of output is the same as in the long run. Finally, as can be seen from examination of Figure 4–5, at an output of 40 units, short-run total cost again exceeds long-run total cost.

In the example illustrated in Figure 4–5, for outputs less than 30 units and for outputs greater than 30 units, short-run total cost will exceed long-run total cost. The fixed quantity of X, X_1, is precisely the quantity that the firm would use in the long run to produce an output of 30, so that at that level of output, short-run total cost will be equal to long-run total cost. The relationship between the short-run total cost curve and the long-run total cost curve will then be as shown in Figure 4–6.[5] At outputs below 30

---

[5] In the example that we have used the long-run total cost curve does not have its conventional shape. This is because of the way in which we labeled the curves of Figure 4–5.

units the short-run total cost curve lies above the long-run total cost curve. At 30 units of output the two curves are tangent so that short-run total cost equals long-run total cost. At larger outputs short-run total cost again exceeds long-run total cost.

Suppose that X is some sort of heavy capital input or plant. The short-run total cost curve of Figure 4–6 then illustrates the fact that a plant of size X_1 is ideally suited to the production of 30 units of output. If the production process is such that some sort of fixed plant *must* be used, and if the firm decides that it should

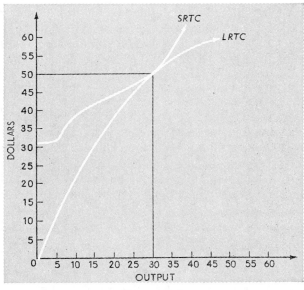

FIGURE 4–6

produce 30 units of output, then to do so in the cheapest possible way, it will build a plant of size X_1, a plant *designed* to produce 30 units of output. In general, there is a different short run for each possible level of each input and for each possible combination of inputs. If the set of factors that is fixed in a particular short-run situation is the same set that the firm would use in order to produce a given output in the long run (all factors variable), then at that level of output the particular short-run total cost curve will be tangent from above to the long-run total cost curve. At other levels of output the short-run curve will normally lie above the long-run curve. If there does not exist a level of output for which the given set of fixed factors would be appropriate in the long run, then the short-run total cost curve associated with the fixed set of factors will lie above the long-run total cost curve at all levels of output.

Consider now a particular firm's long-run total cost curve and the set of all its short-run total cost curves. All points on any short-run total cost curve will lie either above or on the firm's long-run total cost curve. That is, no point on any short-run total cost curve may lie below the long-run total cost curve. If some such short-run curve did lie below the long-run curve then it would be possible to produce some level of output more cheaply in the short run than in the long run. The short run is simply a situation in which some input is in fixed supply, while in the long run all inputs may be varied. If some method were available for producing a given output at a very low cost with some factor being held in fixed supply, then, at worst, one could produce the output at the same cost when the quantity of all factors used was variable simply by using the same quantities of all inputs as one did when the one input was fixed. Similarly, every point on the long-run total cost curve is on *some*

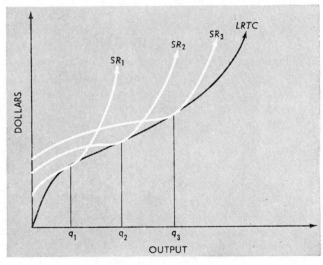

FIGURE 4–7

short-run total cost curve. Points on the long-run curve show the costs of particular input combinations. In order to find a short-run curve which will be tangent to the long-run curve at some output, we need only fix some input at the level at which it would be used in producing that output in the long run. Then the cheapest way to produce that output in the short run will be (as with an output of 30 in Figures 4–5 and 4–6) to produce it exactly as it would be produced in the long run. The long-run total cost curve is simply the minimum bound of all possible short-run total cost curves. This is illustrated in Figure 4–7 where the long-run total cost curve is labeled *LRTC* and *SR*$_1$, *SR*$_2$, and *SR*$_3$ are short-run total cost curves. The "plant" giving rise to *SR*$_1$ produces an output of q_1 as cheaply as possible, that associated with *SR*$_2$ produces q_2 as cheaply as possible, and the plant for which *SR*$_3$ is drawn is ideally suited to the production of q_3. There would exist an infinity of such short-run total cost curves. Each such curve would lie above *LRTC*, or, at best, would be tangent to *LRTC*. A curve having the relationship that *LRTC* has to the set of all possible short-run total cost curves for this firm is said to be the *envelope* curve of the set.

Short-Run and Long-Run Average Cost Curves

Just as an (long-run) average cost curve is associated with the long-run total cost curve so an (short-run) average cost curve is associated with each short-run total cost curve. Moreover, since we would attribute to the short-run total cost curve a shape similar to that of the long-run total cost curve, we must draw the short-run average cost curve as we do the long-run average cost curve, with a **U** shape. In order to establish the relationship between the long-run average cost curve and the short-run average cost curve, study Figure 4–8 in which we have shown a long-run total cost curve with a short-run total cost curve tangent to it. It is fairly simple to establish the relationship between the long-run average cost curve and this particular short-run average cost curve. The slope of a straight line from the origin to the point on *SRTC* corresponding to

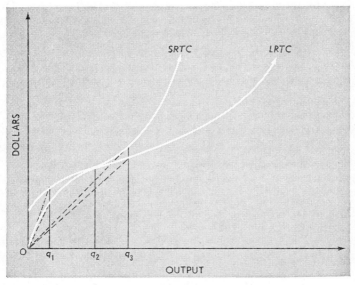

FIGURE 4–8

an output of q_1 is greater than that of a straight line from the origin to the point on *LRTC* corresponding to an output of q_1. Thus, for an output of q_1 short-run average cost will exceed long-run average cost, by the definition of average cost. Similarly, at an output of q_3 short-run average cost must exceed long-run average cost. At the point of tangency between *SRTC* and *LRTC*, q_2, a straight line from the origin to one of the curves will also reach the other curve. Thus, at this point, the short-run average cost curve must touch the long-run average cost curve. The short-run average cost curve must, in fact, lie above the long-run average curve for all outputs either less than or greater than q_2 (as the reader may easily see). At the output q_2, short-run average cost must equal long-run average cost. Thus at the output q_2 the short-run average cost curve must be tangent from above to the long-run average cost curve.

Every short-run total cost curve must lie above or be tangent to the long-run total cost curve. So long as the short-run total curve lies above the long-run total curve so will the short-run average cost curve lie above the long-run average cost curve. When the total curves are tangent so will the average cost curves be tangent. Just as there is at least one short-run total cost curve tangent to the long-run total cost curve at every point on the long run total cost curve, so there is at least one short-run average cost curve tangent from above to the long-run average cost curve at every point on the latter. Just as no short-run total cost curve may ever lie below the long-run total cost curve, no short-run average cost curve may ever lie below the long-run average cost curve. In fact, just as the long-run total cost curve is the lower envelope of the set of all possible short-run total cost curves so the long-run average cost curve is the lower envelope of the set of all possible short-run average cost curves. This is illustrated in Figure 4–9 where *LRAC* is the long-run average cost curve and $SRAC_1$ through $SRAC_6$ are various short-run average cost curves.

If the short-run average cost curve is tangent to the long-run average cost curve at some level of output, then the quantity of fixed factors particular to this short-run is the best available for the production of that output (i.e., no other bundle of factors could produce it more cheaply). This does not mean that the given fixed factors could not be used to produce another level of output still more cheaply. The level of output at which the short-run average cost curve, associated with a particular "plant," is tangent to the long-run average cost curve is an output that no "plant" could be utilized to produce more cheaply. The particular "plant" associated with the short-run average cost curve will typically be able to produce some other (nontangency) output yet more cheaply than the tangency output. The long-run average cost curve does not connect the minimum points of all the short-run average cost curves; it connects the points which are the lowest attainable, for each level of output. Thus, in Figure 4–9, the "plant" associated with $SRAC_1$ can be utilized to produce an output of q_1 as cheaply as possible. This plant may be utilized to produce output q_2 more cheaply than output q_1. If all factors were variable however, the firm would be foolish to use the "plant" associated with $SRAC_1$ to produce q_2, for this output may be more cheaply produced using the "plant" associated with $SRAC_2$. In fact, since tangent curves have the same slope at the point of tangency, and since, at the minimum

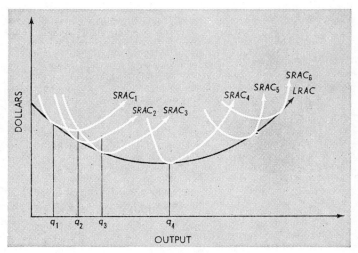

FIGURE 4–9

point of any short-run average cost curve its slope must be zero, the only point on the long-run average cost curve which *can* be tangent to the minimum point of a short-run average cost curve is the minimum point of the long-run average cost curve, output q_4 in Figure 4–9. If *LRAC* were to pass through the minimum point of some *SRAC* at some level of output other than q_4, then the two curves could not be tangent, they would have to cross. Some portion of *SRAC* would then lie below some portion of *LRAC*, but that would imply that some level of output could be produced more cheaply in the short run than in the long run, which is impossible.

Short-Run and Long-Run Marginal Cost Curves

It should be obvious to the reader that having defined long- and short-run total cost curves and long- and short-run average cost curves, we can also define long- and short-run marginal cost curves. The general relationship between the short-run marginal cost curve and the long-run marginal cost curve is neither as clear nor as important as the two relationships discussed above. One characteristic of this relationship, however, will be of central importance to the chapters that follow. In examining Figure 4–8, above, we showed that at the output, at which the short- and long-run total cost curves were tangent, the short- and long-run average cost curves were also tangent. Thus at the level of output at which the short- and long-run average curves are tangent, the short- and long-run *total* cost curves must have the same slopes (because they are also tangent). The slope of the total cost curve is equal to

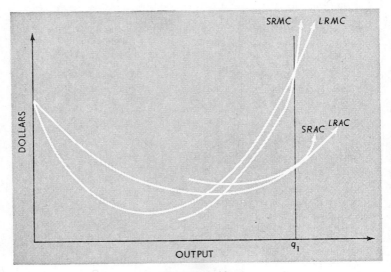

FIGURE 4–10

marginal cost. When the short- and long-run total cost curves have the same slopes, the short- and long-run marginal cost curves must intersect. Thus at the level of output at which the short-run average cost curve is tangent to the long-run average cost curve the short-run marginal cost curve will intersect the long-run marginal cost curve. The curves will have the relationship shown in Figure 4–10. At output q_1 short- and long-run average costs are equal and so must short- and long-run marginal costs be equal.

Variable Costs and Fixed Costs

In the short-run the firm is unable to vary its purchases of some commodity (or commodities). As we mentioned above this means that the firm will definitely face some fixed costs in the short run. In the long run all factors are variable. Thus if the firm is faced with any fixed costs in the long run, these costs must be other than payments to factors of production. Suppose that for some reason the firm is faced with certain fixed costs perhaps attributable to some fixed factors of production. Then total cost is the sum of total variable cost and fixed cost, where the latter is some positive constant. This is shown in Figure 4–11.

Since the total variable cost at any output differs from total cost of that output only by a constant, and since this constant is the same for all levels of output, the slope of the total variable cost curve at any level of output will be equal to that of the total cost

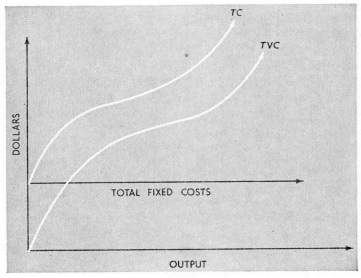

FIGURE 4–11

curve. Thus, the marginal curve associated with the total variable cost curve would be identical with that associated with the total cost curve. This is as it should be since the marginal cost of any output is the rate of change of cost with respect to a change in output at that output level and since, fixed cost being fixed, the rate of change of cost is naught but the rate of change of those costs that change, i.e., variable costs.

The average variable cost is the average curve associated with *TVC* of Figure 4–11. We discussed the average curve associated with such a total curve earlier in the chapter. Furthermore, since the marginal cost curve associated with *TC* is identical with that associated with *TVC* and since *TVC* passes through the origin, the relationship between the average variable cost curve and the marginal cost curve will be exactly the same as the relationship between the marginal cost curve and the average cost curve of Figure 4–4 above.

If there are nonzero fixed costs the total cost curve will not pass through the origin. The total cost of a zero output will be positive. Under these circumstances the reader may satisfy himself that as output approaches zero, average cost will exceed marginal cost. Average cost will be equal to average variable cost plus average fixed cost, where the latter is the average curve associated with the total fixed cost curve of Figure 4–11. Since fixed costs are constant, average fixed costs will fall monotonically as output increases. All these relationships are summarized in Figure 4–12.

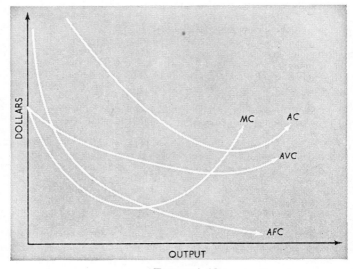

FIGURE 4–12

The reason that these curves are of interest is this. By examination of these curves in conjunction with revenue curves to be defined below we will be able to ascertain whether or not a firm's revenue is sufficient to cover its variable costs. So long as the firm's revenue is sufficient to cover these costs and to make some contribution, however small, to the payment of fixed costs, it will pay the firm to remain in business. If the firm's revenue is not sufficient even to cover variable costs, then the firm loses money in the actual production process as well as losing its fixed costs. The latter losses are unavoidable, but the firm could avoid losses incurred in the production process by stopping production. If the firm's revenue does not cover its variable cost, it would lose less money by closing its doors. That is precisely what a profit-maximizing firm would do.

SELECTED BIBLIOGRAPHY

JOHNSTON, J. *Statistical Cost Analysis.* New York: McGraw-Hill, Inc., 1960.

STIGLER, G. J. *The Theory of Price.* Rev. ed. New York: Macmillan Co., 1952.

VINER, J. "Cost Curves and Supply Curves." Reprinted in *Readings in Price Theory* (eds. G. J. STIGLER AND K. BOULDING). Homewood, Ill.: Richard D. Irwin, Inc., 1952.

PART III

The Theory of Market Forms

By Behavioral Assumption 2 the firm will produce that output for which its profit is a maximum. The profit associated with a given level of output is the difference between the cost of producing that output and the revenue gained from selling it. In the last two chapters we have developed the theory of least cost production. On the basis of this, the firm may find the minimum cost of producing each level of output. In order to ascertain the level of output for which profit will be a maximum, we need only see what revenue can be gained from the sale of each level of output. We must establish the firm's revenue function. This function associates an amount of revenue with each possible level of sales. This revenue will be equal to the number of units sold multiplied by the price each unit will command.

What price a unit of the commodity that a firm sells will command depends upon the firm's demand curve. The demand curve facing a firm may sometimes be derived from the demand function developed in Chapter 1 for the commodity that the firm sells. There we developed a commodity demand function of the form

$$D_i = D_i(P_1, \ldots, P_n, Y_1, \ldots, Y_k) \, ,$$

where D_i is the demand for commodity i, P_i is the price of commodity i (there are n commodities), and Y_j is the purchasing power of individual j (there are k persons). We have already discussed (Chapter 2) how we might solve the single equation

$$D_i(P_1, \ldots, P_n, Y_1, \ldots, Y_k) = S_i$$

for the equilibrium value of P_i if all other prices are fixed at their equilibrium values and all Y_i, $i = 1, \ldots, k$, are fixed. Taking all these variables as fixed, we can write the demand function as

(1) $$D_i(P_i) = D_i,$$

a function of P_i only (because every other variable on which it depends is fixed). We will refer to equation (1) as the *demand curve* for commodity i because, since it is a function of one variable, we can represent it as a curve. We assume that the relationship (1) can also be written

(2) $$P_i = P_i(D_i).$$

Equation (1) tells us what quantity will be demanded at each price. Equation (2) gives the same information, turned around. It says how the price that a unit of commodity i will command varies with the quantity of commodity i sold.[1] Consider the illustration below.

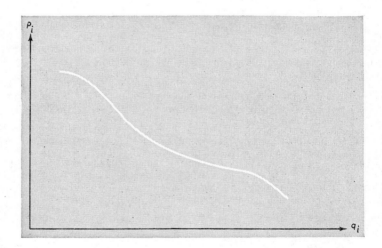

If the curve in this illustration shows how price and quantity sold are related, then it is the demand curve, equation (1). Considered as a demand curve it tells us what quantity will be purchased at each price. If we take quantity as the independent variable, then the

---

[1] Notice that when we draw a demand curve for a firm, we assume that it sells each unit of the quantity depicted, at the same price. Later we will discuss price discrimination, cases in which different purchasers are charged different prices. In this eventuality the firm will face several demand curves each one of which will have the property that all units depicted are sold at the same price.

curve in the illustration shows what price may be charged for each quantity; that is, it depicts equation (2). Equation (2) is said to be the inverse[2] of equation (1), and we shall refer to it as the *average revenue curve* (function).

Unfortunately the information contained in equations (1) and (2) (both, of course, yield the same information) may not be sufficient to determine the revenue function for a single firm. Equation (2) is the revenue function for a commodity. In order for a single firm to be possessed of this revenue function it must be the only firm selling the commodity and it must have no barriers to its selling. In general, given the information in equation (1) or (2), we would need to know, in addition, how the marketing institutions facing the firm affect the firm's ability to vary its price by changing the quantity that it offers to sell. In the chapters that make up this part we will discuss various market forms which may follow from different marketing institutions. We will derive conditions for profit maximization by firms operating under these market forms.

---

[2] If $Y = f(X)$ is a one-to-one relationship between Y and X, that is, if for each value of X in the domain of $f(X)$ only one Y exists in the relationship $f(X)$ to X, and for each value of Y in the range of $f(X)$ only one X exists such that $Y = f(X)$, then a function $X = f^{-1}(Y)$ exists and is called the inverse of the function $f(X)$.

Chapter 5

COMPETITIVE MARKETS

The farmer is the man, The farmer is the man
Lives on credit till the fall
With the interest rate so high it's a wonder he don't
die
For the mortgage man's the one who gets it all.
—*"The Farmer Is the Man"**

Pure Competition

A *market* is an institution through which commodities are traded. We will limit our use of the term market to apply only to institutions in which a single homogeneous commodity is traded. If a group of commodities is said to be in a given market, this will be taken to imply that no differences between the elements of the group exist which would cause *any* consumer to differentiate between them. A market will be said to be *purely competitive* if each firm in the market is able to sell all that it likes at the given price, and every firm in the market sells at the same price. Thus if a market is purely competitive the firms selling commodities in the market all take the same price as given regardless of the quantities that they sell. We will refer to firms which sell in a purely competitive market as purely competitive firms.

Purely competitive firms are price takers. It is usually supposed that if the number of firms selling in a given market is large and if the firms are of roughly the same size, then the market will be purely competitive. That is, each firm in the market will be able to sell all that it likes at the given price, and all firms will charge the same price. This, it is thought, would follow because each firm is, in effect, an insignificantly small part of the total. Whether or not it follows, it is true that the reason that the market would be purely competitive is the fact that all firms take the same price as given and each firm is able to sell all it likes at that price. Now it is

---

* To the best of my knowledge, "The Farmer Is the Man" is in the public domain.

clearly possible for firms to behave in this way even if only a few of them are competing in a given market; accordingly, we make no assumptions regarding the number of firms in a purely competitive market.

The purely competitive firm cannot change its selling price by varying the quantity that it offers—the price that it may charge is fixed. The demand curve (or average revenue curve) for the firm will be a line parallel to the quantity axis through the point on the price (dollars) axis corresponding to the given market price, as $P = AR$ in Figure 5–1. In Chapter 4 we discussed the relationship between average curves and marginal curves. The average revenue curve of Figure 5–1 is neither increasing nor decreasing. Marginal revenue may not exceed average revenue without causing the average to rise, nor may it be less than the average without causing it to fall; thus, so long as average revenue is constant, as in Figure 5–1, marginal revenue must be equal to average revenue. The

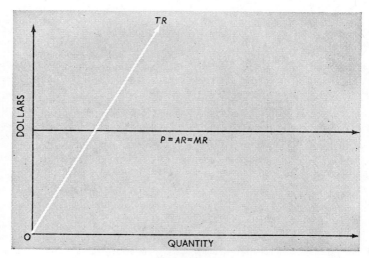

FIGURE 5–1

marginal revenue curve of a purely competitive firm coincides with the horizontal average revenue curve, as shown in Figure 5–1.

The total revenue accruing to the firm from the sale of any particular quantity of output is equal to the unit price (average revenue) that that quantity will command multiplied by the quantity. If the firm is purely competitive then the unit price that it may charge does not vary with quantity. Thus the total revenue function is of the form

$$\text{Rev.} = P \cdot q \,,$$

where P is a constant. This is the equation of a straight line having a slope P. If the firm sells nothing, it receives no revenue from the sale; accordingly the total revenue curve for a purely competitive firm will be a positively sloped straight line from the origin as TR in Figure 5–1.

We will suppose that the purely competitive firm has cost curves of the shapes derived in the preceding two chapters. On the basis of these and the revenue curves of Figure 5–1, we will determine what output the firm will produce in order to maximize its profits. In order to see one way in which long-run and short-run considerations may enter into the determination of the profit-maximizing level of output, we will discuss a firm in the process of entering into a purely competitive market. We will suppose that if the firm is to produce at all, it must construct some sort of plant. Accordingly there will be two types of decisions to be made. How large a plant should the firm build? Having built a plant, how should the firm utilize it?

Suppose that the firm is considering entering into the production of a particular commodity. Suppose further that the commodity is sold in a purely competitive market, and that the firm knows what price it will be able to charge. In order to decide how much it must produce to maximize its profits, and what plant it should build to produce this amount, the firm will need to know how much it will cost to produce each possible level of output. Notice that the firm is in the planning stage, able to plan to utilize any amount of any input that it sees fit to use. Accordingly the relevant cost information is contained in the firm's long-run cost curves. As pointed out above, all the long-run cost information is contained in either the long-run total cost curve or the long-run average cost curve. Let us utilize the average cost curve. Later on we will establish the firm's profit-maximizing output utilizing total cost and revenue curves.

In Figure 5–2 we have drawn the firm's long-run average cost curve, $LRAC$, with the shape established in Chapter 4. This, of course, implies that the long-run total cost curve and long-run marginal cost curve will also have the shapes discussed in Chapters 3 and 4. If the $LRAC$ has the shape shown, and if the long-run total cost curve passes through the origin (i.e., if it costs the firm nothing in the long run to produce nothing) as we will suppose, then the long-run marginal cost curve, $LRMC$, will also have the shape shown. Suppose that the price that the firm will be able to charge is P in Figure 5–2. Then the firm will face the average revenue curve (and marginal revenue curve), $\overline{P} = AR = MR$, shown.

The information in Figure 5–2 is sufficient to determine the level of output for which profit will be a maximum. In fact, as we will now show, the profit-maximizing output will be $\bar{q}$, at which output long-run marginal cost is equal to marginal revenue, and the long-run marginal cost curve cuts the marginal revenue curve from below. At an output of $\bar{q}$ the rate of change of cost with respect to output is exactly equal to that of revenue (by the definitions of marginal cost and marginal revenue). If the firm were to produce more than $\bar{q}$, long-run marginal cost would exceed marginal revenue. Thus each unit beyond $\bar{q}$ would add more to the firm's costs than it would add to the firm's revenue. The firm would lose profit on each additional unit of output in excess of $\bar{q}$. Thus the firm

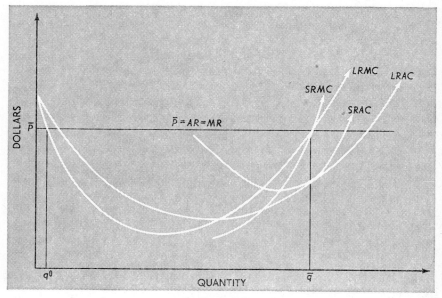

FIGURE 5–2

cannot be maximizing its profit at a level of output greater than $\bar{q}$.

If the firm were to produce less than $\bar{q}$ units of output but more than q^0 units, then its marginal revenue curve would lie above its long-run marginal cost curve. Thus each additional unit of output would add more to the firm's revenue than it would add to its costs. So long as this is true, the firm may increase its profit by increasing the quantity that it produces and sells. Clearly, if it is possible for the firm to increase its profit by increasing its production, profit is not maximized. It will continue to pay the firm to expand its output until a level $\bar{q}$ is reached at which cost changes exactly as rapidly with output as does revenue.

We have only to consider production levels less than or equal to q^0. At any level of production less than q^0, each addition to output adds more to the firm's costs than it does to the firm's revenue. Moreover, below quantity q^0, costs exceed revenue (since *LRAC* is above *AR*). In fact, so long as *LRAC* is above *AR*, costs exceed revenues; however, to the right of q^0 additional units of output add more to *revenues* than they do to costs. Thus to the left of q^0 costs exceed revenues and the difference between the two is growing, while to the right of q^0 costs may still be greater than revenue (so long as *LRAC* is above *AR*), but revenue is growing faster than costs (so long as *MR* lies above *LRMC*). Therefore at an output of q^0 profits are a *minimum*.[1]

Having determined that its profit will be a maximum if it produces and sells an output of $\bar{q}$ at the price $\bar{P}$, the profit-maximizing firm will arrange so to do. To this end, the firm must (under our supposition) build a plant appropriate to this level of production. As we saw in Chapter 4, this will be a plant, the short-run average cost curve associated with which will be tangent from above to the long-run average cost curve of Figure 5–2 at an output of $\bar{q}$. Such a short-run average cost curve, *SRAC*, and the short-run marginal cost curve, *SRMC*, associated with it are drawn into Figure 5–2. As was shown in Chapter 4, at the level of output at which the short-run average cost curve is tangent to the long-run average cost curve, the short-run marginal cost curve will intersect the long-run marginal cost curve. The firm has chosen a plant such that the short-run average cost curve associated with it will be tangent to the long-run average cost curve at the level of output at which the marginal revenue curve intersects the long-run marginal cost curve. Thus the short-

---

[1] At any output at which marginal cost is equal to marginal revenue the profit function will possess an extremum. If the marginal cost curve cuts the marginal revenue from above, the extremum will be a minimum. If the marginal cost curve cuts the marginal revenue curve from below, the extremum will be a maximum. The profit function may be written,

$$\pi(q) = R(q) - C(q),$$

where q is quantity, $R(q)$ is the total revenue function, and $C(q)$ is the total cost function. For an extremum of this function

$$\pi'(q) = R'(q) - C'(q) = 0,$$
$$R'(q) = C'(q),$$

marginal revenue equals marginal cost. For a maximum

$$R''(q) - C''(q) < 0,$$

so that

$$R''(q) < C''(q).$$

If they are to be equal, then the marginal cost curve must cut the marginal revenue curve from below. For a minimum

$$R''(q) > C''(q),$$

so that the marginal cost curve must cut the marginal revenue curve from above.

run marginal cost curve will intersect the marginal revenue curve at $\bar{q}$ in Figure 5–2. This is really quite important. If it were not so, then the firm, having decided to produce an output of $\bar{q}$ and having built the plant appropriate to that level of output, would find that the profit-maximizing level of output for that plant was other than $\bar{q}$, in which case the firm would have been advised to build a different plant. Since the appropriate short-run marginal cost curve intersects the marginal revenue curve at the *same* output level as the long-run marginal cost curve, the firm, having built the appropriate plant, will maximize profit by using the plant to produce an output of $\bar{q}$.

It is sometimes convenient to ignore average and marginal curves and establish the profit-maximizing output of a firm from an analysis of its total cost curve and its total revenue curve. In order to illustrate how such analysis might be carried out we will employ the total revenue curve and long-run total cost curve to determine the profit-maximizing output of a purely competitive firm. The long-run average cost curve of Figure 5–2 will lead to a long-run total cost curve of the elongated S-shape discussed in Chapters 3 and 4. Such a curve, *LRTC*, is shown in Figure 5–3. In Figure 5–1 above, we pictured the total revenue curve of a purely competitive firm. Such a curve, *TR*, also appears in Figure 5–3. The profit associated with any quantity of output will be the amount by which the total revenue associated with that level of output exceeds the total cost associated with that output. This is shown in Figure 5–3 by the vertical distance between the total revenue and total cost curves. Where the total revenue curve is above the total cost curve, profit is positive; where total costs exceed total revenue, profit is clearly negative. Our task is to find the quantity such that the total revenue curve is furthest above the total cost curve.

To the left of quantity q_1 in Figure 5–3 and to the right of quantity q_2, costs exceed revenues. Between q_1 and q_2 revenue exceeds costs. It is in this latter region that profit must reach its maximum, because here alone it is positive. Consider the quantity $\bar{q}$. At this output *LRTC* is parallel to *TR*. Between q_1 and $\bar{q}$ the total revenue curve is steeper than the total cost curve so that revenue is increasing faster with output than is cost. Thus the positive vertical distance between *TR* and *LRTC*, profit, is growing with output. Between $\bar{q}$ and q_2 the long-run total cost curve is steeper than the total revenue curve so that in this region, profit is falling. To the left of $\bar{q}$ profit is increasing. To the right of $\bar{q}$ profit is decreasing. At $\bar{q}$ profit is neither rising nor falling—it is at a maximum. Thus $\bar{q}$ is the firm's equilibrium output.

The profit-maximizing output $\bar{q}$ is that output at which revenue exceeds cost and the total cost curve is parallel to the total revenue curve. At this point, that is, the two curves have the same slope. The slope of the total revenue curve at any level of output is the marginal revenue associated with that level of output. The slope of the total cost curve at any level of output is the marginal cost associated with that level of output. Thus at an output of $\bar{q}$, marginal cost is equal to marginal revenue. The output $\bar{q}$ of Figure 5–3 corresponds to the output $\bar{q}$ in Figure 5–2. Notice that at an output of q^0 in Figure 5–3 the two curves are also parallel. Here, however, costs are greater than revenue. Moreover, it should be clear that the difference between costs and revenue is larger at q^0 than at any

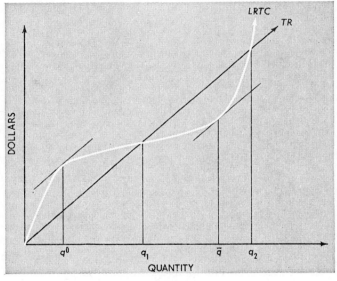

FIGURE 5–3

other quantity in the vicinity of q^0. At this output profits are a minimum. The output q^0 in Figure 5–3 corresponds to the output q^0 in Figure 5–2.

The reader should extend the analysis of Figure 5–3 by showing the appropriate short-run total cost curve and using that curve to establish $\bar{q}$ as the short-run profit-maximizing output.

Perfect Competition

A market is said to be *perfectly competitive* if (*a*) it is purely competitive, (*b*) all firms (in or out of the market) have complete knowledge of profits being earned by firms in the market, and (*c*) all firms (in or out of the market) are free to enter (or leave) the market. We will assume that any two firms producing a given commodity face the same cost functions.[2]

A perfectly competitive market is, among other things, purely competitive. Accordingly any position of equilibrium for a firm in a perfectly competitive market must at least satisfy the conditions for equilibrium of a purely competitive firm. *Given* the firm's revenue functions and cost functions, the output for which the firm's profit will be a maximum will not be changed by the fact that other firms know what profits are, nor by the fact that these other firms are free to enter the market. Suppose that a perfectly com-

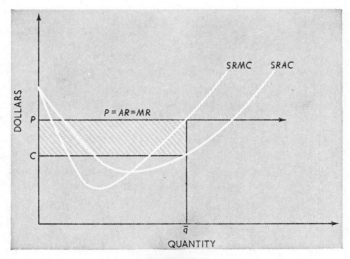

FIGURE 5–4

petitive firm faces the average revenue curve, $P = AR = MR$, of Figure 5–4. Suppose further that the firm has some fixed plant such that its short-run average cost curve and its short-run marginal cost curve are as shown (*SRAC* and *SRMC* respectively) in Figure 5–4. Then the firm will maximize its profits by producing and selling a

---

[2] This assumption will simplify our presentation, but it is in no way essential to our analysis. If we did not make this assumption we would need to take frequent explicit notice of the phenomenon of economic rent. To clarify what economic rent is, consider a firm possessed of a particularly clever file clerk. So efficiently does this unique clerk run the firm's filing system that he is able to observably lower the firm's costs below those of firms less fortunate in their choice of file clerks. This difference in costs is an economic rent attributable to the very productive file clerk. Any differences in costs between firms could be accounted for in terms of such economic rents. Rather than be concerned with such matters, we shall assume the file clerks, *et al.*, are much the same the market over. The cost of a factor (i.e., file clerk) is here taken to be what it can get elsewhere, its opportunity cost.

quantity $\bar{q}$. If the firm's long-run cost curves are such that it would continue to produce $\bar{q}$ if all factors of production were variable, then the firm will be quite content (under our behavioral assumption) to sit tight so long as it is unmolested and things (cost and revenue things) stay as they are.

In a perfectly competitive market it is easy to see that things will not in general stay as they are. The firm in Figure 5–4 is onto a good thing. It is making abnormal profits. Costs include payments to all factors of production, including management, entrepreneurship, and what have you. The firm's average cost curve shows how much it costs the firm per unit to produce each level of output when it pays all that it needs to pay to employ all factors necessary to this production. Average costs include sufficient profits to keep the firm going (called *normal profits*). Thus if the firm gets revenue in excess of costs, it is making more than enough to pay all those involved for what they are doing. It is making profits in excess of the normal profits that the owners involved could expect to earn in some other pursuit. In Figure 5–4 the per-unit cost of producing $\bar{q}$ is C. The revenue per unit gained from the sale of $\bar{q}$ is P. On each unit sold the firm realizes an excess or abnormal profit of $P - C$. By selling $\bar{q}$ units the firm realizes a total abnormal profit equal to the shaded area in Figure 5–4. Since this firm operates in a perfectly competitive market, other firms are aware of these abnormal profits and are free to enter the market and try to get a slice of abnormal profits for themselves. Moreover, since firms maximize profits, firms will tend to enter this market where profits are greater than normally can be achieved. In order to ascertain the effect that such entry will have on the situation facing firms in the perfectly competitive market, we must determine the effect that entry will have on the market price and on costs.

The Determination of Competitive Prices[3]

In competitive markets (both purely competitive and perfectly competitive) firms take prices as given. The obvious question is, given by whom or by what? If firms do not determine prices, how are prices determined? We have discussed this topic above in Chapter 2. There we determined the set of prices which would lead consumers to demand exactly the set of commodities that existed (we called this set the equilibrium set of prices). Later in Chapter 2 we discussed partial equilibrium analysis. We showed that (under appropriate circumstances) if all prices save one were to take on

---

[3] Before beginning this section the reader would be well advised to review that section of Chapter 2 which deals with the relationship between general equilibrium and partial equilibium analysis.

their equilibrium values then, substituting these values into the demand functions, we could find the equilibrium value of the last price by solving any one of equations (1) of Chapter 2. In the current discussion we will follow this procedure. In particular, under the supposition that all other prices are set at their equilibrium values, we will use the demand and supply information about the competitive market under consideration to determine, for the commodity there traded, a price such that consumers will choose to purchase precisely as much as firms will choose to supply. In a later chapter we will return to the discussion of the general equilibrium of the entire economic system.

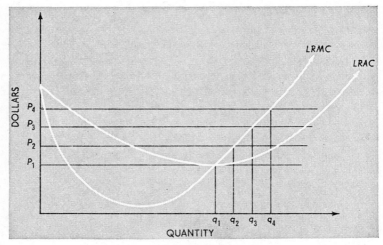

FIGURE 5–5

In the introduction to this part of the book we defined the demand curve for a commodity. For competitive firms we may define a supply curve. Taking all prices other than that of the commodity under consideration (i.e., the commodity traded in the particular competitive market under discussion) as fixed (as their equilibrium values[4]), this supply curve shows the quantity that will maximize the firm's profit at each alternative value of the price of the commodity that it sells. There will be one such supply curve for each firm, and the sum of all these curves will be the supply curve for the commodity.

In order to see how the profit-maximizing output of a competi-

----

[4] In fact all other prices need only be fixed at some levels, however, if the price that we determine for the competitive market is to be the true equilibrium price, then all other prices must be at their equilibrium levels. See Chapter 2.

tive firm varies with the market price facing the firm, let us reconstruct part of one of the diagrams we have used above (Figure 5–2) to determine the firm's profit-maximizing output. As one might suspect, the profit-maximizing output of a firm will vary differently with price in the long run than it will in the short run. We will show the firm's long-run supply curve. In Figure 5–5 the firm's long-run average cost curve and long-run marginal cost curves are appropriately labeled. At any price below P_1 the firm cannot earn normal profits. Accordingly, below this price it will supply nothing in the long run. At a price of P_1 the firm maximizes its profit by supplying q_1 units. At P_2 the firm will supply q_2 units.

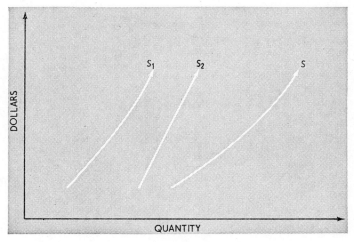

FIGURE 5–6

At P_3 it supplies q_3, and at P_4 it supplies q_4. In general, as the price given to the firm varies upward from P_1, the long-run profit-maximizing output increases along the firm's long-run marginal cost curve. The long-run supply curve for a competitive firm coincides with that portion of the long-run marginal cost curve that lies above the long-run average cost curve. If the reader will consider Figure 4–12 of Chapter 4 and determine how output will vary as prices vary in the short run, he will see that the short-run supply curve for a competitive firm coincides with that portion of the short-run marginal cost curve that lies above the average variable cost curve.

Suppose, for purposes of exposition, that there are two firms in a given competitive market and that they have the supply curves S_1 and S_2 shown in Figure 5–6. Then the supply curve for the market will be the horizontal sum of S_1 and S_2 labeled S in Figure 5–6. Under our supposition that all firms have the same cost curves S_1 would, of course, coincide with S_2 and S would simply be twice S_1.

In the competitive market for commodity i[5] there exists a supply curve showing the total quantity forthcoming at each price, P_i, when all firms in the market are in equilibrium supplying that quantity which maximizes their profits at each price. From the theory of consumer equilibrium, we may derive the market demand curve for commodity i. This curve shows the total quantity purchased at each price, P_i, when all consumers are allocating their expenditure in such a way as to maximize their utility. At a price

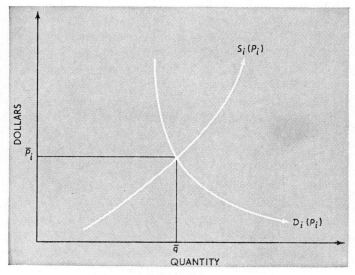

FIGURE 5–7

for commodity i at which the market supply curve intersects the market demand curve, firms will maximize their profits by supplying exactly the quantity which, when properly distributed, will allow every consumer to maximize his utility subject to his budget restraint. This equilibrium price is shown in Figure 5–7 as $\overline{P}_i$, where $S_i(P_i)$ is the market supply curve for commodity i and $D_i(P_i)$ is the market demand curve for commodity i.

For $S_i(P_i)$ and $D_i(P_i)$ to be defined as functions of the single variable P_i, all prices other than P_i must be fixed at some levels, $P_1^0, P_2^0, \ldots, P_{i-1}^0, P_{i+1}^0, \ldots, P_n^0$. Suppose the price set $P_1^0, \ldots, P_{i-1}^0, \overline{P}_i, P_{i+1}^0, \ldots, P_n^0$ is such that in *all* markets the

---

[5] We include the subscript i to explicitly draw the reader's attention to the fact that we are discussing *one* of n commodities.

quantities demanded (by utility-maximizing consumers) are equal to the quantities supplied (by profit-maximizing firms), then $\overline{P}_i$ is said to be the equilibrium price for commodity i (see Chapter 2). What this amounts to is what was discussed in Chapter 2. If all prices except one (i.e., P_i) are set at their equilibrium values, then we may use any supply and demand equation (i.e., $D_i = S_i$) to determine the equilibrium value of the remaining price. If $S_i(P_i)$ and $D_i(P_i)$ were constructed as of some nonequilibrium price set, $P_1^*, \ldots, P_{i-1}^*, P_{i+1}^*, \ldots, P_n^*$, then the value P_i^* such that $D_i(P_i^*) = S_i(P_i^*)$ would, by this equality, clear the market for commodity i at the given price set, but it would not, in general, be the equilibrium value $\overline{P}_i$. This is so for two reasons: varying any prices other than P_i will shift $S_i(P_i)$ and $D_i(P_i)$ (since the supply *function* and demand *function* depend upon the other prices) so that a different point of intersection would result, and the price set $P_1^*, \ldots, P_{i-1}^*, P_i^*, P_{i+1}^*, \ldots, P_n^*$ will clear the market for commodity i (since P_i^* is so determined given the other prices) but it will not, in general, clear the markets for other commodities. To rid ourselves of these complications we will assume, unless otherwise stated, that whenever we are discussing partial equilibrium analysis, the prices of all commodities, other than the one under discussion, are set at their equilibrium levels.

The Effect of Entry on the Perfectly Competitive Firm

We are now in a position to see what will happen to the price facing the perfectly competitive firm earning abnormal profits as depicted in Figure 5–4. It should be mentioned that the firm may be subjected to more than price changes alone. As new firms enter the market they might bid up the costs of factors of production. Thus not only will the average revenue–marginal revenue curve of Figure 5–4 shift, but the cost curves of the firm may shift as well. Having mentioned this possibility we will abstract from it. The form of our analysis would not be changed by shifts in the firm's cost curves that arise as the costs of factors are bid up by new firms. Thus there is no gain in introducing such complications. Accordingly we assume that as firms enter the industry the costs of factors remain constant.

In Figure 5–8(i) we again show the equilibrium position of a competitive firm earning excess profits. In Figure 5–8(ii) the market demand and supply curves are drawn. Originally the market curves intersect at the price P_1 which results in the firm's earning abnormal profits. At the market-clearing price, P_1, the firm will maximize its profit by producing q_1 units of output. At this level of production it costs the firm C_1 per unit to produce goods that it sells at P_1 per unit. Thus the firm will be earning excess profits. By the defining characteristics of perfectly competitive markets these excess profits will tempt new firms to enter the market. The result of this entry will be that at each price more of the commodity will be offered for sale (this may be seen from our derivation of the market supply curve above). The supply curve will shift to the right, say to S_2. This will result in a fall in the market-clearing price to P_2. At this price the firm will produce q_2 units at a cost of C_2 per unit. Clearly, since C_2 is less than P_2, this cannot be a position of long-run market equilibrium because the firm still earns excess profits. Thus new firms will still be tempted into the market. The market supply curve will continue to shift to

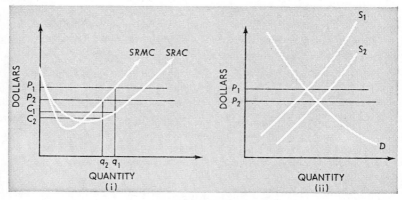

FIGURE 5–8

the right, and a new market-clearing price will be determined. If at this price the firm is earning excess profits, new firms will continue to enter, etc.

In order to examine the outcome of this process we consider Figure 5–9. In Figure 5–9 the firm's long-run average and marginal cost curves are shown. So long as the market price is such that the firm's average revenue curve lies above $\bar{P}$, then the firm and like firms will earn excess profits and other firms will be tempted into the market driving the price down. So long as the market price is such that the firm's average revenue curve is below $\bar{P}$, then the firm and like firms will earn less than normal profits. Accordingly they will leave the market seeking the normal profits which, by definition, may be earned elsewhere. In long-run equilibrium, under perfect competition, the market price must be such that firms earn exactly normal profits which will neither tempt new firms into the market nor drive old firms out. If this is not the case, then variations in the number of firms in the market will result causing the market equilibrium price to vary. In long-run equilibrium the perfectly competitive firm will produce $\bar{q}$ units and sell them at a price of $\bar{P}$.

Notice that in long-run perfectly competitive equilibrium the firm's average revenue curve will be tangent to the firm's long-run average cost curve. This is the reason that we could not depict long-run equilibrium in Figure 5–8. The cost curves shown there are short-run curves, and it is quite likely that the short-run average cost curve shown is not tangent to the long-run average cost curve at its minimum point. If the firm should begin at P_1 in Figure 5–8

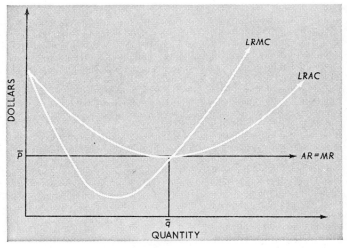

FIGURE 5–9

with a plant other than one which corresponds to the minimum point of the long-run average cost curve, then as firms enter (or leave) the industry, causing the price to come to $\bar{P}$ in Figure 5–9, the firm under discussion must adjust its plant size until ultimately it produces $\bar{q}$ in Figure 5–9 using the plant appropriate to that level of production. If it used another plant associated with a short-run average cost curve not tangent to *LRAC* of Figure 5–9 at output $\bar{q}$, then it would not be maximizing its profits at price $\bar{P}$, and only a price of $\bar{P}$ can be maintained.

One final point must be made before we turn to a mathematical analysis of the competitive firm. The firm does not *choose* to move from an excess profit-making position producing q_1 at price P_1 in Figure 5–8 to a normal profit-earning position producing $\bar{q}$ at price $\bar{P}$ in Figure 5–9; it is forced to do so by market conditions. Students sometimes become confused and argue that the firm will move to a production of $\bar{q}$ at price $\bar{P}$ in order to minimize its costs. This is clearly wrong for several reasons. To begin with, since the firm takes price as given, it could not set the price at $\bar{P}$ on its own. Secondly, the firm does not choose that output such that its costs are a minimum. It chooses the minimum costs associated with each level of output, and using this information it chooses that output for which profits are maximized. Finally notice that costs are not a minimum at point $\bar{q}$, average costs are. Costs would be a minimum at a zero level of output which is pretty dull. In a perfectly competitive market the firm is so beset by the ruinous rigors of competition that in long-run equilibrium an output of $\bar{q}$ at a price of $\bar{P}$ is the best that it can do, and normal profits are the best that it can earn. If the firm must be competitive, it is to its profit to be pure but imperfect.

MATHEMATICAL APPENDIX TO CHAPTER 5

A firm that buys all its inputs and sells its products in competitive markets will, by definition, take the prices of both the things that it buys and the things that it sells as given. In what follows, we will deal with a multiproduct firm, that is, a firm that produces and sells several different commodities. If all these commodities are sold under competitive conditions, we are able to deal with a multiproduct firm as easily as with a single-product firm. We will suppose that the firm produces m different commodities the quantities of which shall be designated $X_1, X_2, \ldots, X_m$. The reader who really insists upon thinking in terms of a single-product firm may suppose that m is equal to 1. Let us further suppose that in producing these m commodities the firm employs k factors of production. Let $m + k = n$ and designate the quantities of the k inputs $Y_{m+1}, Y_{m+2}, \ldots, Y_n$. Then, since the firm takes the prices of both its inputs and its products as given, its profit function will be given by

$$\Pi = \sum_{i=1}^{m} X_i P_i - \sum_{j=m+1}^{n} Y_i P_i \,,$$

where $P_1, \ldots, P_n$ are the given constant prices. For notational convenience define[6]

$$X_{m+1} \equiv - Y_{m+1} \,, \quad i = 1, \ldots, k \,.$$

The firm's profit function may then be written

(1) $$\Pi = \sum_{i=1}^{n} X_i P_i \,.$$

The firm wishes to choose a set of X's for which (1) will be a maximum. Notice, however, that just any set of X's will not do. The firm must choose its profit-maximizing set of X's so that the inputs chosen will produce the outputs chosen. The firm must choose a set of X's consistent with what can be produced. We may write the production function in implicit form as follows:

(2) $$f(X_1, \ldots, X_n) = 0 \,,$$

which designates the set of inputs and outputs which may feasibly be attained at the same time. If, for the set of X's, $\overline{X}_1, \ldots,$ $\overline{X}_m, \overline{X}_{m+1}, \ldots, \overline{X}_k$, it is true that

$$f(\overline{X}_1, \ldots, \overline{X}_m, \overline{X}_{m+1}, \ldots, \overline{X}_k) = 0 \,,$$

---

[6] Thus we consider inputs to be negative outputs.

173

then by using the inputs $\overline{X}_{m+1}, \ldots, \overline{X}_k$, it would be possible to produce the outputs $\overline{X}_1, \ldots, \overline{X}_m$.

The set of X's satisfying (2) is *defined* by the property that it is consistent with the production possibilities facing the firm. In order to determine the signs of the derivatives of the implicit production function (2) let us consider a simple example. Suppose that the firm produces a commodity X_1 by employing two factors of production Y_2 and Y_3. Writing the production function explicitly as in Chapter 3 we have

$$X_1 = X_1(Y_2, Y_3)$$

where

$$\frac{\partial X_1}{\partial Y_2} > 0, \quad \frac{\partial X_1}{\partial Y_3} > 0.$$

Rewriting this in implicit form we have

$$g(X_1, Y_2, Y_3) = X_1 - X_1(Y_2, Y_3) = 0$$

and

$$g_1 > 0, \quad g_2 = -\frac{\partial X_1}{\partial Y_2} < 0, \quad g_3 = -\frac{\partial X_1}{\partial Y_3} < 0.$$

Employing our notational convention

$$X_2 \equiv -Y_2, \quad X_3 \equiv -Y_3,$$

we have

$$g(X_1, -X_2, -X_3) = X_1 - X_1(-X_2, -X_3) = 0,$$

or

$$h(X_1, X_2, X_3) = 0.$$

Moreover $h_1 > 0$, and, since

$$\frac{\partial X_1}{\partial X_2} = -\frac{\partial X_1}{\partial Y_2}$$

and

$$\frac{\partial X_1}{\partial X_3} = -\frac{\partial X_1}{\partial Y_3},$$

$$h_2 = -\frac{\partial X_1}{\partial X_2} = -\left(-\frac{\partial X_1}{\partial Y_2}\right) > 0,$$

and

$$h_3 = -\frac{\partial X_1}{\partial X_3} = -\left(-\frac{\partial X_1}{\partial Y_2}\right) > 0.$$

Thus in the general implicit case of equation (2)

$$f_i > 0 , \quad i = 1, \ldots, n .$$

We shall also suppose that the implicit production function, equation (2), is such that

$$f_{ij} = f_{ji} , \quad i, j = 1, \ldots, n .$$

The firm chooses from the set of all X's satisfying (2), that set such that (1) is a maximum. That is, it maximizes (1) subject to (2). To this end, form the Lagrangian function

$$g = \sum_{i=1}^{n} X_i P_i + \mu \cdot f(X_1, \ldots, X_n) .$$

The first-order conditions for (1) to be a maximum subject to (2) are that the set of $n + 1$ equations

(3) $$\begin{cases} P_i + \mu f_i = 0 , & i = 1, \ldots, n , \\ f(X_1, \ldots, X_n) = 0 , \end{cases}$$

be simultaneously satisfied. The second-order conditions for (1) to be a maximum subject to (2) are that the quadratic form

$$d^2 g = \mu d^2 f$$

be negative definite for all dX_i, $i = 1, \ldots, n$, not all zero such that the constraint (2) is satisfied. That will be for the set of dX_i, $i = 1, \ldots, n$, such that

(4) $$\sum_{i=1}^{n} f_i dX_i = 0 .$$

The first-order conditions for a maximum include

$$P_i + \mu f_i = 0 , \quad i = 1, \ldots, n .$$

Since $P_i > 0$ and $f_i > 0$ this implies that

$$\mu < 0 .$$

Thus, if $\mu d^2 f$ is negative definite under the constraint (2) then

$$d^2 f > 0$$

for all dX_i not all zero such that equation (4) is true. The conditions necessary and sufficient for this form to be *positive* definite under the constraint are

(5) $$\begin{vmatrix} 0 & f_1 & f_2 & f_k \\ f_1 & f_{11} & f_{12} & f_{1k} \\ \hdotsfor{4} \\ f_k & f_{k1} & f_{k2} & f_{kk} \end{vmatrix} < 0 , \quad k = 2, \ldots, n .$$

Call this determinant F when $k = n$ and let F_{ij} be the cofactor of f_{ij} in F.

To determine the comparative statics properties of the theory of profit maximization for competitive markets, we differentiate conditions (3) with respect to some price, P_r. The results may be written

$$\sum_{j=1}^{n} f_j \frac{\partial X_j}{\partial P_r} = 0 ,$$

$$-\frac{P_i}{\mu^2} \frac{\partial \mu}{\partial P_r} + \sum_{j=1}^{n} f_{ij} \frac{\partial X_j}{\partial P_r} = 0 , \qquad i = 1, \dots , n \neq r ,$$

$$-\frac{P_r}{\mu^2} \frac{\partial \mu}{\partial P_r} + \sum_{j=1}^{n} f_{rj} \frac{\partial X_j}{\partial P_r} = -\frac{1}{\mu} .$$

Solving this system of equations by Cramer's rule[7] and making use of the fact that conditions (3) imply

$$-\frac{P_i}{\mu^2} = \frac{f_i}{\mu} ,$$

we get

(6)
$$\frac{\partial X_s}{\partial P_r} = -\frac{F_{rs}}{\mu F} .$$

a) By conditions (5) and the assumption that $F \neq 0$ we have $F_{rr} < 0$ and $F < 0$. This with $\mu < 0$ yields

(7)
$$\frac{\partial X_r}{\partial P_r} = -\frac{F_{rr}}{\mu F} > 0 .$$

If commodity r is an output, the quantity that the firm will produce of it will increase when its price increases. If commodity r is an input then since $X_r = -Y_r$, the quantity of r used in the production process will fall when its price increases.

b) Since $f_{ij} = f_{ji}$, $F_{ij} = F_{ji}$, $i, j = 1, 2, \dots , n$, so that

(8)
$$\frac{\partial X_s}{\partial P_r} = \frac{\partial X_r}{\partial P_s} .$$

Since X_s may represent either the output of a commodity or minus the input of a factor, equation (8) has several interpretations. If, for example, commodity s is produced by the firm and commodity r is used in the production process, then (8) may be written

$$\frac{\partial X_s}{\partial P_r} = -\frac{\partial Y_r}{\partial P_s} .$$

---

[7] We assume that $F \neq 0$, i.e., that we have a *regular* maximum.

This implies, among other things, that if the output of commodity s decreases when the price of input r rises, then more of input r will be employed when the price of output s increases. Interpretation of (8) when both s and r are outputs or when both are inputs should be clear to the reader from the similarity of (8) with symmetry properties derived in earlier chapters.

   c) The determinant F is of the form

$$F = \left| \begin{array}{c|c} 0 & f_i \\ \hline f_i & f_{ij} \end{array} \right| .$$

In view of (6) and (8)

$$\sum_{s=1}^{n} P_s \frac{\partial X_s}{\partial P_r} = - \sum_{s=1}^{n} \frac{P_s}{\mu} \frac{F_{rs}}{F} = \sum_{s=1}^{n} P_s \frac{\partial X_r}{\partial P_s}$$

and

$$\frac{P_s}{\mu} = - f_s$$

so that

(9)
$$\sum_{s=1}^{n} P_s \frac{\partial X_s}{\partial P_r} = \frac{1}{F} \sum_{s=1}^{n} f_s F_{rs} = 0$$

by alien cofactors. Also

(10)
$$\sum_{s=1}^{n} P_s \frac{\partial X_r}{\partial P_s} = 0 .$$

Result (10) would be difficult to test since it would require observations of the firm's adjustment to n price changes. Result (9) on the other hand would require observation of all the firm's quantity reactions to a *given* price change only and could quite feasibly be tested.

   d) As discussed in the mathematical appendix to Chapter 1 the second-order conditions for a constrained maximum imply that the substitution effects of consumer equilibrium theory are the elements of a negative definite quadratic form. Exactly similarly, conditions (5) imply that

$$- \frac{1}{\mu} \sum_{r=1}^{m} \sum_{s=1}^{m} \frac{F_{rs}}{F} Z_r Z_s > 0 , \qquad m < n .$$

Thus the terms

$$- \frac{1}{\mu} \frac{F_{rs}}{F}$$

are the elements of a *positive* definite quadratic form. This yields

$$
\begin{vmatrix} \dfrac{\partial X_r}{\partial P_r} & \dfrac{\partial X_s}{\partial P_r} \\[2mm] \dfrac{\partial X_r}{\partial P_s} & \dfrac{\partial X_s}{\partial P_s} \end{vmatrix} > 0 \,, \qquad
\begin{vmatrix} \dfrac{\partial X_r}{\partial P_r} & \dfrac{\partial X_s}{\partial P_r} & \dfrac{\partial X_\tau}{\partial P_r} \\[2mm] \dfrac{\partial X_r}{\partial P_s} & \dfrac{\partial X_s}{\partial P_s} & \dfrac{\partial X_\tau}{\partial P_s} \\[2mm] \dfrac{\partial X_r}{\partial P_\tau} & \dfrac{\partial X_s}{\partial P_\tau} & \dfrac{\partial X_\tau}{\partial P_\tau} \end{vmatrix} > 0 \,, \qquad \ldots, \text{etc.} \,,
$$

so that

$$
(11) \qquad \frac{\partial X_r}{\partial P_r}\frac{\partial X_s}{\partial P_s} - \frac{\partial X_s^2}{\partial P_r} > 0 \,,
$$

and so on for larger determinants, the elements of which are the firm's quantity adjustments to price changes.

The reader's attention is drawn to the similarity of the results of this appendix to those of earlier mathematical appendices. The reasons for this similarity have already been discussed in previous chapters. As with the theory of cost minimization, no income type effect arises in the theory of competitive profit maximization because no price type terms enter the implicit production function constraint. We have also attached no economic significance to the Lagrange multiplier, μ. This multiplier is equal to the rate of change of the function we are maximizing with respect to a change in the constraint. Thus in the current context With its implicit production constraint, this simply leads to a restatement of the first n of equations (3). Note that the results derived in this appendix refer to the firm's *profit-maximizing* adjustment to price changes. There is no assumption like that in the mathematical appendix to Chapter 3 that the firm holds its output constant.

SELECTED BIBLIOGRAPHY

HENDERSON, J. M., AND QUANDT, R. E. *Microeconomic Theory*. New York: McGraw-Hill, Inc., 1958.

HICKS, J. R. *Value and Capital*. 2d ed. Oxford: Clarendon Press, 1946.

LEFTWICH, R. H. *The Price System and Resource Allocation*. Rev. ed. New York: Holt, Rinehart & Winston, 1960.

MARSHALL, A. *Principles of Economics*. 8th ed. London: Macmillan Co., 1920.

SAMUELSON, P. A. *Foundations of Economic Analysis*. Cambridge, Mass.: Harvard University Press, 1948.

STIGLER, G. J. *The Theory of Price*. Rev. ed. New York: Macmillan Co., 1952.

Chapter 6

MONOPOLISTIC MARKETS

It's the syme the whole world over,
It's the poor what gets the blyme,
While the rich 'as all the plysure,
Now, ain't it a blinkin' shyme
—"It's the Syme the Whole World Over"*

The word "monopolist" means, literally, "single seller," and it is usual to suppose that a monopolistic firm is one which is alone in selling the commodity that it deals in. It is not the loneliness of the seller, however, which makes the behavior of the monopolistic firm different from that of the competitive firm. Rather it is the fact that when the monopolist increases the quantity that he offers to sell, the price that he is able to charge for each unit that he sells falls. It is conceivable that a single seller (perhaps a regulated seller) would find himself unable to change his price and able to sell all that he chose to at the given price. That is, a single seller could be purely competitive.

> **Definition:** *A monopolist is a single seller who does not take price as given.*

The average revenue curve for the monopolistic firm is the inverse of the market demand curve for the commodity that it sells. We will continue to suppose that this demand curve is negatively sloped. Thus the average revenue curve of a monopolist will slope downward from left to right as *AR* in Figure 6–1. When the quantity sold increases, the price per unit falls. The average revenue associated with a level of sales will be lower the larger the level of sales.

The marginal revenue curve associated with *AR* of Figure 6–1 must lie below *AR* for familiar reasons. Since *AR* is always falling,

---

* "Its the Syme the Whole World Over" is, to the best of my knowledge, in the public domain. The version quoted here is from Carl Sandburg, *The American Songbag* (New York: Harcourt, Brace & World, Inc., 1927).

MR must always lie below it causing it to fall. Since no revenue will be earned if nothing is sold, the marginal revenue curve will cut the dollars axis at the same point as the average revenue curve (see Chapter 4). Thus the marginal revenue curve will share a dollars intercept with the average revenue curve and will lie below the average revenue curve at all other levels of quantity sold. Such a marginal revenue curve is depicted in Figure 6–1 as *MR*. On the basis of these curves it is a simple matter to establish the nature of the firm's total revenue curve. As mentioned above, no revenue is to

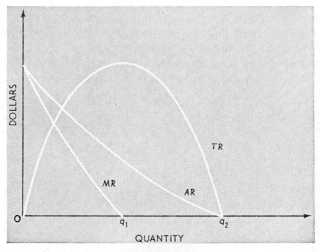

FIGURE 6–1

be gained or lost by selling nothing, so that the total revenue curve will pass through the origin. The marginal revenue curve shows the slope of the total revenue curve at each level of output. Where *MR* is positive the total revenue curve will be positively sloped. Thus, starting at the origin the total revenue curve, *TR*, rises to the right until sales reach a level of q_1. At q_1, *MR*, the slope of the total revenue curve is zero. Accordingly, at this quantity *TR* is flat; it is at a maximum. To the right of q_1, *MR* (which we have not extended beyond q_1) would be negative, so that *TR*, having a negative slope, would fall. The total revenue associated with any level of sales is equal to the quantity sold multiplied by the price per unit (average revenue). At an output of q_2 the price per unit is zero. As a result, the total revenue associated with sales of q_2 must be zero. The total revenue curve must start at the origin, rise monotonically to a maximum at a quantity q_1, and fall thereafter to cut the quantity axis at sales of q_2. Such a curve is shown as *TR* in Figure 6–1.

The average revenue curve of the firm may also be called the demand curve as discussed above. In accordance with the definition of elasticity given in the mathematical appendix to Chapter 1, the own-price elasticity of demand would be given by $-\dfrac{P}{q}\dfrac{dq}{dP}$. In connection with the theory of monopoly, it can be shown that so long as the elasticity of demand is greater than 1, total revenue will rise when the quantity sold increases (in this event demand is said to be *elastic*). If the elasticity of demand is equal to 1 (demand is then said to be of *unitary elasticity*), an increase in quantity will not change total revenue. If the elasticity of demand is less than 1 (called *inelastic* demand), then total revenue will fall as the quantity sold increases.[1] Thus in Figure 6–1, to the left of q_1 demand is elastic, at q_1 demand is of unitary elasticity, and to the right of q_1 demand is inelastic. Notice that this information may be gained by examination of the marginal revenue curve alone, so that while the concept of elasticity of demand may be of interest and may be convenient for certain purposes, it is not essential to our analysis, and we will not discuss it further.

We will suppose that the monopolistic firm faces cost curves of the forms derived in Chapters 3 and 4. These are shown in Figure 6–2. In particular *LRAC* is the firm's long-run average cost curve and *LRMC* is the long-run marginal cost curve. As in Figure 6–1, we depict *AR* the firm's average revenue curve and *MR* its marginal revenue curve. We consider a firm planning to begin production and trying to determine what output it should produce in order to maximize its profits. Accordingly it may vary the quantity that it will employ of all inputs, and the relevant cost functions are the long-run cost curves. Having determined a profit-maximizing output the firm will then need to construct an appropriate plant which will have a set of short-run cost curves associated with it.

At an output of q_1 the long-run marginal cost curve cuts the marginal revenue curve from below. The price that the firm may charge at this output is shown by *AR* to be P_1. At this price and

---

[1] These propositions may be established in several ways—perhaps the most informative of which is as follows. Total revenue is given by $q \cdot P(q)$, where q is quantity sold and $P(q)$ is the average revenue curve. Thus marginal revenue, *MR* is given by

$$MR = \frac{d}{dq}[q \cdot P(q)] = P + q\frac{dP}{dq}$$

$$= P\left(1 + \frac{q}{P}\frac{dP}{dq}\right) = P\left(1 - \frac{1}{-\dfrac{P}{q}\dfrac{dq}{dP}}\right).$$

Thus if the elasticity of demand, $-\dfrac{P}{q}\dfrac{dq}{dP}$, is more than 1, *MR* must be positive since P is positive. If *MR* is positive, total revenue is increasing, etc.

output, profit will be a maximum. This may be easily seen by considering the marginal increment to profits made by each addition to output. At outputs to the left of q_1, marginal revenue exceeds marginal cost so that each additional unit of output adds to the firm's total profits. Additional units continue to add to the firm's profits until a level q_1 is reached, at which output, the rate of change of profits with respect to a change in output, is zero. This can be seen by the fact that at this level the rate of change of cost

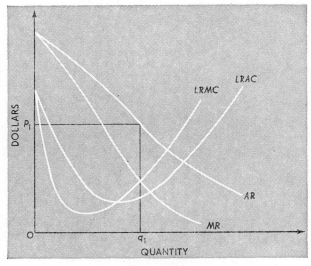

FIGURE 6–2

with respect to output is equal to the rate of change of revenue with respect to output, that is, marginal cost equals marginal revenue. At levels of output and sales in excess of q_1, marginal cost is greater than marginal revenue. Each additional unit adds more to costs than it does to income. As a result, to the right of q_1, profits decrease as quantity increases. As was seen to be the case with competitive firms, for a monopolist, profits will be a maximum at that output at which the marginal cost curve cuts the marginal revenue curve from below.[2]

In order to utilize this information the firm must construct a plant designed to produce q_1 units. This plant will have a short-run average cost curve associated with it, and this curve will be tangent to the *LRAC* of Figure 6–2 at point q_1. As discussed above (see

---

[2] Note that, marginal cost being positive throughout the relevant range, this means that the monopolist will always produce where its demand curve is elastic.

Chapters 4 and 5), the fact that this particular short-run average cost curve is tangent to *LRAC* at the output q_1 means that the short-run marginal cost curve associated with this short-run average curve will cut *LRMC* at an output of q_1. Thus, having built the plant appropriate to an output of q_1, the firm, so long as the revenue curves facing it hold still, will maximize its profits by utilizing this plant to build the output for which it was designed. We have not drawn in these short-run curves, since they would be exactly like

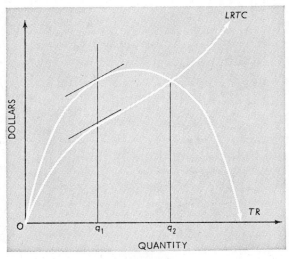

FIGURE 6–3

those drawn in Chapter 5. The reader, so inclined, might seek amusement by reproducing and completing Figure 6–2.

As with competitive firms, we may establish the equilibrium output of a monopolist by examination of his total revenue and total cost curves only. In Figure 6–3 we have the firm's total revenue curve, *TR*, and its long-run total cost curve, *LRTC*. The profit-maximizing output will be that output for which the difference between revenue and costs is greatest, and revenue exceeds costs. This will be the output for which the vertical distance between *LRTC* and *TR* is greatest, and *TR* is above *LRTC*. Revenues exceed costs at quantities below q_2, and costs exceed revenues at larger quantities; thus the equilibrium quantity will be less than q_2. At quantities below q_1, *TR* is above *LRTC* and the former is steeper than the latter. Thus, in this region, the two curves are going apart, profits are increasing. Between q_1 and q_2, *TR* exceeds *LRTC*, but the latter has a greater slope so that the curves are coming together —profits are positive but decreasing. At an output of q_1, revenue is greater than cost and the slope of TR is equal to that of $LRTC$. Profits are neither falling nor rising; they are at a maximum. Since the slope of TR is marginal revenue and that of $LRTC$ is the long-run marginal cost, q_1 in Figure 6–3 corresponds to q_1 in Figure 6–2. The reader may reproduce Figure 6–3 and sketch in an appropriate short-run total cost curve showing that in the short-run also q_1 will be the profit-maximizing output.

The reader should, by this time, have noticed that the only difference between our analysis of a single purely competitive firm and that of a single monopolist is that the latter has a negatively sloped demand curve while the former has a horizontal demand curve. The form of the analysis is unchanged by this difference. In what follows we will continue to analyze monopolistic markets along lines similar to those employed in our analysis of competitive markets.

Monopolistic Competition

Consider a large group of markets for closely competing commodities in which all firms are monopolistic. Let the number of firms be large enough that the action of any *single* firm will not significantly affect the profit position of any other single firm. Suppose that all firms in or out of this set of markets have complete knowledge of the profits earned by firms in the markets. Suppose further that firms are free to enter or to leave the set of markets. Then the firms in this set of markets will be competing monopolists, or, more traditionally, they will be said to be engaged in *monopolistic competition*. It should be obvious to the reader that monopolistic competition bears the same relation to monopoly that perfect competition bears to pure competition. Monopolistic competition is simply a special sort of monopoly. Monopolistic competition is a relationship between closely competing single seller markets. New firms will create, by their entry into production, new markets which will become additions to the set of closely competing markets. Firms engaged in monopolistic competition will be said to be monopolistically competitive.

A monopolistically competitive firm is, among other things, monopolistic, the price that it may charge for the good that it sells will fall as the quantity sold increases. Thus the equilibrium of the firm must at least satisfy the conditions for equilibrium for a monopolist. Suppose that a monopolistically competitive firm is at a position of monopolistic equilibrium, as q_1 in Figure 6–4. It costs the firm C_1 per unit to produce q_1 units of output, and demand conditions are such that this quantity will command a price of P_1 per unit. Since P_1 is greater than C_1 and since C_1 includes normal profits, the firm is realizing $P_1 - C_1$ in abnormal profits for each unit that it sells. Because it sells q_1 units, the firm will earn abnormal profits equal to the shaded area of Figure 6–4.

At this position, producing q_1 units and selling them at a price P_1, the firm, if its short-run plant is appropriate to an output of q_1, is perfectly content to remain as it is. In fact, given the extent of its abnormal profits, the firm would, more than likely, be elated to be allowed to stay put. However, since the firm is engaged in monopolistic competition, other firms are aware of its enviable profit

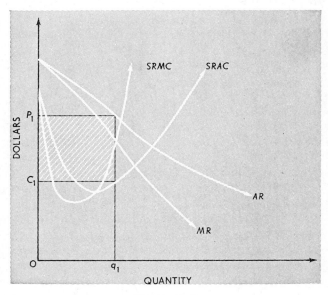

FIGURE 6–4

position and, moreover, they are able to enter into close competition with the abnormally profitable firm. Because these other firms are profit-maximizers at least some of them will begin to compete with this profitable firm in order to become abnormally profitable themselves. In general this will require that they vary their use of all or nearly all factors of production. Entry is a long-run proposition. Accordingly we will refer to the situation shown in Figure 6–4 as one of *short-run equilibrium* for the monopolistically competitive firm.

Price Determination in Monopolistic Markets

Before turning to an examination of the results of entry in monopolistically competitive markets, we will briefly discuss the determination of equilibrium prices in monopolistic markets generally. To begin with, note that equilibrium prices in monopolistic markets cannot be determined by supply and demand as in competitive markets because no supply curve can be defined for a monopolist. To see why this is true consider what a supply function or supply curve is. The supply function for a firm shows for any set of prices, what quantity the firm will offer for sale in order to maximize its profits. Taking the prices of all other commodities as given at their equilibrium values, a firm's supply *curve* for commodity i shows what quantity of commodity i the firm will offer to sell in order to maximize its profits at each alternative level of price P_i. For a competitive firm this curve is perfectly well defined. Given any price, there are an infinity of possible levels of sales open to the firm. From this infinite set the firm chooses that quantity that maximizes its profit, and this is the quantity supplied at the given price.

For a monopolistic firm the supply curve is not so easy to come by. The firm's average revenue curve associates a unique quantity which can be sold with any given price. Moreover, given an arbitrary price, it is not likely that a profit-maximizing output exists consistent with that price. This is clear if one considers any given price above P_1 in Figure 6–4. If the firm is to maximize its profits, it must produce at that quantity at which its marginal revenue is equal to its marginal cost. This will typically be a unique quantity (q_1 in Figure 6–4). Associated with any price there is also a unique quantity, and (in Figure 6–4) it usually is not q_1. For a monopolistic firm we are not able to associate a profit-maximizing output with *each* possible level of price. In order to maximize its profits the monopolist chooses that output such that his marginal cost is equal to his marginal revenue. His average revenue curve associates a particular price with this output. He cannot charge a higher price than is shown by his average revenue curve, and if he is to maximize his profits, he will not charge a lower one. The equilibrium price then is that unique price associated with the profit-maximizing output by the average revenue curve, not one determined by the intersection of a supply curve and a demand curve. Notice, however, that in equilibrium the monopolist does supply a particular output and, moreover, he sets a price such that this quantity will just be purchased. Thus, even in monopolistic equilibrium, supply is equal to demand, although we are not able to utilize this fact alone in establishing where the equilibrium point will be.

The Effects of Entry in Monopolistic Competition

The monopolistically competitive firm whose situation is depicted in Figure 6–4 is in short-run equilibrium earning abnormally high profits. These abnormal profits will tempt other firms to engage in activities that compete closely with those of the profitable firm. As these new firms enter production they will presumably tempt some buyers away from older firms. Then, at each price, the older firms would find that they were able to sell less. Suppose that the firm was originally in short-run equilibrium with the average revenue curve AR_1 in Figure 6–5. Then since P_1 is greater than C_1 the firm will be realizing abnormal profits. This will result in the entry of new firms causing the original firm's average revenue

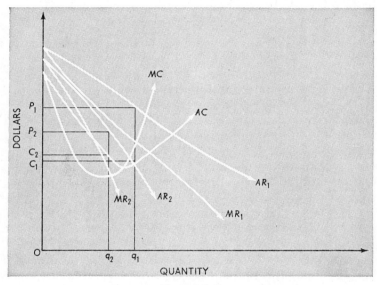

Figure 6–5

curve to shift to the left, say to AR_2 in Figure 6–5. This will result in a profit-maximizing output of q_2. This output has a per-unit cost of C_2 and a per-unit price of P_2 associated with it. P_2 being greater than C_2 this leaves the firm realizing abnormal profits which will continue to tempt in new firms. In fact, so long as the price associated with the firm's profit-maximizing output is greater than the per-unit cost associated with that output, new firms will be tempted into production and the firm's average revenue curve will continue to shift to the left. New firms will cease to enter into competition with existent monopolistically competitive firms only when a position such as that depicted in Figure 6–6 is reached.

If the firm faces an average revenue curve such as AR_1 in Figure 6–6 it will maximize its profits by producing $\bar{q}$ units and selling them at a price $\bar{P}$. Notice that the per-unit cost of producing $\bar{q}$ is $\bar{C} = \bar{P}$ so that no excess profits are being made and no new firms will be tempted into competition with the existing firm. Whenever some portion of the firm's average revenue curve lies above the firm's long-run average cost curve, there will exist levels of output (at which the profit-maximizing firm will operate) at which price exceeds per-unit costs and abnormal profits may be realized. Accordingly new firms will continue to be tempted into the production of commodities that compete with those of the monopolistic competitor until the latter's average revenue curve is shifted to a level at which no portion of it lies above the firm's long-run average

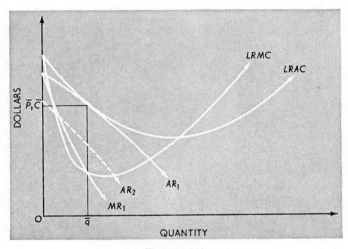

FIGURE 6-6

cost curve. Should this entry process go too far, an average revenue curve such as AR_2 in Figure 6-6 will result. This curve lies *below* LRAC at all levels of output. A firm faced with such an average revenue curve cannot realize normal profits at any output. In such circumstances firms will find it advantageous to quit production of closely competing commodities in order to earn normal profits elsewhere. Thus the average revenue curves of firms remaining in production will shift to the right. This shift will continue until firms in production earn at least normal profits.

If the average revenue curves of monopolistically competitive firms lie below the firms' long-run average cost curves, there will be an exodus of firms from the competing markets. If any portions of the average revenue curves lie above the firms' long-run average cost curves, new firms will enter the competing markets. Thus, the number of firms will remain constant and the average revenue curves of these firms will cease to shift about only if positions such as $\bar{q}$ in Figure 6–6 are reached. In this situation the average revenue curve of the monopolistically competitive firm is just tangent to the firm's long-run average cost curve. As shown in Chapter 4, when two average curves are tangent at a particular quantity, the marginal curves associated with them will intersect at that quantity. Thus in long-run equilibrium for a monopolistically competitive firm the firm's average revenue curve will be tangent to its long-run average cost curve and the firm will produce the output associated with the point of tangency because at that output marginal cost will equal marginal revenue. The firm will thus realize exactly normal profits.

I hope that the reader has been disturbed by this analysis, because something has been left unexplained. In general, different monopolistically competitive firms, even though they compete with each other, will not produce identical commodities. As a result they need not have identical cost curves (even abstracting from rent phenomena). What is to prevent a situation in which some competing firms make less than normal profits and other make extra profits? In such an event, do new firms enter production, or do old firms leave production? Clearly such a situation could develop. If firms are then to maximize profits, they will attempt to cut back on the production of competing commodities which are making less than normal profits and expand production of competing commodities more and more similar to those that are earning abnormally high profits. This process will continue until a situation is reached at which all firms are in long-run equilibrium as $\bar{q}$ in Figure 6–6. Should no such situation ever be reached, the firms will simply never get into long-run equilibrium.

Discriminating Monopoly

Suppose that a monopolistic firm finds that it is, in effect, supplying several different markets. That is, suppose that a monopolist finds that there are different groups of people buying the commodity that it sells and that these groups are somehow separated from, and do not trade with, each other so that it is possible for the monopolist to charge different prices to the different groups. A monopolistic firm in such a situation is said to be a *discriminating monopolist,* and the act of charging different groups of buyers different prices for the same commodity is called *price discrimination.* A classic example of this sort of thing would be a railroad serving several isolated communities. Different communities might be dependent upon the railroad to different degrees. Thus, one might be located on a navigable stream, another might be served by inadequate roads, and a third might be entirely dependent upon the railroad. Similarly, one might earn its livelihood by transporting its produce by rail while another might be relatively self-sufficient. Under these conditions the monopolist (the railroad) may be faced by several distinct and dissimilar demand functions for its product, one such function for each different group of buyers.

A monopolist faced with the possibility of charging different prices to different groups of buyers may find it to his profit so to do. In general such a monopolist's revenue function will be a sum of revenue functions, one for each of the groups facing him. He will be free to deal with these markets separately or collectively, whichever is most profitable. To deal with them collectively he would simply charge the same price in each market and satisfy the total demand at that price by supplying all that each market would buy at that price. In any case, in order to ascertain what total quantity he should offer for sale, how much of this quantity should be sold to each group (hereafter called submarkets), and at what price or prices, the monopolist must be able to consider simultaneously all the submarkets facing him.

In order to keep our analysis within easily manageable proportions we will consider a discriminating monopolist selling its output in two submarkets. Call the average revenue function associated with submarket 1 AR_1 and that associated with submarket 2 AR_2. Similarly let MR_1 denote the marginal revenue function of submarket 1 and MR_2 denote that of submarket 2. Suppose that a particular level of output is distributed between the two submarkets in such a way that the marginal revenue in one submarket exceeds that in the other. Then, irrespective of the level of costs, it is clear that profits will not be a maximum. This is true because by taking some output away from the submarket with the lower marginal revenue and selling it in the market with the higher marginal revenue the monopolist will increase his total revenue by the difference between the two marginal revenues. Thus if $MR_1 > MR_2$ by taking one unit of output from submarket 2 the firm foregoes revenue equal to MR_2. By then selling this unit of output in submarket 1 the firm gains revenue equal to MR_1 so that the resultant gain in revenue is positive. In order to gain the maximum revenue from a given total output, the firm must distribute this output to the various submarkets so that all the marginal revenues are equal. Thus a necessary condition for profit maximization by a discriminating monopolist is that his output be distributed so that the marginal revenue gained from each submarket is the same.

The above considerations tell us how to distribute a given

output among the various submarkets. Two questions then remain open. What total quantity should the firm offer for sale, and what price should it charge in each submarket? To close these questions consider Figure 6–7. Let AR_1 and AR_2 represent the average revenue functions mentioned above, and MR_1 and MR_2 represent the associated marginal revenue functions. Since it is a necessary condition for equilibrium that $MR_1 = MR_2$, we may construct a curve showing the marginal revenue associated with each level of total output. At any level of output the marginal revenue which may be gained will equal that which may be gained either by selling the last unit of output in submarket 1 or by selling it in submarket

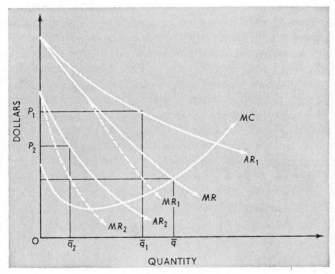

FIGURE 6–7

2. MR_1 shows what quantity sold in submarket 1 is associated with each level of marginal revenue. MR_2 shows the quantity sold in submarket 2 for each level of marginal revenue. Thus, at any level of marginal revenue if the marginal revenues earned in each submarket are to be equal, the total quantity sold will be that sold at that marginal revenue in submarket 1 plus the quantity sold at that level of marginal revenue in submarket 2. This is shown by the horizontal sum of MR_1 and MR_2, the solid line labeled MR in Figure 6–7.

If the firm is to maximize its profits, it must distribute its sales so that in each submarket the same marginal revenue is realized. If the same marginal revenue is realized in each submarket, then the marginal revenue associated with each level of total output is the curve designated MR in Figure 6–7. Thus if the firm is to maximize its profits, then MR, the horizontal sum of the marginal revenue curves for the various submarkets, will be its marginal revenue curve. As shown in previous discussion, the firm's profit will be a maximum when it produces and sells that output at which its marginal cost curve cuts its marginal revenue curve from below. Since the firm produces a single commodity, each level of total output will have a single marginal cost associated with it. In Figure 6–7 the firm's marginal cost curve is shown by the curve MC. Thus the profit-maximizing output will be $\bar{q}$.

This leaves us with two questions to answer. How should $\bar{q}$ be distributed between the two submarkets? What price should be charged in each submarket? Actually we have already answered the first of these questions. $\bar{q}$ should be distributed so that $MR_1 = MR_2$. Since MR is simply the horizontal sum of MR_1 and MR_2, when MR_1 and MR_2 are both equal to the level of MR associated with an output of $\bar{q}$ the outputs, $\bar{q}_1$ associated with this level of MR_1 and $\bar{q}_2$ associated with this level of MR_2 will sum to $\bar{q}$. Thus in Figure 6–7, $\bar{q}_1$ should be sold in submarket 1 and $\bar{q}_2$ sold in submarket 2. Once these quantities are determined, it is a simple matter indeed to ascertain the prices that should be charged in each submarket. $\bar{q}_1$ sold in submarket 1 will command a price of P_1 as is shown by the average revenue curve for submarket 1, AR_1. Similarly $\bar{q}_2$ sold in submarket 2 will, according to AR_2, command a price of P_2. The firm can get no higher prices for these levels of sales, and it would forego profits by accepting lower prices. Accordingly the firm will maximize its profits by producing $\bar{q}$ units of output, selling $\bar{q}_1$ of these units in submarket 1 at a price P_1 and $\bar{q}_2$ in submarket 2 at a price of P_2.

Since the discriminating monopolist produces a single commodity to be sold in several submarkets, it has a well-defined set of cost functions associating various costs with different levels of total output. Since the revenue gained from a given level of output will be less than it could be so long as the marginal revenues in different submarkets are not equal, we are able to define a marginal revenue curve for total output (by summing horizontally the marginal revenue curves for the various submarkets). This, with the firm's marginal cost curve, determines the level of total output that will maximize profits. Distributing this total output so that the marginal revenues in the various submarkets are equal, we ascertain what quantity is appropriate to each submarket. This information in conjunction with the various average revenue functions determines what prices should be charged in each submarket.

MATHEMATICAL APPENDIX TO CHAPTER 6

The competitive firm takes the price at which it can sell its output as given. If a firm is monopolistic the price that it may charge will depend upon the quantity that it means to sell. In any case, however, the *revenue* that the firm earns will depend upon the quantity that it produces and sells. The quantity that the firm produces will depend, through the production function (see Chapter 3), upon the quantities of inputs that it employs. Thus for *any* firm having a defined revenue function, this function may be written

$$(1) \qquad R = R[X_n(X_1, \ldots, X_{n-1})]$$

where R is revenue, X_n is the commodity that the firm produces and sells, and $X_1, \ldots, X_{n-1}$ are the inputs used in producing commodity X_n.

We may assume as in Chapter 3 that the monopolistic firm like the competitive firm discussed in Chapter 5 purchases its inputs competitively. That is, the firm takes the prices of its inputs as given. For any firm that purchases its inputs competitively the expenditure function may be written

$$(2) \qquad E = B + \sum_{i=1}^{n-1} X_i P_i$$

where B is some constant (possibly zero), X_i is as above, and P_i is the price of commodity (input) i. This linear expenditure function which associates a level of expenditure with each set of inputs and input prices should not be confused with the firm's cost function which associates a least cost with each level of output and which need not be linear.

Using equations (1) and (2) we may state the profit earned by any single-output firm that purchases its factors of production competitively as a function of the inputs used in production, and their prices.

$$(3) \qquad \Pi(X_1, \ldots, X_{n-1}, P_1, \ldots, P_{n-1}) = R[X_n(X_1, \ldots, X_{n-1})] - B$$
$$- \sum_{i=1}^{n-1} X_i P_i .$$

The profit-maximizing firm, given any set of input prices $P_1, \ldots, P_{n-1}$, will employ the factors $X_1, \ldots, X_{n-1}$ so that (3) is as large as possible.[3] Equation (3) may, in particular, describe the profit function of a single-product monopolistic firm which purchases its factors of production competitively.

Since the constraint that the output that the firm chooses to produce be consistent with the inputs that it chooses to employ is already built into the revenue portion of equation (3) (this is illustrated in footnote 3), the firm seeks an unconstrained maximum of equation (3). The first-order conditions for (3) to be a maximum are

$$\frac{dR}{dX_n}\frac{\partial X_n}{\partial X_i} = P_i, \quad i = 1, \ldots, n-1,$$

since

$$\frac{dR}{dX_n}\frac{\partial X_n}{\partial X_i} = \frac{\partial R}{\partial X_i} = R_i$$

we will write these first-order conditions

(4) $$R_i = P_i, \quad i = 1, \ldots, n-1,$$

where $R_i = R_i[X_n(X_1, \ldots, X_{n-1})]$.

The second-order conditions for profit to be a maximum are that

$$d^2\Pi = d^2R$$

be negative definite. Necessary and sufficient conditions for d^2R to be negative definite are that the principal minors of the determinant A,

(5)
$$R_{ii} < 0, \quad \begin{vmatrix} R_{ii} & R_{ij} \\ R_{ji} & R_{jj} \end{vmatrix} > 0, \quad \begin{vmatrix} R_{ii} & R_{ij} & R_{ik} \\ R_{ji} & R_{jj} & R_{jk} \\ R_{ki} & R_{kj} & R_{kk} \end{vmatrix} < 0, \ldots, \text{etc.} \quad i,j = 1, \ldots, n-1$$

---

[3] In the mathematical appendix to Chapter 5 we dealt with an m-product competitive firm. If m is equal to 1, it is easy to see that the analysis in that appendix was a special case of maximization of equation (3) here.

Maximize
$$X_n P_n - \sum_{i=1}^{n-1} Y_i P_i$$

subject to
$$X_n = X_n(Y_1, \ldots, Y_{n-1}).$$

Substituting the production constraint into the revenue function we get

Maximize
$$X_n(Y_1, \ldots, Y_{n-1}) \cdot P_n - \sum_{i=1}^{n-1} Y_i P_i$$

which is a special case of (3) where $R(X_n) = P_n X_n$ and $B = 0$.

alternate in sign as shown, where

$$A = |R_{ij}|, i, j = 1, \ldots, n - 1.$$

We also denote A_{ij} as the cofactor of R_{ij} in A. Notice that since we are working with an unconstrained maximum, A is simply the Hessian of $R[X_n(X_1, \ldots, X_{n-1})]$ and is not bordered. Also, we suppose that $A \neq 0$.

Conditions (4), the first-order conditions for profit to be a maximum, form a system of $n - 1$ equations which may be solved to express the $n - 1$ variables $X_1, \ldots, X_{n-1}$ as functions of the $n - 1$ prices, $P_1, \ldots, P_{n-1}$, as below

$$(6) \qquad X_i = X_i(P_1, \ldots, P_{n-1}), \quad i = 1, \ldots, n - 1.$$

These equations show the firm's demand for factors of production. In order to ascertain the nature of these factor demand functions we differentiate conditions (4) with respect to a particular price P_s. This yields $n - 1$ equations

$$\sum_{i=1}^{n-1} R_{ji} \frac{\partial X_i}{\partial P_s} = 0, \quad j = 1, \ldots, n - 1 \neq s,$$

$$\sum_{i=1}^{n-1} R_{si} \frac{\partial X_i}{\partial P_s} = 1,$$

in the $n - 1$ variables,

$$\frac{\partial X_1}{\partial P_s}, \ldots, \frac{\partial X_{n-1}}{\partial P_s},$$

which may be solved by Cramer's rule to yield

$$(7) \qquad \frac{\partial X_r}{\partial P_s} = \frac{A_{sr}}{A}, \quad r, s = 1, \ldots, n - 1.$$

1. It should be immediately obvious to the reader that the second-order conditions for profits to be maximized, conditions (5), imply that the sign of any principal minor of A of order $n - 2$ will be opposite to that of A itself which is a principal minor of order $n - 1$. Accordingly,

$$(8) \qquad \frac{\partial X_r}{\partial P_r} = \frac{A_{rr}}{A} < 0, \quad r, s = 1, \ldots, n - 1.$$

2. It is perhaps less obvious but no less true that conditions (5) imply (by the theorem on reciprocal determinants cited in the mathematical appendix to Chapter 1) that the terms A_{ij}/A are the elements of a negative definite quadratic form. Thus

$$\sum_{i=1}^{m} \sum_{j=1}^{m} \frac{A_{ij}}{A} \delta_i \delta_j < 0 , \qquad m < n - 1 .$$

This yields

(9) $\dfrac{A_{ii}}{A} < 0 , \qquad \begin{vmatrix} \dfrac{A_{ii}}{A} & \dfrac{A_{ij}}{A} \\ \dfrac{A_{ji}}{A} & \dfrac{A_{jj}}{A} \end{vmatrix} > 0 , \qquad \begin{vmatrix} \dfrac{A_{ii}}{A} & \dfrac{A_{ij}}{A} & \dfrac{A_{jk}}{A} \\ \dfrac{A_{ij}}{A} & \dfrac{A_{jj}}{A} & \dfrac{A_{jk}}{A} \\ \dfrac{A_{ki}}{A} & \dfrac{A_{kj}}{A} & \dfrac{A_{kk}}{A} \end{vmatrix} < 0 , \qquad \ldots , \text{etc.}$

The first of these inequalities with result (7) yields result (8) ; the second yields

(10) $\qquad \dfrac{\partial X_i}{\partial P_i} \dfrac{\partial X_j}{\partial P_j} - \dfrac{\partial X_i}{\partial P_j} \dfrac{\partial X_j}{\partial P_i} > 0 , \qquad i, j = 1, \ldots, n - 1 .$

The third yields a more complicated sum, etc.

3. It should not be at all obvious that $R_{ij} = R_{ji}$ for all i and all j, but we will show that it is nonetheless true.

$$R_{ji} = \frac{\partial^2 R}{\partial X_i \partial X_j} = \frac{\partial}{\partial X_i} \left(\frac{\partial R}{\partial X_j} \right) = \frac{\partial}{\partial X_i} \left(\frac{dR}{dX_n} \frac{\partial X_n}{\partial X_j} \right)$$

$$= \frac{dR}{dX_n} \cdot \frac{\partial^2 X_n}{\partial X_i \partial X_j} + \frac{\partial X_n}{\partial X_j} \frac{\partial}{\partial X_i} R_n[X_n(X_1, \ldots, X_{n-1})] ,$$

where

$$R_n[X_n(X_1, \ldots, X_{n-1})] = \frac{dR}{dX_n} .$$

$$\frac{\partial}{\partial X_i} R_n[X_n(X_1, \ldots, X_{n-1})] = \frac{dR_n}{dX_n} \frac{\partial X_n}{\partial X_i} = \frac{d^2 R}{dX_n^2} \frac{\partial X_n}{\partial X_i} .$$

Thus

$$R_{ji} = \frac{dR}{dX_n} \frac{\partial^2 X_n}{\partial X_i \partial X_j} + \frac{\partial X_n}{\partial X_j} \frac{\partial X_n}{\partial X_i} \frac{d^2 R}{dX_n^2} .$$

In the mathematical appendix to Chapter 3 we assumed that the production function

$$\Phi = \Phi(X_1, \ldots, X_n)$$

was such that $\Phi_{ij} = \Phi_{ji}$. In the above notation this would yield

$$\frac{\partial^2 X_n}{\partial X_i \partial X_j} = \frac{\partial^2 X_n}{\partial X_j \partial X_i} .$$

Thus

$$R_{ji} = R_{ij} ,$$

so that the determinant A is symmetrical and

$$A_{ij} = A_{ji}.$$

Accordingly

(11)
$$\frac{\partial X_r}{\partial P_s} = \frac{\partial X_s}{\partial P_r}, \qquad r, s = 1, \ldots, n - 1.$$

We have left to the reader the task of interpreting the empirical meaning of results (8), (10), and (11). If he finds this difficult he may refer to earlier mathematical appendices in which results of similar form have been interpreted. The results here, of course, refer to rates of changes of the profit-maximizing employment of various factors of production with respect to changes in various factor prices. The reader's attention is drawn to the fact that since the determinant A is not bordered we have not established any results by expanding A by alien cofactors. The results here derived hold for any firm having a defined revenue function and buying its inputs competitively.

Discriminating Monopoly

The discriminating monopolist produces a single commodity which he distributes between several submarkets so as to maximize his profits. Suppose that the firm is faced with n such submarkets. If q_i is the quantity sold in submarket i and $R_i(q_i)$ is the revenue function associated with the ith submarket, then the firm's profit function is given by

(12)
$$\sum_{i=1}^{n} R_i(q_i) - C\left(\sum_{i=1}^{n} q_i\right).$$

The problem is to choose $q_1, \ldots, q_n$ so that (12) is a maximum. Differentiating (12) with respect to $q_1, \ldots, q_n$ yields n equations

$$R_i'(q_i) = \frac{dC}{dq_i}, \qquad i = 1, \ldots, n.$$

Since the quantities $q_1, \ldots, q_n$ enter the cost function as a sum

$$C'\left(\sum_{i=1}^{n} q_i\right) = \frac{dC}{dq_1} = \frac{dC}{dq_2} = \cdots = \frac{dC}{dq_n}$$

so that the conditions for (12) to be a maximum may be written

(13)
$$R_i'(q_i) = C'\left(\sum_{i=1}^{n} q_i\right), \qquad i = 1, \ldots, n.$$

These n equations may be solved to yield $q_1, \ldots, q_n$ such that profit is maximized. This set of quantities, chosen so as to maximize (12), will also be such that

$$R_1'(q_1) = R_2'(q_2) = \ldots = R_n'(q_n) = C'\left(\sum_{i=1}^{n} q_i\right),$$

so that the marginal revenue earned in each market is equal, as shown in the verbal discussion above.

SELECTED BIBLIOGRAPHY

See those works listed in the Bibliography of Chapter 5. The following works are also useful:

CHAMBERLIN, E. *The Theory of Monopolistic Competition.* 6th ed. Cambridge, Mass.: Harvard University Press, 1950.

COURNOT, A. *Researches into the Mathematical Principles of the Theory of Wealth.* New York: Macmillan Co., 1929.

HICKS, J. R. "Annual Survey of Economic Theory: The Theory of Monopoly," *Econometrica,* 1935. Reprinted in STIGLER, G. J., AND BOULDING, K. E. (eds.). *Readings in Price Theory.* Homewood, Ill.: Richard D. Irwin, Inc. 1952.

TRIFFIN, R. *Monopolistic Competition and General Equilibrium Theory.* Cambridge, Mass.: Harvard University Press, 1956.

Chapter 7

LIFE AMONG THE OLIGOPS

*"The Trouble with Me Is You"**

The theory of competitive markets has traditionally been considered somewhat descriptive of institutional situations in which a large number of sellers of similar size and economic power compete in selling a particular commodity. The theory of monopoly is associated with single seller markets and that of monopolistic competition with large numbers of competing single seller markets. An obvious question is, what theory does one employ to describe the behavior of a small group of sellers of the same or closely competing goods. One might suppose that in their actions a very few sellers could approximate the behavior of a single seller so that an appropriate theory of the behavior of a small group of competing sellers might be very like the theory of monopoly. If an individual seller should increase the quantity that he offered for sale, the price that a unit of his commodity would command may be expected to fall. Thus, his average revenue curve would be negatively sloped, and this we have said above is a characteristic of a monopoly. Consider, however, the effect of such an increase in the quantity offered by one firm upon the profit-maximizing output of one of his few competitors. Such a competitor would find that the change in quantity offered and/or price charged by the original firm would cause his own average revenue curve to shift. Accordingly, in keeping with the theory of monopoly, he would choose a new price and/or quantity in order to maximize his profits. This action would, of course, shift the average revenue curve of the original firm who, in reaction to this shift, would choose a new price and/or quantity in order that his profit be a maximum. This would, once again, shift his competitor's average revenue curve, and so *ad infinitum.*

* "The Trouble with Me Is You," written by Frank Reardon and Bill Genna. Copyright, 1955, Hamilton Music Corp. USED BY PERMISSION.

We shall call the theory that is supposed to describe the behavior of firms with a small number of competitors, the theory of oligopoly. From the above discussion, it should be clear that if the oligopolist is a single seller and thus a sort of monopolist, he is certainly a monopolist with a problem.

Definition: *A firm is said to be an oligopoly (or an oligopolist) if any unilateral action with respect to selling price or output which the firm takes will provoke a reaction by its competitors, which reaction will affect the original firm's revenue function.*

Markets in which all the firms are oligopolies will be called *oligopolistic markets*.

The oligopoly problem is that any action that a firm might take will have a significant effect on the profit positions of other firms. These other firms will react to this, and their reactions will affect the profitability of the original firm's action. Oligopolistic firms, being profit-maximizing, will react only to changes in their profit functions, that is, to changes in their cost functions or in their revenue functions. Relationships between firms' cost functions will arise from the competitive situation in the markets for factors of production. We will discuss the markets for factors in the chapter that follows; here we are concerned with the firms' output market. Oligopolistic interactions arise through the relationship between firms' revenue functions. If two firms are so related that each of them can affect the revenue function of the other by its quantity and price decisions, then we will suppose that each of them can cause the price that its own commodity will command to vary by varying its output. We will confine our attention to cases in which each firm's average revenue function is, if defined, negatively sloped over its entire range.

A philosopher once said that only mathematicians are bothered by contradiction, and then presumably only when these contradictions arise in their mathematics. Economists, on the other hand, appear uncomfortable in the presence of mere disagreement. Thus, one frequently hears it said that we have no determinate theory of oligopoly. The problem really is that we have so many such theories that there is none which is generally accepted—none, that is, which all economists believe. As we noted before, belief is the business of churchmen. If physicists can live in a world lighted both by particles and by waves, it seems little to ask of the economist that he work with theories that imply that when the few compete, they do so in a variety of ways. To the author of a textbook, such as this one, however, the real problem of oligopoly is the embarrassment of riches, which theories of oligopoly should one discuss, and which theories should one exclude. To discuss them all completely would require a separate volume, to discuss only one or two would be a disservice to the reader. We shall attempt a selection in keeping with our title and discuss those theories of oligopoly which, in some sense, appear to be traditional in character. Of course, one man's tradition is another's outrage, and so, before the fact, we apologize both to the proponents of those theories excluded and to the opponents of those theories included.

Introductory Comment

In the introduction to Part III, we discussed briefly the derivation of demand curves and average revenue curves for commodities. The latter, we saw, was the inverse of the former. Thus, if the demand curve for a commodity is written $D = D(P)$, then the average revenue function can be written $P = D^{-1}(D)$. The total revenue that may be gained by selling a certain quantity of the commodity at a certain price will be equal to the product of the quantity times the price. Taking price as the independent variable, this revenue is given by

$$(1) \qquad\qquad R = P \cdot D(P) \,,$$

the demand function multiplied by price. Taking quantity as the independent variable total, revenue is given by

$$(2) \qquad\qquad R = D \cdot D^{-1}(D) \,,$$

the average revenue function multiplied by the quantity demanded. The total revenue function (either for a commodity, or for a firm) may thus be written either as a function of price, as in (1), or as a function of quantity, as in (2). This inversion process has led to something of a proliferation of classical oligopoly, or more accurately duopoly (two seller), models. The Cournot model is a natural development of the theory of duopoly when revenue is taken as a function of quantity. The Bertrand-Edgeworth model is a similar natural development where revenue is considered a function of price. Finally, the Stackelberg-Bowley model is simply a sophisticated version of the Cournot model.

COURNOT DUOPOLY

Antoine Augustin Cournot was perhaps the most original economic theorist who ever lived. He was born in 1801 in France and was trained as a mathematician. In addition to his work in mathematics and economics, Cournot wrote on philosophy and did translations. In 1838, he published *Researches into the Mathematical Principles of the Theory of Wealth*[1] in which he developed, among a great many other things, the theory of duopoly which we shall discuss below. His book was many years ahead of its time and was widely ignored until late in the nineteenth century when it was studied and its methods and suggestions employed by such writers as Jevons, Walras, Marshall, and Edgeworth.

Cournot imagines two identical mineral springs supplying a given market. Each spring is owned by a firm intent upon maximizing its profits, and there are no costs associated with drawing mineral water from the springs. In his theory of duopoly, Cournot treats revenue as a function of quantity. In fact, he explicitly deals with the inverse of the industry demand function and writes the revenue function of firm 1 as

$$(1) \qquad\qquad D_1 \cdot f(D_1 + D_2)$$

and that for firm 2 as

$$(2) \qquad\qquad D_2 \cdot f(D_1 + D_2)$$

where D_1 is the quantity sold by firm 1 and D_2 is the quantity sold by firm 2. The function $f(D_1 + D_2)$ is, of course, the average revenue function for the commodity. Firm 1 is able to control the quantity that it sells, but cannot control what firm 2 sells. Since it costs the firms nothing to offer water for sale, firm 1 will choose the value of D_1 such that (1) is maximized, given the value taken by D_2. Firm 2, on the other hand, will choose D_2 so that (2) is as large as possible given D_1. Each firm chooses that output which will maximize its profit if the other firm holds its output constant.

Consider Figure 7–1. Along the horizontal axis, we measure quantities sold. Along the vertical axis, we measure price. The decision facing firm 1 is to maximize its profits given the quantity that firm 2 is producing. Let the curve denoted $D_1 + D_2$ represent the demand curve for the commodity that the two firms sell. So long as firm 2 is selling D_2, firm 1 can consider any demand in excess of D_2, at any price, as its own to exploit. Thus, firm 1's demand curve (or average revenue curve) is simply the commodity demand curve with D_2 subtracted horizontally from it. The average revenue curve for firm 1 is thus D_1 in the figure. Associated with this average revenue curve is the marginal revenue curve, MR_1. Since it costs the

---

[1] This book has recently been republished in paper back by R. D. Irwin, Inc., of Homewood, Ill., in their *Paperback Classics in Economics Series* in 1963.

firm nothing to allow consumers to dip water from its spring, the firm will expand its output until marginal revenue is equal to zero, its marginal cost. Thus, firm 1 will offer a quantity, $\bar{q}_1$, for sale. This plus the quantity, D_2, that firm 2 is offering will command a price of $\bar{p}$ as shown by the average revenue curve for the commodity, $D_1 + D_2$ (since we have subtracted D_2 from $D_1 + D_2$ to get the curve D_1, this curve, too, associates a price $\bar{p}$ with the quantity $\bar{q}_1$).

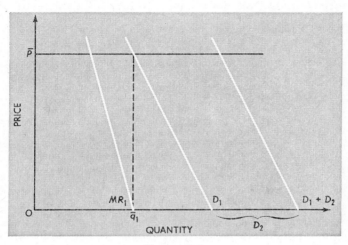

FIGURE 7–1

Before proceeding with our analysis of Cournot duopoly, let us reflect a moment about the nature of Cournot's assumption that each firm supposes that the other will hold its output constant. This is an extremely natural assumption to make if one contemplates a profit-maximizing duopolist and treats revenue as a function of quantity. If revenue is a function of quantity, i.e., if we work with average revenue functions rather than demand functions, then it is by variations in quantity that the firm is able to affect its profit position. Since both duopolists sell the same goods in the same market, their total revenue will depend upon the total quantity that they sell. Firm 1 cannot influence the quantity that its competitor will offer for sale; accordingly it treats this quantity as datum, just as it takes the commodity average revenue function (which it is also powerless to change) as datum. Given this datum, it does what it can do, varies its own offering, in order to maximize its profits.[2]

---

[2] This is not intended as an explanation of Cournot's development of the theory of duopoly. In fact, Cournot originally discusses industry demand functions and switches to analysis of average revenue functions when he begins his discussion of duopoly.

Clearly, Figure 7–1 does not tell the entire story. What, after all, is firm 2 doing with itself? By assumptions, it is doing exactly what firm 1 is doing, trying to adjust its sales so as to maximize its profits given its competitor's sales. In order to discuss the behavior of both firms simultaneously, consider Cournot's reaction function diagram, Figure 7–2. Along the horizontal axis, we measure the quantity offered for sale by firm 1. Along the vertical axis, we measure the quantity offered for sale by firm 2. From equations (1)

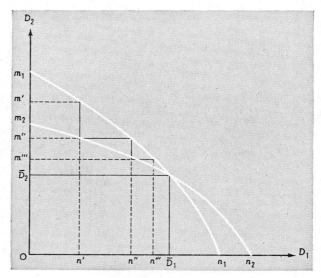

FIGURE 7–2

and (2), it can be seen that each firm, in deciding what quantity it will offer for sale, must take cognizance of the amount that the other firm is offering. We will suppose that the average revenue function is such that associated with each level of D_2, there is one unique level of D_1 which will yield firm 1 maximum profits and, conversely, for each D_1 there is only one D_2 such that firm 2's profits will be a maximum. In Figure 7–2, the curve m_1n_1 shows, for each level of D_2, what level of output D_1 will yield maximum profits for firm 1. Similarly, m_2n_2 associates with each level of D_1 that level of D_2 which will maximize firm 2's profits. If a situation can be reached at which firm 1 is selling $\bar{D}_1$ and firm 2 is selling $\bar{D}_2$, then each firm will be maximizing its profits given the other firm's output because m_1n_1 associates $\bar{D}_1$ with $\bar{D}_2$ while m_2n_2 associates $\bar{D}_2$ with $\bar{D}_1$, i.e., the two curves cross at the point $(\bar{D}_1, \bar{D}_2)$.

Before we discuss the process by which the point $(\bar{D}_1, \bar{D}_2)$ might be reached, let us further examine the derivation of m_1n_1 and

m_2n_2. Since neither firm is subjected to any costs of production, each wishes to maximize its profits by maximizing its revenue given the other firm's output. Thus, firm 1 wishes to choose D_1 so as to maximize

(1) $\qquad\qquad\qquad\qquad D_1 \cdot f(D_1 + D_2)$

while firm 2 wishes to maximize

(2) $\qquad\qquad\qquad\qquad D_2 \cdot f(D_1 + D_2)$.

If equation (1) is to be a maximum, then

$$f(D_1 + D_2) + D_1 \frac{\partial f}{\partial D_1} = 0$$

while (2) being a maximum requires

$$f(D_1 + D_2) + D_2 \frac{\partial f}{\partial D_2} = 0 .$$

Now

$$\frac{\partial f}{\partial D_1} = \frac{\partial f}{\partial D_2} = \frac{df}{d(D_1 + D_2)} = f'(D_1 + D_2) .$$

Thus a necessary condition for both firms to be simultaneously maximizing their profits would be that D_1 and D_2 take on values such that the two equations

(3) $\qquad\qquad\quad f(D_1 + D_2) + D_1 f'(D_1 + D_2) = 0$

(4) $\qquad\qquad\quad f(D_1 + D_2) + D_2 f'(D_1 + D_2) = 0$

are simultaneously satisfied. These are the first-order conditions for each firm's profits to be a maximum. The second-order conditions are that each firm's marginal revenue function be negatively sloped. We will assume these latter conditions to be satisfied. The curve m_1n_1 in Figure 7–2 is drawn by plotting equation (3) showing D_1 as a function of D_2. Similarly m_2n_2 is drawn by plotting equation (4) with D_2 as a function of D_1.

    As we will see in a moment, it is important to our analysis that m_1 lie above m_2 and n_2 lie to the right of n_1. In order to see that we are justified in having drawn these curves as we have, let us examine the relationship between m_1 and m_2. Equation (3) associates a value of m_1 for D_2 with a value of zero for D_1. Letting D_1 equal zero, equation (3) yields

$$f(D_2) = 0 .$$

Thus, m_1 is that level of D_2 such that if firm 1 sold nothing, price would be driven to zero. Equation (4) associates a value of m_2 for D_2 with a zero value of D_1. Letting D_1 equal zero in (4), we get

$$f(D_2) + D_2 f'(D_2) = 0 .$$

The average revenue function is, by assumption, negatively sloped, so that

$$f'(D_2) < 0 .$$

Thus m_2 must be a level of D_2 such that the price associated with a total output of D_2 will be positive (because it, plus a negative number, sums to zero). Since the average revenue function is negatively sloped, a zero price is associated with a larger output than is a positive price. Accordingly, m_1 must lie above m_2. By an exactly symmetrical argument, n_2 must lie to the right of n_1. Thus, the curves $m_1 n_1$ and $m_2 n_2$ must look somewhat similar to those shown in Figure 7–2.

The reason that we have been concerned with the somewhat correctness of Figure 7–2 may be seen if we consider the sequence of instantaneous adjustments that Figure 7–2 would imply. Starting with an arbitrary value of output by firm 2 at m', curve $m_1 n_1$ shows that firm 1 would react to such a level of D_2 by producing n'. According to $m_2 n_2$, firm 2 would produce m'' if D_1 were set at n'. An offer to sell m'' by firm 2 would lead firm 1 to sell n'', etc. This sort of sequence would lead continually toward the point $(\bar{D}_1, \bar{D}_2)$. Similarly, should we start with $D_2 < \bar{D}_2$ or $D_1 > \bar{D}_1$ the subsequent sequence would lead the two firms back toward the point $(\bar{D}_1, \bar{D}_2)$ at which both firms are simultaneously maximizing their profits. This consideration led Cournot to assert that the point $(\bar{D}_1, \bar{D}_2)$ is a position of stable equilibrium.

The very mention of the word "stable" brings us far closer to the study of dynamics than the author has any intentions of our remaining. There are three types of analysis employed in microeconomics: statics, comparative statics, and dynamics. Statics, as we said in Chapter 1, is equilibrium-defining analysis. Comparative statics is the study of the changes in the *equilibrium values* of variables which result from parameter changes. Dynamics is the study of the time paths of variables. Thus, while both statics and comparative statics are limited to some sort of analysis of equilibrium situations, dynamics is not. Recall the theory of the determination of competitive prices from Chapter 5. For a single competitive market, all other prices at their equilibrium levels, we may employ the supply and demand functions for the commodity under consideration to determine its equilibrium price. In this context, consider Figure 7–3. The demand function for commodity i is denoted D_i. S_i is the supply function for commodity i. The job of

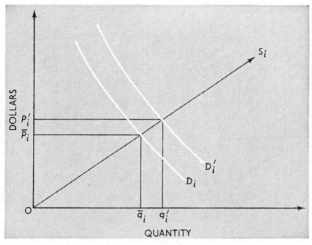

FIGURE 7–3

static analysis is simply to designate $\bar{p}_i$ as the equilibrium price and $\bar{q}_i$ as the equilibrium quantity. Comparative statics is concerned with changes in equilibrium quantities. Thus, if we were told that the demand curve shifted from D_i to D_i', it would be a piece of comparative statics to say that, under these circumstances, equilibrium price would shift from $\bar{p}_i$ to p_i' while equilibrium quantity would shift from $\bar{q}_i$ to q_i'. In order to carry on static analysis, we need certain information. In our example, we need to know the supply curve and the demand curve. For comparative-static analysis, we simply examine the same information further, i.e., by shifting the demand curve in Figure 7–3 or by differentiating the equilibrium conditions with respect to a parameter as in the various mathematical appendices.

Now consider the following problem. Suppose price was at $\bar{p}_i$ and quantity was equal to $\bar{q}_i$ and demand shifted as shown in Figure 7–3. How would price and quantity vary over time? The equilibrium values associated with D_i' and S_i are p_i' and q_i', but starting at $\bar{p}_i$

and $\bar{q}_i$ by what *time path* do the variables move to p_i' and q_i'? Indeed, do they move to these values at all? We may examine Figure 7–3 for so long as we like, but we will not be able to answer these questions. Additional information is required. In general, we need information regarding disequilibrium behavior as well as equilibrium behavior, and we cannot get such information from Figure 7–3. We need something like Figure 7–4 below. Along the horizontal axis we measure time. Along the vertical axis we measure price upward from the origin and quantity downward

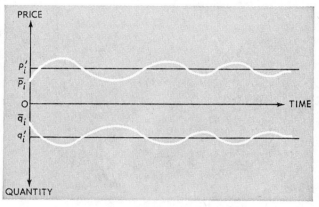

FIGURE 7–4

from the origin. According to Figure 7–4, both price and quantity follow damped oscillatory paths gradually settling down to their new equilibrium values. Dynamic analysis is the analysis of such time paths. Two important things to notice are these: first, in order to examine the dynamic behavior of economic variables, we need explicit information regarding the time paths that these variables follow; second, such information is not contained in traditional static and comparative static analysis. Figure 7–3, which contains all the information necessary to traditional static or comparative-static analysis, does not contain information necessary to dynamic analysis. It has no time dimension and, more importantly, it has no information regarding time paths. Knowledge of where a man is buried tells us little of the life that he lead.

There exist several different, precise concepts of stability, but in spirit, they amount to this: an equilibrium point is said to be stable if when the system is disturbed and moved away from the equilibrium point it will return to it over time. Stability is, thus, a dynamic property. It depends upon the nature of the time paths taken by the variables under consideration. Since stability is a

dynamic property and since the study of dynamics requires information additional to that employed in the study of statics and
comparative statics, we cannot determine the stability of systems
studied without such additional information. Since such additional
information is not usually explicitly dealt with in traditional microeconomics, we will not usually discuss dynamics in this book.

This leads to a bit of a muddle. In our discussion of Figure 7–2,
we have provided no explicit information regarding time paths and
yet we referred to point $(\bar{D}_1, \bar{D}_2)$ as a position of stable equilibrium. How can such a classification be made on the basis of the
information provided? The answer is simply that it cannot. The
assertion that $(\bar{D}_1, \bar{D}_2)$ is a position of stable equilibrium is based
on implicit dynamic assumptions. As an example of the sort of
dynamic adjustment process implicitly assumed, suppose that each
firm sets its quantity first thing in the morning when trading
begins. Suppose that firm 1 opens a few minutes before firm 2.
Letting superscripts denote time and treating a day as a unit of
time, firm 1 begins day 1 by adjusting his offering exactly to the
offering of firm 2 on the previous day. Thus firm 1 on day 1 will
choose $D_1{}^1$ so as to satisfy

$$f(D_1{}^1 + D_2{}^0) + D_1{}^1 f'(D_1{}^1 + D_2{}^0) = 0 \, .$$

The late-sleeping manager of firm 2 will then choose $D_2{}^1$ so as to
satisfy

$$f(D_1{}^1 + D_2{}^1) + D_2{}^1 f'(D_1{}^1 + D_2{}^1) = 0 \, .$$

On day 2, firm 1 will choose $D_1{}^2$ so that

$$f(D_1{}^2 + D_2{}^1) + D_1{}^2 f'(D_1{}^2 + D_2{}^1) = 0$$

and firm 2 will choose $D_2{}^2$ such that

$$f(D_1{}^2 + D_2{}^2) + D_2{}^2 f'(D_1{}^2 + D_2{}^2) = 0 \, .$$

In general, $D_1{}^T$ will be chosen to satisfy

$$f(D_1{}^T + D_2{}^{T-1}) + D_1{}^T f'(D_1{}^T + D_2{}^{T-1}) = 0$$

while $D_2{}^T$ will be chosen so that

$$f(D_1{}^T + D_2{}^T) + D_2{}^T f'(D_1{}^T + D_2{}^T) = 0 \, .$$

Under this sort of dynamic adjustment process, the point $(\bar{D}_1, \bar{D}_2)$
in Figure 7–2 is indeed a position of stable equilibrium. Notice that
while these adjustment processes may seem quite appropriate to the
Cournot model, they are, nonetheless, quite special sorts of dynamic
adjustment assumptions. Each firm adjusts its output completely
and directly to some previous output offered by the other firm. On a

given morning, firm 1 is aware of firm 2's offering of the previous day and adjusts his output correctly to it, etc. Should this adjustment by firm 1 be more complicated, for example, should firm 1 adjust its output gradually during the day and moving first away from and then toward its appropriate output, and should firm 2 adjust quickly to these movements in the wrong direction, or adjust in the wrong direction itself, then it would be possible to devise adjustment processes according to which $(\bar{D}_1, \bar{D}_2)$ was not stable. Thus, the stability of the equilibrium point is a result of the adjustment process assumed, not an intrinsic property of the Cournot model, unless the sort of implicit adjustment process outlined in the previous paragraph is deemed part of that model.

One could pursue the Cournot duopoly model at great length. The model may be generalized to include more than two firms. We could deal with nonzero costs. We could search for explicit dynamic adjustment processes which would lead to the instability of $(\bar{D}_1, \bar{D}_2)$ in Figure 7–2. The reader might profitably amuse himself with any combination of these projects. We shall stop here.

BERTRAND-EDGEWORTH DUOPOLY

If the Cournot model is the natural result of treating revenue as a function of quantity sold in a duopoly situation, the Bertrand-Edgeworth model is the equally natural result of treating it as a function of prices. If there are two firms selling a single commodity, then the demand function facing one seller of that commodity (say firm 1) may be written

$$D_1(P_1, P_2) \, ,$$

the prices of all other commodities being fixed at their equilibrium levels, and P_1 and P_2, respectively, being the prices charged by duopolists 1 and 2. Duopolist 1 will attempt to choose P_1 so as to maximize

$$P_1 \cdot D_1(P_1, P_2) \quad \text{given } P_2 \, .$$

His competitor will seek a value for P_2 such that, given P_1,

$$P_2 \cdot D_2(P_1, P_2)$$

is as large as possible. Given the apparent similarity between these equations and equations (1) and (2) above, one is tempted to apply the methods of Cournot duopoly to the analysis of the Bertrand-Edgeworth approach. Thus, we might set the partial derivatives of the above equations equal to zero and solve the resultant equations for those values of P_1 and P_2 such that both firms would be maximizing their profits.

This is not possible, however. P_1 and P_2 are two different prices being charged for the same commodity in the same market. Should two different prices be charged in the same market for the same commodity, then consumers in that market will, in effect, be allowed to choose between two budget restraints one of which (that associated with the lower price) lies entirely outside the other (except for common end points). Thus, for any person who consumes some of the commodity for which there are two different prices, the budget line associated with the lower price will contain points preferred to any points on the interior budget line. Accordingly, any person who consumes any of the commodity having two prices will buy this at the lower price. Consider firm 1's demand function

$$D_1(P_1, P_2) .$$

Let P_2 be fixed at some level. Should P_1 be ever so slightly greater than P_2, then firm 1 will only be able to sell to those consumers (if any) who are turned away by firm 2. Should P_1 be any less than P_2, then firm 1 will be able to supply either the entire consumer population or all those that it has the capacity to cope with. The demand function

$$D_1(P_1, P_2)$$

will be discontinuous in the region such that $P_1 = P_2$. It will equal the market demand function for $P_1 < P_2$ and the market demand function less firm 2's output for $P_1 > P_2$. A similar statement is true of

$$D_2(P_1, P_2) .$$

Thus, neither function is differentiable where $P_1 = P_2$. As will be seen below it is in the region such that $P_1 = P_2$ that equilibrium points will lie. Accordingly, we cannot apply calculus to the solution of the Bertrand-Edgeworth duopoly model.

Cournot was primarily a mathematician, and some of the earliest attention paid his book was by mathematicians. In 1883, another French mathematician, Joseph Bertrand, reviewed Cournot's work (after 45 years, some nerve!) in the *Journal des Savants*. Bertrand was dissatisfied with Cournot's analysis of duopoly and assumed that each duopolist took the price his rival charged as fixed and adjusted his price so as to maximize his revenue (and hence his profits since costs were taken to be zero). Bertrand took revenue to be a function of price as discussed above. He argued somewhat as follows. Each firm will be able to capture the entire market by undercutting his rival's price by the least observable amount. Thus, firm 1, given any level of P_2, will choose P_1 slightly below P_2, for if P_1 were set above P_2, firm 1 would sell nothing (or only firm 2's discards). If P_1 were set equal to P_2, then firm 1 could only plan on half the market. By setting P_1 ever so slightly below P_2, firm 1 will get either all the market or all that he can supply. Thus, while P_1 will be slightly lower than P_2, D_1 will exceed what it would be with P_1 equal to P_2 by so much that $P_1 D_1$ will be a maximum. It will then pay firm 2 to set P_2 ever so slightly lower than P_1 etc. This process (essentially price warfare) will continue until price is driven to zero. There are things wrong with this analysis, however. What if each firm was able to satisfy only a part of the market?

It was left for the great English mathematical economist, F. Y. Edgeworth, to provide an explicit example of such a price adjustment duopoly model. Edgeworth's contributions to economics are legion. We have already mentioned his name in connection with the Edgeworth box diagram (Chapter 2). He introduced the indifference curve and also a process of "recontracting" very similar to the *tâtonnement* process discussed above. He authored books with delightful titles, the most accessible of which nowadays is *Mathematical Psychics* published in 1881. Edgeworth worked with various explicit price adjusting duopoly models. We will discuss a simple example taken from his *Papers Relating to Political Economy*.[3] For simplicity, several very particular assumptions are made; there are no costs of production but each firm has a definite limit to the amount that it can offer for sale. Moreover, this limit is the same for each firm. There are n consumers each of whom has a demand function of the form

$$x_r = 1 - P, r = 1, \ldots, n.$$

Thus, the demand function for the commodity is

$$x = n(1 - P).$$

Should each duopolist supply half the people, then the demand curves of the two firms would be those shown "back to back," as it were, in Figure 7–5. Price is measured along the vertical axis, and the point R corresponds to a price of 1. The line RC represents one

---

[3] Volume 1, p. 116. Published by Macmillan Co., 1925.

half the market demand function as does RC'. The quantity sold by firm 1 is measured from the origin, 0, to the right along the horizontal axis, and the point B represents firm 1's total capacity. The quantity sold by firm 2 is measured from the origin to the left, the point B' representing the total capacity of firm 2. Given that each firm is supplying half the market, that there are no costs, and that the demand curve is linear, it would pay the firms to set the price $P = \frac{1}{2}$ in Figure 7–5,[4] and sell the quantities A and A'. Given

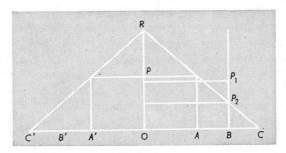

FIGURE 7–5

---

[4] These will be the outputs at which the marginal revenue functions associated with the average revenue functions RC and RC' will cut the quantity axis. The reason for this is that A is $\frac{1}{2} C$ and A' is $\frac{1}{2} C'$, and when a demand function is straight, the marginal revenue function associated with it will be straight and will lie (at each price) half the distance from the vertical axis that the demand curve lies. Let

$$q = a - bP$$

be the *demand function*. Average revenue then is

$$P = \frac{a}{b} - \frac{1}{b} q \text{ ,}$$

and total revenue is

$$TR = \frac{a}{b} q - \frac{1}{b} q^2$$

so that marginal revenue is

$$MR = \frac{a}{b} - 2 \frac{1}{b} q \text{ ;}$$

thus, the dollar value of marginal revenue is

$$P = \frac{a}{b} - 2 \frac{1}{b} q$$

and

$$q = \frac{1}{2} a - \frac{1}{2} bP = \frac{1}{2} (a - bP)$$

is the *quantity associated with each level of marginal revenue*. Note that this quantity is $\frac{1}{2}$ that associated with each level of price (average revenue) by the demand function. Thus, with a marginal revenue of zero, $\frac{1}{2}$ the quantity C in Figure 7–5 will be associated. For any linear average revenue function, the marginal revenue function lies half way between the AR and the price axis at *each* level of price.

this situation, however, it would pay either firm to lower its price slightly, and at that price to supply all that it can produce. Thus, firm 1 would prefer profits equal to the area under the line P_1 to profits equal to that under the line P. Should firm 1 set a price P_1, firm 2 would maximize its profits by offering a lower price still.

One might suspect an outcome similar to that of the Bertrand discussion above, but one would be disappointed, for price will certainly not fall below P_2. Should firm 1 finally be driven to a price of P_2, it will be able to sell all that it produces at that price and *still satisfy only half the market*. Recall, each individual has the same demand curve, and selling on a first-come first-serve basis, firm 1 will have sold all that it can offer at the price P_2 to only half the individuals in the market. Firm 2 then has the remaining half of the market left to exploit, and the demand curve for half the market is precisely RC' in Figure 7–5. So back will go firm 2 to a price of P and sales of A' which maximize his profit for the demand curve. Firm 1 will simply supply himself out of half the market so long as he stays at a price of P_2. Firm 2's having returned to P, it will no longer behoove firm 1 to remain at P_2. Rather, firm 1 will switch to P_1, firm 2 will undercut him and off we go to "again descend, again to mount"[5] as Edgeworth so poetically put it.

We do not pretend that the above is a complete description, even of the special case discussed. At some level above P_2 it will profit one of the firms to stop price warfare, set a price of P, and sell to the part of the entire market that his rival cannot satisfy. Once this is done, up will go the rival's price, etc. Should different consumers have different demand curves, prices may oscillate between different limits depending upon which consumers buy where. Should costs be introduced, they also may affect the limits of oscillation. The point, however, should be clear: given duopolists who adjust their prices on the assumption that the price charged by their rivals will remain fixed, perennial price oscillation is a possible result.

By the 1930's, economists were becoming dissatisfied with models which would have firms basing their actions on the assumption that their rivals would react in a certain way, while time and again the rival's reaction is the same and always quite other than expected (the reader is invited to admire the patience of the profession). Two economists, A. L. Bowley and H. von Stackelberg,[6] attempted to extend the Cournot model to include more

[5] *Economic Journal*, 1922, p. 404.

[6] A. L. Bowley, *Mathematical Groundwork of Economics* (Oxford: Clarendon Press, 1924). Discussions of Stackelberg's model may be found either in William Fellner, *Competition among the Few* (New York: Alfred A. Knopf,

sophisticated behavior on the part of sellers. Thus, firm 1 might recognize the fact that firm 2 behaves as assumed by Cournot. Firm 1 would then choose his output so as to maximize

$$D_1 \cdot f[D_1 + D_2(D_1)]$$

where the variables are defined as above. Numerous obvious variations on this theme exist. Firm 2 might adjust *a la* Cournot, as its rival supposes, or it might attempt to maximize

$$D_2 \ f[D_1(D_2) + D_2] \ .$$

The nature of the assumed dependence of one firm's output upon that of the other firm is subject to variation, etc. It is also possible to construct Bertrand-Edgeworth type models in which one or both firms are cognizant of effects of their own behavior upon that of their rivals. Thus, firm 1 might attempt to maximize

$$P_1 \cdot D_1[P_1, P_2(P_1)]$$

where the variables are defined as above. Numerous different assumptions may govern firm 2's behavior. Models such as these in which firms recognize the fact that their actions will lead to a reaction by their rivals are called models of conjectural variation. Such models may or may not suffer from the weakness mentioned in the opening sentence of this paragraph. We shall discuss only one such model.

THE KINKED DEMAND CURVE

In 1939, two articles were published which independently presented a conjectural variation type oligopoly model.[7] The distinguishing characteristic of this model was that each firm supposed that its rivals would react to a price change differently depending upon whether it was an increase or a decrease. Should the firm raise its price, it imagined that its rivals would simply sit tight, happy in the additions to their sales that resulted as customers deserted the

---

Inc., 1949) ; or in H. V. Stackelberg, *The Theory of the Market Economy* (London: Hodge & Co., Ltd., 1952). The book by Fellner is entirely dedicated to the exposition and discussion of oligopoly theory (the reader is invited to admire the patience of Professor Fellner).

[7] R. J. Hall and C. J. Hitch, "Price Theory and Business Behavior," *Oxford Economic Papers*, No. 2 (May, 1939), pp. 12–45. Paul Sweezy, "Demand under Conditions of Oligopoly," *The Journal of Political Economy*, Vol. XLVII (August, 1939).

price raiser in their favor. Should the firm lower its price, it supposed that its rivals would be forced to lower theirs as well. Thus, the firm imagined that it faced an average revenue curve such as AR in Figure 7–6. If the price is $\bar{P}$ in Figure 7–6, then the firm supposes that for prices above $\bar{P}$, its average revenue curve is relatively flat, while for prices below $\bar{P}$, it is relatively steep. Thus, at the price $\bar{P}$ and quantity $\bar{q}$ there is a kink in the firm's imagined demand (average revenue) curve. The marginal revenue curve associated with a kinked average revenue curve will possess a

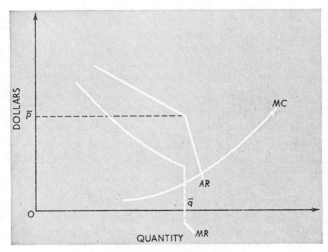

FIGURE 7–6

discontinuity at the quantity $\bar{q}$ associated with the kink. Such a curve is shown by MR in Figure 7–6. Should the firm's marginal cost curve lie anywhere between the upper and lower portions of this discontinuity (along the dotted portion of MR in Figure 7–6) then the firm will continue to sell $\bar{q}$ at a price $\bar{P}$. Thus, the kinked demand curve model predicts price rigidity.

The kink hypothesis has been criticized on the basis of observations of the reactions by firms to actual price changes by rivals.[8] It was found that when a firm raised its price it was as likely to be followed as when it lowered its price. The difficulty with this as a refutation of the kink is that the kinked demand curve is supposed to explain price rigidity, not price changes. A firm will not consider changing its price (except in extreme circumstances) when it imagines that it faces a kink. Thus, according to the

---

[8] George J. Stigler, "The Kinky Oligopoly Demand Curve and Rigid Prices," *The Journal of Political Economy*, Vol. LV (1947).

hypothesis, a firm will not normally raise or lower its price unless it imagines that, for some reason, it is momentarily not faced with a kink. What Professor Stigler's results may indicate is that the firms are usually correct in this supposition. A real problem with the kink hypothesis is, in fact, that in the form presented it is very difficult to subject it to empirical test. It predicts little other than price rigidity, and unless one is convinced by interviews with business-men (on which the hypothesis was originally based), it is not a simple theory to test. A further weakness of the kink hypothesis is its failure to explain how the price $\overline{P}$ in Figure 7–6 was ever determined in the first place. It is a theory of price maintenance rather than one of price determination.

COLLUSION

In 1838, Cournot dismissed the possibility that duopolistic firms might simply join together and become monopolistic. He showed that their profits would be larger should they do so, but argued that given any such collusive agreement it would always pay one of the firms to vary its sales on the assumption that its rival would stand pat, and this temptation to vary the output he thought too great for duopolists to withstand. Cournot felt that, lacking a formal agreement, it was unrealistic to expect duopolists to collude. It says something about the permanency of man's intuition that most modern writers on traditional oligopoly theory feel that it is unrealistic to expect oligopolists (or duopolists) to do anything else.

Should oligopolists collude, the result is a profit-maximizing single seller who does not take price as given. Accordingly, the theory appropriate to the behavior of colluding oligopolists is the theory of monopoly. It would seem rather repetitive here to discuss once more the theory of monopoly, and we shall not do so. The reason that oligopolists might collude is, quite simply, that it would pay them. It should be clear that neither the Bertrand case, which yields zero prices, nor the Edgeworth case, which yields no solution, would lead firms to a very profitable life. Should oligopolists behave according to the kink hypothesis, their profit position will be a bit arbitrary, since, given a going price, they will usually maintain it even though the profits associated with it may not be too great.

It only remains for us to show that collusion leads to greater profits than does the Cournot solution. Firm 1 will choose D_1 so as to maximize

$$D_1 \cdot f(D_1 + D_2)$$

while firm 2 will maximize

$$D_2 \cdot f(D_1 + D_2) \, .$$

For equilibrium then (given that the second-order conditions for maxima are met) we seek D_1 and D_2 such that

$$D_1 \cdot f'(D_1 + D_2) + f(D_1 + D_2) = 0$$

$$D_2 \cdot f'(D_1 + D_2) + f(D_1 + D_2) = 0$$

are simultaneously satisfied. These two equations being simultaneously true, we may add them. This yields

$$(D_1 + D_2) \cdot f'(D_1 + D_2) + 2f(D_1 + D_2) = 0 \, .$$

Since $D_1 + D_2 = D$, total output, we may write this

(5) $$D \cdot f'(D) + 2f(D) = 0 \, .$$

Under Cournot duopoly, the total output of the industry would be such that equation (5) was satisfied.

Should the firms collude, they would combine their efforts so as to maximize

$$D \cdot f(D) \, .$$

This requires that total output, D, be such that

(6) $$D f'(D) + f(D) = 0 \, .$$

When equation (6) is satisfied, the total profit accruing to the two firms jointly will be maximized. But notice that (6) is different from equation (5). The total output produced under the Cournot solution is other than that output which would yield the two firms the greatest profit to split between them. Thus, if firms are profit-maximizing, and if they can arrange to collude, they will do so. On the other hand, if no formal collusive agreement is reached, each firm will have to fight that nagging temptation to increase its profits (temporarily?) by deviating from the collusive solution.

SELECTED BIBLIOGRAPHY

BERTRAND, J. "Théorie Des Richesses," *Journal des Savants* (September, 1883), pp. 499–508.

BOWLEY, A. L. *Mathematical Groundwork of Economics*. Oxford: Clarendon Press, 1924.

CHAMBERLIN, E. *The Theory of Monopolistic Competition*. 6th ed. Cambridge, Mass.: Harvard University Press, 1950.

COURNOT, A. *Researches into the Mathematical Principles of the Theory of Wealth*. New York: Macmillan Co., 1929.

EDGEWORTH, F. Y. *Papers Relating to Political Economy*. London: Macmillan Co., 1925.

FELLNER, W. *Competition among the Few*. New York: Alfred A. Knopf, Inc., 1949.

HALL, R. J. AND HITCH, C. J. "Price Theory and Business Behavior," *Oxford Economic Papers*, II (May, 1939), pp. 12–45.

STACKELBERG, H. V. *The Theory of the Market Economy*. Translated by PEACOCK, A. T. London: William Hodge & Co., 1952.

STIGLER, G. J. "The Kinky Oligopoly Demand Curve and Rigid Prices," *The Journal of Political Economy*, Vol. LV (1947).

SWEEZY, P. "Demand under Conditions of Oligopoly," *The Journal of Political Economy*, Vol. XLVII (August, 1939).

Chapter

8

PAYMENTS TO
FACTORS OF PRODUCTION

*The bosses don't drive Cadillacs or wear silken
B.V.D.s
Because they pay us workingmen such fancy salaries.
—"Put It on the Ground"**

The profit-maximizing firm chooses a level of output such that its profits will be as large as possible. Alternatively, it chooses a set of inputs such that the output associated with them will lead to maximum profits. In Chapters 5, 6, and 7, we have dealt with profit maximization as a choice of output. In the mathematical appendices to Chapters 5 and 6, we have considered profit maximization as a problem in the choice of inputs. In this chapter, we will again deal with profit maximization as input selection. In particular, we shall develop tools for discussing the firm's demand for factors in partial equilibrium terms. Using these tools, we will point out certain results that we have not discussed above. Finally, we will analyze situations in which the firm does not take the prices of inputs as given, as we have supposed above, but, in part, determines them through its actions. Thus, while much of this chapter will be somewhat repetitive in that we will restate certain results derived above, there is a significant change of emphasis. Before, we have been concerned with the firm's adjustment to given factor prices. Here, we turn our attention to the theory of the determination of those factor prices. Of course, the firm's demand for factors is most relevant to the determination of these prices, just as the consumer's demand for final commodities is most relevant to the determination of the prices of final commodities. In fact, the distinction between final commodities and factors of production is frequently entirely illusory so that any complete theory of price determination must

---

* "Put It on the Ground," words by Ray Glaser, music by Bill Wolff. Copyright, 1947, People's Songs, Inc. USED BY PERMISSION. All Rights Reserved.

take into account the way in which firms as buyers of commodities influence commodity prices.

Certain notions which have already arisen in the mathematical appendices above have, thus far, gone unnamed.

Definition: *The marginal revenue product of input* i *is equal to marginal revenue multiplied by the rate of change of output with respect to input* i *(called the marginal product[1] of input* i*).*

In equation (4) of the mathematical appendix to Chapter 6, R_i is the marginal revenue product of input i. Marginal revenue shows the change in revenue that will accompany an output change of one unit. The marginal product of commodity i shows the change in output which will accompany a unit change in the use of input i. Thus, the product of these two quantities, the marginal revenue product of commodity i, measures the rate of change of revenue with respect to a unit change in the employment of input i.

A closely related concept is a measure of the rate of change of the *value* of the firm's output with respect to a unit change in the employment of some input, say input i.

Definition: *The marginal value product of input* i *is equal to output price multiplied by the marginal product of input* i.

Should the firm under discussion sell its output competitively, then (see Chapter 5) its marginal revenue for any level of output will be equal to the given price of its output. Thus, for competitive firms, for any input i, the marginal revenue product of i will equal the marginal value product of i.

In order to avoid confusion, we shall (in this chapter only) refer to the prices of inputs as wages.

Definition: *The average wage of input* i *is the wage that the firm must pay per unit of input* i *employed.*

Definition: *The marginal wage of input* i *is the rate of change of the firm's expenditure on input* i *with respect to a unit change in its employment of input* i.

Notice that the marginal wage of input i is not defined as the rate of change of the wage (average wage) of input i, but rather the rate of change of expenditure on input i with respect to a unit change in the employment of input i. This is quite in keeping with the usual

---

[1] Notice that the average and total products of input i may be defined **in** a way which should be obvious to the reader.

meaning of the concepts of marginals, totals, and averages in economics. We only mention it because the term "marginal wage" is sometimes a bit misleading.[2] In equation (4) of the mathematical appendix to Chapter 6, P_i is the marginal wage of input i. It is also the average wage of input i. This is true because in all our discussion to this point we have supposed that firms purchase their inputs competitively, taking wages as given. The firm's purchases do not affect wages, which are constant, and for each input marginal wage is equal to average wage. This will become clear immediately.

Buying Factors Competitively

Consider a firm that takes both the price of its produce and the wages of inputs as given. That is, a firm that is both a competitive buyer of factors and a competitive seller of its output. In Figure 8–1 below, we plot on the horizontal axis the quantity of input i

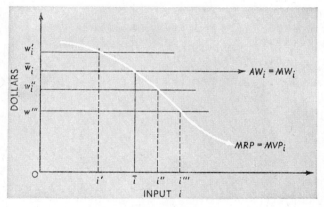

FIGURE 8–1

employed by the firm. Along the vertical axis, we measure in dollars. The firm, buying input i competitively, takes the wage of input i as given. Thus the per-unit wage (average wage) is not under the firm's control. The firm cannot cause per-unit wages to vary by altering the amount of input i that it purchases. The firm's average wage curve is, therefore, horizontal at the given level, as AW_i in Figure 8–1. As shown in Chapter 4, if an average curve is horizontal, then the marginal curve associated with it will also be horizontal at the same level. The two curves are identical. The

---

[2] Because of the form of the firm's expenditure function (Chapter 3) the marginal wage of input i is equal to the partial derivative of the firm's expenditure function with respect to input i.

marginal wage curve is denoted MW_i in Figure 8–1 and is identical with AW_i. If the firm purchases input i competitively, then its marginal wage and average wage curves for input i are identical and horizontal.

Since the firm sells its output competitively, it takes the price at which it may sell as given. Thus, the firm's average revenue (price) curve is also horizontal. Accordingly, the firm's marginal revenue curve will be identical with its average revenue curve as in Chapter 5 and price will equal marginal revenue. From this it follows that the marginal revenue product of input i will equal the marginal value product of input i. If we denote the marginal product of input i by Φ_i as in the mathematical appendix to Chapter 3, then both the marginal revenue product of input i and the marginal value product of input i are given by

$$P \cdot \Phi_i .$$

We wish to plot $P \cdot \Phi_i$ in Figure 8–1. The only question is, how does $P \cdot \Phi_i$ vary as the use of input i varies. Now P is externally given and does not vary with input i. On the other hand,

$$\Phi_i = \Phi_i(X_1, \ldots, X_n)$$

where $X_1, \ldots, X_n$ are the quantities of inputs 1 through n employed by the firm. In order to plot $P \cdot \Phi_i$ meaningfully, we must hold the use of all these other inputs fixed. Then the question is, how does Φ_i vary as the amount of input i employed by the firm varies? That is, what is the sign of Φ_{ii}? We shall leave it to the reader to prove that for a competitive firm to be maximizing its profits Φ_{ii} must be negative.[3] Thus, the marginal revenue product curve of input i as well as the marginal value product curve of input i will be negatively sloped, as the curve $MRP_i = MVP_i$ in Figure 8–1.

The negatively sloped curve in Figure 8–1 associates with each level of employment of input i a certain rate of change of revenue,

---

[3] Directions: Define the firm's profit function as

$$P \cdot \Phi(X_1, \ldots, X_n) - \sum_{i=1}^{n} W_i X_i$$

where P is the price of output, $\Phi(X_1, \ldots, X_n)$ is the production function, X_i is the quantity of input i, and W_i is the wage of input i. We seek the set of inputs which will render this function an unconstrained maximum (see footnote 3, mathematical appendix to Chapter 3). The second-order conditions for this unconstrained maximum imply $\Phi_{ii} < 0$ for all i. For further clues, the reader's attention is drawn to the fact that this is simply a special case of the general unconstrained profit maximization problem worked out in the mathematical appendix to Chapter 6. In particular, it is a case in which $R_{ii} = P \cdot \Phi_{ii}$.

namely, the change in revenue which would result from a unit increase in the firm's employment of input i, all other inputs fixed. The horizontal marginal wage curve similarly associates with each level of employment the change in the total wage bill (costs) which would result from a unit change in the amount of input i employed, all other inputs fixed (see footnote 2 above). If less than $\bar{i}$ is employed then each additional unit of input i adds more to the firm's revenue than it does to the firm's cost. Thus, each additional unit of input i employed, up to the level $\bar{i}$ is profitable for the firm. To the right of $\bar{i}$ each additional unit of input i adds more to the firm's costs than to its revenue. Thus, the profit-maximizing firm will employ $\bar{i}$ of input i. The firm will employ input i up to that level at which the firm's marginal revenue product curve cuts its marginal wage curve from above. The reader should ascertain for himself why the former curve must cut the latter from *above*.

Since the firm buys factor i competitively, the wage at which it will purchase $\bar{i}$ is the given wage, $\overline{W}_i$. The firm's demand curve for factor i would associate with each level of W_i a given level of employment of factor i. If we consider various wages for input i, say W_i', W_i'', and W_i''', it is clear from Figure 8–1 that the quantities of input i that the firm will employ are respectively i', i'', and i'''. In fact, for each possible level of W_i, the quantity that the firm will employ of input i is the quantity associated with the given level of W_i by the firm's marginal revenue product curve. This is true because the firm buys input i competitively. Thus, in this case, the firm's demand curve for input i is simply the inverse of its marginal revenue product curve (just as the demand curve for its output is the inverse of its average revenue curve). In deriving the *market* demand for input i, we add to the demand by consumers and by other firms the demand by this firm. Should all other prices (and wages) be fixed, should the firm's employment of all other inputs be fixed, and should the firm purchase input i competitively, then in deriving the market demand curve for input i, we would add in the inverse of the firm's marginal revenue product curve.

The reader's attention is drawn to the fact that the results from Figure 8–1 have already come up in our study. In particular, in the mathematical appendix to Chapter 6, by examining the argument leading to equation (4), the reader will note that what is there denoted R_i is the marginal revenue product of input i while what is denoted P_i is the marginal wage of input i. Thus, equation (4) says the same thing as Figure 8–1 of this chapter. Moreover, equation (6) of the mathematical appendix to Chapter 6 is the firm's demand *function* for input i, and this demand function must be added to all other individual demand functions for input i to derive the market demand function. The equilibrium price for input i will be determined as discussed in Chapter 5 by the interaction of the market demand function for i and the market supply function. In the chapter that follows, we will turn to a more complete discussion of the determination of equilibrium prices.

In the analysis connected with Figure 8–1, the firm sold its output competitively. As a result, its price was equal to its marginal revenue so that the marginal value product of input i was exactly the same as the marginal revenue product of input i. What is more, since the wage of input i was equal to the marginal wage, the equilibrium wage of input i was equal to its marginal value product. In other words, input i received wages exactly equal to the *value* of its marginal addition to production. For a firm which sells its output monopolistically, the marginal revenue product of input i will no longer be equal to its marginal value product. As shown in Chapter 6, the monopolistic firm will sell its product at a price in excess of marginal revenue. Thus, for the monopolist, the marginal value product of each input will be greater than the marginal revenue product.

Still, the above analysis is not significantly changed if we suppose that the firm sells its produce monopolistically while buying its inputs competitively. The firm, in choosing how much of an input to employ, is not concerned with the contribution that the input will make to the *value* of its output. Rather it is concerned with the contribution that the input will make to its *revenue*. Consider Figure 8–2. The marginal value product curve for input i is labeled MVP_i. MRP_i is the marginal revenue product curve of input i.[4] The marginal wage (equals average wage) curve is labeled MW_i. Along the horizontal axis, we plot the amount of input i employed. Along the vertical axis, we measure in dollars. To the left of $\bar{i}$ it pays the firm to expand its use of input i as argued above in connection with Figure 8–1. Similarly, to the right of $\bar{i}$, it pays the firm to cut back on its use of i. To employ input i in such a way as to maximize its profits, the firm will hire $\bar{i}$ and pay it a wage of $\overline{W}_i$. Moreover, the firm's demand curve for input i will still be the inverse of its marginal revenue product curve. In effect, because the firm is concerned with the contribution that employment of i makes to its revenue and not with the contribution to the value of its

---

[4] The reader's attention is drawn to the negative slope of MRP_i in Figure 8–2. In footnote 3 of this chapter, the reader was directed to prove that Φ_{ii} must be negative for a profit-maximizing competitive firm. It was pointed out that we were discussing a special case of what had been worked out in the appendix to Chapter 6, in particular, the case in which $P \cdot \Phi_{ii} = R_{ii}$. The reader should satisfy himself that we are now dealing with a less special case in which the slope of the marginal revenue product curve of input i is R_{ii}.

output, as soon as the marginal value product curve ceases to coincide with the marginal revenue product curve, it ceases also to be of concern to us. It is the marginal revenue product curve which (with the marginal wage curve) determines the quantity employed, and so it is the marginal revenue product curve, the inverse of which is the firm's demand curve for factor i (all other factors fixed).

And yet one can see that Figures 8–1 and 8–2 differ. In particular, if the firm sells its output competitively, then its inputs

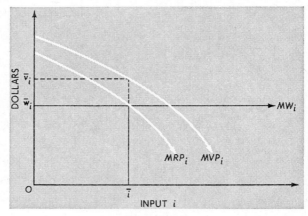

FIGURE 8–2

receive wages equal (in equilibrium) to the value of their marginal contribution to output. Not so should the firm be a monopolist. The wage $\overline{W}_i$ in Figure 8–2 is less than the value of the marginal product of input i when $\bar{i}$ is employed. The latter is equal to $\overline{V}_i$. In the old days, when economists had consciences and businessmen did not, there were fewer philanthropic organizations to support research, but there was a well-developed theory of the exploitation of labor by monopolists. An input was said to be exploited if it was paid less than the value of its marginal product. Thus, input i would be being exploited to the extent $\overline{V}_i - \overline{W}_i$. Since under monopoly, the marginal revenue product of any input is less than the marginal value product, it follows that, under monopoly, all inputs will, by this definition, be exploited. This definition has not proven very useful, however, and accordingly, we will not discuss it further. Since the notion of the marginal value product of an input is primarily of use in determining whether or not the input is being exploited, we shall also cease to allude to that concept.

So long as we are not concerned with possible exploitation of labor, it matters little how a firm which buys its inputs competitively, sells its produce. For any competitive buyer, the conditions for equilibrium in the purchase of factors of production are given regardless of how the firm sells its output. As both Figures 8–1 and 8–2 indicate, the firm will purchase any input i up to that level at which the MRP_i curve intersects the MW_i (AW_i) curve. This invariance of the conditions governing factor demand with respect to differences in the conditions governing the sales of produce has been anticipated in the mathematical appendix to Chapter 6. As pointed out there, the analysis of that appendix applies to *any* firm buying its inputs competitively so long as the firm has a defined revenue function. Thus, equation (4) of the appendix to Chapter 6 applies to all such firms, monopolistic or competitive, and equation (4) says exactly what we have shown in Figures 8–1 and 8–2.

MONOPSONY

Thus far, we have done little in this chapter other than restate graphically results obtained earlier and view these results from a slightly different perspective. We are now prepared to extend our analysis to include situations not dealt with before.

Definition: *A firm is said to be a monopsonist if it is the only buyer of an input and does not take the price as given.*

A firm may be a monopsonist with respect to certain inputs while it purchases other inputs competitively. Monopsony plays the same role in the sale of factors of production that monopoly plays in the sale of output. Just as monopoly is associated with a single seller of a commodity so monopsony is associated with a single buyer. The significant characteristic of the monopsonistic buyer, however, is not his solitude, but the power that he has to change the price of what he purchases by varying the quantity.

Monopsony is really a property of the firm's expenditure function. The reader will recall our discussion of expenditure functions in Chapter 3. There we assumed that the firm took the prices (wages) of inputs as given so that the expenditure function was linear as

$$E = P_x X + P_y Y$$

where E is the level of expenditure, P_x is the price (wage) of input X, P_y is the price (wage) of input Y, and X and Y are quantities of the two inputs. Should the firm be a monopsonistic buyer of input X, the price (wage) that it will have to pay for X will depend upon the quantity of X that it employs, thus

$$P_x = P_x(X) ,$$

all other prices being fixed (see Chapter 9). The firm's expenditure function will then be

$$E = P_x(X) \cdot X + P_y \cdot Y .$$

The linear expenditure function of Chapter 3 led to the systems of linear isoexpenditure curves depicted in that chapter. Thus, in the linear case, an isoexpenditure curve is the locus of all combinations of X and Y such that

$$\bar{E} = P_x X + P_y Y$$

for a given $\bar{E}$, P_x, and P_y. This yields a curve having the equation

$$Y = \frac{\bar{E}}{P_y} - \frac{P_x}{P_y} X$$

which is the equation of a straight line with Y intercept equal to $\bar{E}/P_y$ and a slope of $- P_x/P_y$. In the monopsonistic case

$$Y = \frac{\bar{E}}{P_y} - \frac{P_x(X)}{P_y} X$$

is the equation of the isoexpenditure curve associated with an expenditure of $\bar{E}$. This is not a linear equation because the coefficient of X is itself dependent upon the value of X. The slope of this curve is given by

$$\frac{dY}{dX} = - \frac{1}{P_y} [P_x'(X) \cdot X + P_x(X)] .$$

Since P_y, $P_x'(X)$, $P_x(X)$, and X are all positive, this slope is clearly negative though it will vary with X. Thus, the isoexpenditure curves of a monopsonist will be other than linear, perhaps as in Figure 8–3. There is no implication that these curves will be concave to the origin as shown however.

Suppose that a particular firm sells its production competitively but buys input i monopsonistically. Then the wage that it will pay for input i will increase with the quantity of input i that it purchases. Thus, the average wage curve for input i will be positively sloped as AW_i in Figure 8–4. Note that, like the average revenue curve which can also be considered a demand curve, the average wage curve can be viewed in two ways. If we take quantity

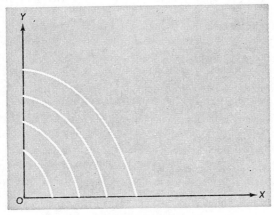

FIGURE 8–3

employed as the independent variable, the average wage curve associates, with each quantity, the per-unit wage required to bring forth that quantity. If we take wage as the independent variable, the curve associates with each wage the quantity that would be offered to the firm at that wage. Thus, the average wage curve for input i may also be called the supply curve of input i for the firm. The marginal curve associated with the average wage curve of Figure 8–4 must lie above it, causing it to rise. Moreover, should none of X_i be bought, no money would be spent on purchasing it. Thus, the total wage curve for input i, were we to draw it, would pass through the origin of Figure 8–4. As shown in Chapter 3, the

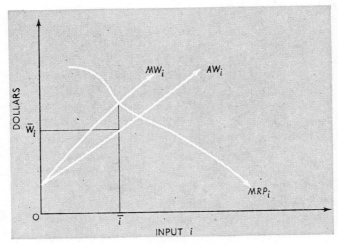

FIGURE 8–4

marginal and average curves associated with a total curve that passes through the origin will cut the vertical axis at a single point. Thus, the marginal wage curve associated with AW_i of Figure 8–4 must start at the same point as AW_i and rise to the right remaining always above AW_i. Such a curve is MW_i in the diagram. As shown above (by the reader) the marginal revenue product curves of a competitive seller will be negatively sloped, as MRP_i in Figure 8–4. As before, the profit-maximizing employment of input i is the level $\bar{i}$ at which the curve MRP_i cuts the curve MW_i from above (why?). Thus, the profit-maximizing firm will employ $\bar{i}$ units of input i. At what wage? According to the average wage curve for input i, a quantity $\bar{i}$ of input i will be forthcoming to the firm at a per-unit wage of $\overline{W}_i$. Should the firm pay less, it will not be able to employ the profit-maximizing amount of input i (because, the firm being monopsonistic, it must pay more to hire more). Should it pay more, the firm would be squandering its substance, for $\bar{i}$ units will be made available to it at $\overline{W}_i$. Thus, the profit-maximizing firm will employ $\bar{i}$ units of input i and pay each unit a wage of $\overline{W}_i$.

The monopsonistic firm, like its monopolistic counterpart, takes on itself many of the characteristics of the marketplace. One tends to think of the marketplace as the institution in which prices are set. That being the case, both the monopsonistic and the monopolistic firm are marketplaces, because both are institutions in which prices are set. In the competitive marketplace, a price (or set of prices) is determined such that consumers will choose to purchase exactly as much as producers will choose to supply. In the monopolistic firm an output which will maximize profits is determined and a price is set so that that output will be sold. In the monopsonistic firm, a level of employment for the input in question is determined such that the firm's profit will be a maximum. A level of wage for the factor is then chosen which is exactly sufficient to get those who supply the factor to offer this amount to the firm.

Should we consider a monopolistic seller who was also a monopsonistic buyer of a particular input, the analysis would be just as above except that were one concerned with the marginal value product of the input, a marginal value product curve lying above MRP_i in Figure 8–4 would be included. The reader's attention is drawn to the fact that by the definition of exploitation dismissed above, the monopsonistic and competitive seller of Figure 8–4 would be exploiting input i. The reader is invited to show that were the firm a monopolistic rather than a competitive seller, exploitation of input i would be increased. He is also invited to note that the quantity purchased of input i and the wage paid to input i are determined in the same way regardless of whether the monopsonistic firm sells its output competitively or monopolistically.

OLIGOPSONY

Purely linguistic considerations would lead one to expect there to be a theory of oligopsony, and indeed one's worst fears would be realized. It is quite possible for the number of buyers of a particular commodity to be such that any action by one, regarding the wage or quantity of the factor employed, would significantly change the average wage functions of the others. An oligopsonistic buyer of an input might well imagine, for example, that, were he to raise the wage of the input, those competing with him for it would be forced to follow suit so that only a small increase in the quantity of the input offered him would be forthcoming and his average wage curve would be relatively steep above the going wage. He might further imagine that should he lower the wage of the input, his competitors would simply be grateful to him and hold the going wage so that he would lose a great deal of the input and his average wage curve would be relatively flat below the going wage. The reader may show that this kinked average wage curve would lead to a discontinuity in the firm's marginal wage curve so that wages would be held constant for limited shifts in the firm's marginal revenue product curve.

Just as the firm's revenue may be shown to be dependent (as in Chapter 7) either upon the quantities sold by the various firms or upon the prices charged by the various firms, so the total expenditure on input i by firm j may be shown to be dependent either upon the wages paid to input i by the various firms or upon the quantities employed by the various firms (the reader should exhibit these different statements of firm j's expenditure on input i). It is, accordingly, possible to develop a theory of "Cournot duopsony" in which each firm supposes that the other will hold its employment of input i fixed and thus adjusts its own employment of i so as to maximize its profits, given its rival's employment of i. Alternatively, it is possible to develop "Stackelberg duopsony," or "Bertrand-Edgeworth duopsony" (the behavioral characteristics of both of which the reader may state for himself). The possibilities are legion. One could discuss a "kinky" oligopsony average wage curve. One could discuss "Cournot duopsonists," their wisdom growing heavy upon them, craftily converting themselves into "Stackelberg duopsonists." One could consider whether or not "Bertrand-Edgeworth duopsonists" were so volatile as their selling counterparts. One could consider all these things and many more as well. One could, but we shall not, for moderation in the pursuit of oligopsony theory is clearly a virtue, and never has it been more truly the case that virtue is its own reward.

MATHEMATICAL APPENDIX TO CHAPTER 8

It is the purpose of this appendix briefly to discuss a problem that has not been explicitly mentioned in the text. Suppose that the firm determines its employment of the various factors of production so as to maximize its profits. Will the total of what is thus paid out to factors be equal to the value of what is produced? That is, will the value of all that is produced be paid out to *some* factor? In the vernacular of the profession, will the product be exhausted? Having asked this question three times it behooves us to answer it at least once.

The reader will recall that the function $f(X_1, \ldots, X_n)$ is said to be homogeneous of degree h if

$$f(\lambda X_1, \ldots, \lambda X_n) \equiv \lambda^h f(X_1, \ldots, X_n).$$

Since this is an identity, we may differentiate both sides with respect to λ and it will remain true. Taking

$$Z_i = \lambda X_i$$

we have

(1) $$f(Z_1, \ldots, Z_n) \equiv \lambda^h f(X_1, \ldots, X_n).$$

By the chain rule

$$\frac{df}{d\lambda} = \sum_{i=1}^{n} \frac{\partial f}{\partial Z_i} \frac{\partial Z_i}{\partial \lambda} = \sum_{i=1}^{n} f_{Z_i} X_i.$$

Differentiating the right-hand side of (1) with respect to λ yields

$$h f(X_1, \ldots, X_n) \lambda^{h-1}.$$

Thus

$$\sum_{i=1}^{n} f_{Z_i} X_i \equiv h f(X_1, \ldots, X_n) \lambda^{h-1}.$$

Evaluating this at a particular point, we let $\lambda = 1$, so that

$$Z_i = X_i,$$

and we get,

$$f_1 X_1 + f_2 X_2 + \ldots + f_n X_n \equiv h f(X_1, \ldots, X_n),$$

Euler's theorem on homogeneous functions.

Consider a firm which buys its inputs competitively and sells

232

its output competitively. As shown above, such a firm will pay input i a wage W_i such that

$$W_i = P\Phi_i$$

where P is the price of output, marginal revenue, and Φ_i is the marginal product of input i. Thus

(2)
$$\sum_{i=1}^{n} W_i X_i = \sum_{i=1}^{n} P\Phi_i X_i = P \sum_{i=1}^{n} \Phi_i X_i .$$

If the firm's production function is homogeneous of degree 1, then

$$\sum_{i=1}^{n} \Phi_i X_i = \Phi(X_1, \ldots , X_n)$$

by Euler's theorem. Then the value of the firm's output will be

(3)
$$P \cdot \Phi(X_1, \ldots , X_n) = P \sum_{i=1}^{n} \Phi_i X_i = \sum_{i=1}^{n} W_i X_i ,$$

by equation (2). A firm which buys and sells competitively and which has a production function homogeneous of degree 1 will, by equation (3), pay its factors of production in total exactly the value of what it produces. Production will be exhausted in payments to factors.

Should the firm buy monopsonistically or sell monopolistically, then

$$W_i < P\Phi_i .$$

Equation (2) becomes an inequality

$$\sum_{i=1}^{n} W_i X_i < P \sum_{i=1}^{n} \Phi_i X_i ,$$

so that, should the production function be homogeneous of degree 1, equation (3) becomes

$$\sum_{i=1}^{n} W_i X_i < P \cdot \Phi(X_1, \ldots , X_n) .$$

Having paid all factors, the firm will have money left over in the form of excess profits.

If the firm's production function is other than homogeneous, we cannot apply Euler's theorem to determine whether or not the firm will pay all that it earns to factors of production. The reader will recall, however, that in long-run equilibrium, both monopolistically competitive firms (Chapter 6) and perfectly competitive firms (Chapter 5) earn zero profits. Consider any such firm in long-run equilibrium. The profit function will be

$$\Pi = R[\Phi(X_1, \ldots, X_n)] - \sum_{i=1}^{n} W_i X_i$$

if the firm has no fixed cost, attributable to nonfactors. For profits to be zero

$$(4) \qquad R[\Phi(X_1, \ldots, X_n)] = \sum_{i=1}^{n} W_i X_i .$$

The left-hand side of equation (4) is the value of the firm's output. The right-hand side is the total of payments to factors by the firm. Thus, any monopolistically competitive or perfectly competitive firm having no fixed payments to make to nonfactors will, in long-run equilibrium, pay out all that it earns to factors of production. So will *any* firm making zero profits, and indeed, one would have it no other way.

SELECTED BIBLIOGRAPHY

HICKS, J. R. *Value and Capital.* 2d ed. Oxford: Clarendon Press, 1946.

LEFTWICH, R. H. *The Price System and Resource Allocation.* Rev. ed. New York: Holt, Rinehart & Winston, 1960.

SAMUELSON, P. A. *Foundations of Economic Analysis.* Cambridge, Mass.: Harvard University Press, 1948.

STIGLER, G. J. *The Theory of Price.* Rev. ed. New York: Macmillan Co., 1952.

———. *Production and Distribution Theories.* New York: Macmillan Co., 1941.

PART IV
All Together Now

Chapter 9

THE GENERAL EQUILIBRIUM OF THE ENTIRE SYSTEM

The little wheel runs by faith and
The big wheel runs by the grace of God.
—*"Ezekial Saw the Wheel"**

In Chapter 2, we introduced the notion of general equilibrium in the context of a pure exchange economy. In the chapters since 2, we have developed the theory of production under various types of market organization. In this chapter, we shall return to our discussion of general equilibrium introducing production and non-competitive markets. Earlier, we presented the theory of consumer equilibrium which presumes to describe the way in which the consumer chooses the quantities that he will purchase of the various commodities. Later, we stated the components of the theory of production which would describe the ways in which firms under alternative market organizations determine how much to offer for sale. In this chapter, we bring all this together to exhibit a theory of the way in which a set of prices may be defined such that firms, maximizing their profits, will choose to offer for sale precisely that quantity of each commodity that consumers, maximizing their utility subject to their budget restraints, will choose to purchase.

The equilibrium configuration of prices and quantities which we shall derive has no particular properties other than those mentioned in the last sentence of the previous paragraph. There is no implication that the configuration is stable in the sense that prices and quantities will somehow tend, over time, to approach these equilibrium values. Such implications of stability would require explicit dynamic analysis which we have not provided. If our theories of the ways in which economic units behave are correct, then the equilibrium configuration that we derive will be one such that no economic unit would have reason to move from it

---

* "Ezekial Saw the Wheel" was first published in Thomas P. Fenner, *Religious Folk Songs of the Negro As Sung on the Plantation.* Copyright, Hampton Institute, 1909. USED BY PERMISSION.

unless something governing its choices were to change. One sometimes sees references to this sort of equilibrium as equilibrium at a
point in time. This is, at best, misleading. We will derive a set of
prices and quantities appropriate (in the sense of the preceding
paragraph) to a given "economic situation," i.e., to given consumers' tastes, production functions, organization of markets, etc.
So long as this "economic situation" does not change, the equilibrium price-quantity configuration will not vary either, and time has
nothing to do with it. Whether or not the equilibrium configuration
will *ever* be attained is quite another question, the answer to which
depends upon the correctness of our theory and the dynamics of
actual behavior, both of which topics are outside the competence of
this book.

A general equilibrium model of production and exchange will
serve two functions. First, if, in fact, "everything depends upon
everything else," then it is well that we be able to describe or at
least characterize this interdependence. This is what a general
equilibrium model attempts to do. In addition, we have supposed
that economic units strive for their various goals in different ways.
Is it possible for them all to achieve these goals? Is profit
maximization by firms consistent with utility maximization by
consumers, or will the one somehow frustrate the other? In a
general equilibrium model, we exhibit a set of equations having the
property that when the variables of the model take on values such
that all of these equations are simultaneously true, then each
economic unit will be achieving its assumed goal. We further show
(at least under the equation counting untheorem of Chapter 2) that
the set of equations *may be* simultaneously solved. Thus, the
construction of a general equilibrium model enables us, in part, to
check the mutual consistency of the models employed to describe the
behavior of the various economic units.

Pure Competition Again

The reader will recall our discussion in Chapter 2 of the
general equilibrium of a competitive pure exchange economy. In
particular, he will recall that we directed our attention to the set of
market demand functions

$$X_1(P_1, \ldots, P_n) = S_1$$
$$X_2(P_1, \ldots, P_n) = S_2$$
$$\cdots\cdots\cdots\cdots\cdots\cdots$$
$$X_n(P_1, \ldots, P_n) = S_n,$$

where S_i is the given supply of commodity i, $X_i(P_1, \ldots, P_n)$ is the
market demand function for commodity i, and P_i is the price of
commodity i. We sought a set of P's such that these equations

should be simultaneously true. This set of P's would provide for each commodity a market demand that was exactly equal to the given market supply. Implicitly, we supposed that the consumers could see to the distribution of this quantity so that not only was the market supplied with precisely the quantity that the consumers *in the aggregate* desired of each commodity, but each individual consumer took home that bundle which he most preferred among those that he could afford. In the more complex general equilibrium system to which we are about to turn, it is no longer feasible to leave such matters implicit. Nor is it wise to turn directly from the simple implicit model of Chapter 2 to the significantly more complex model that we have here to consider. Accordingly, before turning to our model of the general equilibrium of production and exchange, we will again examine the competitive pure exchange model of Chapter 2, this time dealing explicitly with the distribution of commodities among consumers.

Suppose that there are n commodities and L consumers. Let $\overline{X}_{ij}$ represent consumer j's initial endowment of commodity i. Let X_{ij} represent the amount of commodity i that he has after trading. Finally, let P_i be the price of commodity i. Suppose that commodity n is the numéraire (money) so that $P_n = 1$. Consumer j will attempt to maximize his utility function,

$$U_j = U_j(X_{1j}, \ldots, X_{nj})$$

subject to his budget restraint,

$$\sum_{i=1}^{n} P_i(\overline{X}_{ij} - X_{ij}) = 0 .$$

As in the mathematical appendix to Chapter 1, the first-order conditions for this maximization are

(1)
$$\begin{cases} U_{ij} - \lambda P_i = 0 , & i = 1, \ldots, n \\ \sum_{i=1}^{n} P_i(\overline{X}_{ij} - X_{ij}) = 0 , \end{cases}$$

where

$$U_{ij} = \frac{\partial U_j}{\partial X_{ij}} .$$

Since $P_n = 1$,

$$U_{nj} = \lambda .$$

Thus, we may eliminate the Lagrange multiplier from equations (1) by substituting U_{nj} for it to obtain the diminished set of equations

$$(2) \quad \begin{cases} U_{ij} = U_{nj}P_i, & i = 1, \ldots, n-1, \\ \sum_{i=1}^{n} P_i(\overline{X}_{ij} - X_{ij}) = 0. \end{cases}$$

Equations (2) are n in number, and (supposing that the second-order conditions for a maximum are satisfied) they may be solved to find the values of the n variables $X_{1j}, \ldots, X_{nj}$ which consumer j would prefer given his budget restraint. A similar set of equations may be written for each consumer.

In order that each market be cleared, it is necessary that

$$(3) \quad \sum_{j=1}^{L} X_{ij} = \sum_{j=1}^{L} \overline{X}_{ij}, \quad i = 1, \ldots, n;$$

that is, that the consumers, in total, shall have, after trading, the same amount of each commodity that they, in total, had at the beginning of trading. The act of trading neither creates nor destroys commodities, it simply redistributes them. The sums in equations (3) are taken over all consumers. We shall refer to equations (3) as market-clearing conditions.

We wish to determine how much each of L consumers will demand of each of n commodities. Thus, there are $L \cdot n$ variables

$$X_{ij}, \quad \begin{aligned} i &= 1, \ldots, n, \\ j &= 1, \ldots, L, \end{aligned}$$

the equilibrium values of which are to be established. In addition to these, we are interested in the equilibrium values of the $n-1$ prices, $P_1, \ldots, P_{n-1}$ ($P_n = 1$). This gives us a total of

$$L \cdot n + n - 1 = n(L+1) - 1$$

variables to determine. According to the untheorem of Chapter 2, we need $n(L+1) - 1$ equations with which to determine them. Each of L consumers will select their purchases of commodities so as to satisfy a system of equations like (2). In addition, n market-clearing equations (3) must be satisfied if supply is to equal demand in each market. We, therefore, have the following system of $n(L+1)$ equations:

$$(4) \quad \begin{cases} U_{ij} = U_{nj}P_i, & i = 1, \ldots, n-1, \\ \sum_{i=1}^{n} P_i(\overline{X}_{ij} - X_{ij}) = 0, & j = 1, \ldots, L, \\ \sum_{j=1}^{L} X_{ij} = \sum_{j=1}^{L} \overline{X}_{ij}, & i = 1, \ldots, n. \end{cases}$$

It is easy to see that the last $L + n$ of equations (4) are dependent. We need only utilize Walras' Law for this system.

Suppose that for $j = 1, \ldots, L$

$$\sum_{i=1}^{n} P_i(\overline{X}_{ij} - X_{ij}) = 0.$$

Then

$$\sum_{j=1}^{L} \sum_{i=1}^{n} P_i(\overline{X}_{ij} - X_{ij}) = 0.$$

Since we may add these terms in any order, we have

(5) $$\sum_{i=1}^{n} P_i \sum_{j=1}^{L} (\overline{X}_{ij} - X_{ij}) = 0,$$

Walras' Law in the form of an equality. Suppose further that all but one (say the last) of the market-clearing conditions are satisfied, then

$$\sum_{j=1}^{L} X_{ij} = \sum_{j=1}^{L} \overline{X}_{ij}, \qquad i = 1, \ldots, n - 1.$$

Thus

$$\sum_{i=1}^{n-1} P_i \sum_{j=1}^{L} (\overline{X}_{ij} - X_{ij}) = 0,$$

simply because each of the terms

$$\sum_{j=1}^{L} (\overline{X}_{ij} - X_{ij}) = 0, \qquad i = 1, \ldots, n - 1.$$

Walras' Law, equation (5), then implies that

$$\sum_{j=1}^{L} (\overline{X}_{nj} - X_{nj}) = 0.$$

If all but one of the market-clearing conditions of the last $L + n$ of equations (4) are satisfied then so must that one be true. Thus we may drop any one of the last n of equations (4). This leaves us with, at most, $n(L + 1) - 1$ independent equations, say (dropping the nth equation)

(6) $$\begin{cases} U_{ij} = U_{nj}P_i, & \begin{aligned} i &= 1, \ldots, n - 1, \\ j &= 1, \ldots, L, \end{aligned} \\[2ex] \displaystyle\sum_{i=1}^{n} P_i(\overline{X}_{ij} - X_{ij}) = 0, & j = 1, \ldots, L, \\[2ex] \displaystyle\sum_{j=1}^{L} X_{ij} = \sum_{j=1}^{L} \overline{X}_{ij}, & i = 1, \ldots, n - 1. \end{cases}$$

which may, by our untheorem, be solved to yield those values of the variables

$$X_{ij}, \quad \begin{aligned} i &= 1, \ldots, n, \\ j &= 1, \ldots, L, \end{aligned}$$

and

$$P_i, \quad i = 1, \ldots, n - 1,$$

which will have each consumer maximizing his utility given his budget, and each market cleared.

The General Equilibrium of the Entire System

Equations (6) comprise an example of a complete general equilibrium system albeit for a very simple economy. The equilibrium values of all prices and quantities purchased may be determined by the simultaneous solution of these equations. We now wish to develop such a model of a more complex economy. Particularly, we desire such a model of production consumption and exchange in an economy having elements of monopoly and monopsony, as well as competitive firms and consumers who take prices as given. We shall not talk of oligopoly; however, the model that we shall present could include firms behaving according to certain of the oligopolistic models of Chapter 7 (clearly, since collusive oligopolists would behave like monopolists). We require only that each monopolistic demand function and each monopsonistic supply function be defined and differentiable.

Suppose that there are n commodities, the nth being the numéraire so that $P_n = 1$. Let there be L consumers all of whom take prices as given. Finally, let there be m firms. Our problem is to exhibit a set of equations with which to establish the net demand (supply) for each commodity by each consumer, the net supply (demand) by each producer for each commodity and a set of market clearing prices.

Because the arguments will be of a familiar form, we shall begin by discussing the consumer sector. We shall use j subscripts to refer to consumers, i subscripts to refer to commodities, and k subscripts to refer to firms. Thus, consumer j will choose his final consumption bundle so as to maximize

(7) $$U_j = U_j(X_{1j}, \ldots, X_{nj})$$

subject to

(8) $$\sum_{i=1}^{n} P_i(X_{ij} - \overline{X}_{ij}) = R_j$$

where P_i is the price of commodity i, X_{ij} is j's consumption of commodity i, $\overline{X}_{ij}$ is his initial endowment of i, and R_j is his receipt of excess profits. This last variable is included because of considerations introduced in the mathematical appendix to Chapter 8. In general, the initial endowment vector of consumer j, $\overline{X}_{1j}, \ldots, \overline{X}_{nj}$, will include some factors of production. The consumer will receive purchasing power by selling such inputs as his budget restraint, equation (8), indicates. However, there is no reason to believe that for each firm, production is exhausted. Some firms may realize profits over and above their payments to factors of production. These excess profits are distributed to the owners of such firms. Should consumer j be such an owner, he will receive such income in addition to whatever he may earn by selling his initial endowment. In this case, $R_j > 0$. Should consumer j not be such an owner, his total purchasing power will be from the sale of his initial endowment and $R_j = 0$. Should consumer j be so ill advised as to be an owner of firms which earn less than enough to pay the factors that they employ, then $R_j < 0$. R_j is simply a notational convenience. We suppose that individual j owns a fixed proportion λ_{jk} of firm k. Thus, if Π_k is the profit of firm k, then

$$R_j \equiv \sum_{k=1}^{m} \lambda_{jk} \Pi_k, \qquad j = 1, \ldots, L.$$

We shall continue, for a time, to use the shorthand, R_j, to denote the profit income of individual j.

The first-order conditions for (7) to be a maximum subject to (8) are

$$U_{ij} - \lambda P_i = 0, \qquad i = 1, \ldots, n,$$

$$\sum_{i=1}^{n} P_i(X_{ij} - \overline{X}_{ij}) = R_j,$$

where U_{ij} is as defined in the preceding section of this chapter. Since $P_n = 1$, these conditions imply

$$U_{nj} = \lambda.$$

Employing this equality to delete λ from the above system yields n equations

(9)
$$U_{ij} = U_{nj} P_i, \qquad i = 1, \ldots, n - 1,$$
$$\sum_{i=1}^{n} P_i(X_{ij} - \overline{X}_{ij}) = R_j.$$

Each of the L consumers will choose his consumption bundle so as to satisfy a set of n equations of this sort.

We wish to include in our model monopolistic, monopsonistic, and competitive firms. It will, thus, be convenient for us to develop a theory of profit maximization for a multiproduct multi-input firm which sells some of its products monopolistically and some competitively and buys some of its inputs monopsonistically and some competitively. We shall refer to commodities traded monopolistically or monopsonistically as *monops*. We shall refer to firms that sell some commodities monopolistically and/or buy some monopsonistically as *monopic* firms. We suppose that any monopic firm trades exclusively with consumers and nonmonopic firms. In other words, the buyers of all monopolistically sold commodities and the sellers of all monopsonistically purchased commodities take all prices as given. In a phrase, monopic firms do not trade with other monopic firms. This assumption allows us to define unambiguously the market demand (supply) function for each monop.

Equations (9) may be solved to yield consumer demand functions as in the mathematical appendix to Chapter 1. For consumer j, these would be of the form[1]

$$X_{ij} = X_{ij}(P_1, \ldots, P_n, \overline{X}_{1j}, \ldots, \overline{X}_{nj}, R_j), \qquad i = 1, \ldots . n.$$

From the mathematical appendix to Chapter 5, we have the demand (supply) functions for a competitive firm k

$$X_{ik} = X_{ik}(P_1, \ldots, P_n), \qquad i = 1, \ldots, n.$$

Since we suppose that monopic firms trade only with consumers and competitive firms, we add together the demand (supply) functions of consumers and competitive firms to derive the market demand (supply) function for any monop. If firm k is monopic in commodities $1, \ldots, s_k$ and competitive in commodities $s_k + 1, \ldots, n$, then we may employ the notational convention introduced in the mathematical appendix to Chapter 5 to write its profit function

$$(10) \qquad \Pi_k = \sum_{i=1}^{s_k} P_i X_{ik}(P^*, \overline{X}^*, R^*) + \sum_{i=s_k+1}^{n} P_i X_{ik},$$

where $P^* = (P_1, \ldots, P_n)$ is the vector of prices, $\overline{X}^* = (\overline{X}_{11}, \overline{X}_{21}, \ldots, \overline{X}_{n-1L}, \overline{X}_{nL})$ is the vector of initial endowments of all consumers, and $R^* = (R_1, \ldots, R_L)$ is the vector of all consumers' profit receipts. The function $X_{ik}(P^*, \overline{X}^*, R^*)$ is the market demand function for commodity i and is formed by adding together the demand functions of all consumers and all nonmonopic firms. Π_k is firm k's profit, and X_{ik}, if it is positive, is firm k's production of commodity i, and if it is negative, is firm k's input of commodity i. Should firm k be nonmonopic, it may yet buy from or sell to monopic firms, but it will take all prices as given.

---

[1] The reader's attention is drawn to the fact that individual j begins trading with $\overline{X}_{ij}$ of commodity i and ends it with X_{ij}. Should $\overline{X}_{ij} > X_{ij}$, then individual j is a net supplier of commodity i, i.e., his excess demand for i is negative.

Its profit function would then be as shown in the mathematical appendix to Chapter 5. The s_k of equation (10) would be zero for such a firm.

Because the independent variables of the market demand functions in equation (10) are the prices, it is convenient to consider firm k as a price setter in its monopic markets. By this, we mean that rather than choosing $X_{1k}, \ldots, X_{nk}$ so as to maximize its profit, it is convenient to suppose that the firm selects $P_1, \ldots, P_{s_k}, X_{s_k+1}, \ldots, X_{nk}$ so as to maximize profit. Prices $P_{s_k+1}, \ldots, P_n$ are given to the firm. On the basis of these prices and the market situation by which it is faced the firm chooses those values of the variables under its control, $P_1, \ldots, P_{s_k}$, $X_{s_k+1k}, \ldots, X_{nk}$, which will render its profit a maximum.

It is necessary that the inputs that the firm chooses to employ be sufficient to produce the outputs that it chooses to sell. As in the mathematical appendix to Chapter 5, the firm will maximize its profit function, equation (10), subject to an implicit production function,

(11) $f_k[X_{1k}(P^*, \bar{X}^*, R^*), \ldots, X_{s_kk}(P^*, \bar{X}^*, R^*),$
$$X_{s_k+1k}, \ldots, X_{nk}] = 0\,.$$

This function is an efficiency frontier, associating with each set of outputs those sets of inputs which will just produce it.

Firm k will choose those values of $P_1, \ldots, P_{s_k}, X_{s_k+1k}, \ldots, X_{nk}$ (hereafter called *control variables*) that maximize

(10) $$\Pi_k = \sum_{i=1}^{s_k} P_i X_{ik}(P^*, \bar{X}^*, R^*) + \sum_{i=s_k+1}^{n} P_i X_{ik}$$

subject to

(11) $f_k[X_{1k}(P^*, \bar{X}^*, R^*), \ldots, X_{s_kk}(P^*, \bar{X}^*, R^*),$
$$X_{s_k+1k}, \ldots, X_{nk}] = 0\,.$$

Form the Lagrangian function

(12) $$H_k = \Pi_k - \lambda f_k\,.$$

The firm seeks values for the control variables and for λ which will render (12) a maximum. For convenience we will utilize the following notation:

$$\Pi_{rk} = \frac{\partial \Pi_k}{\partial X_{rk}},$$
$$f_{rk} = \frac{\partial f_k}{\partial X_{rk}},$$
$$\Pi_{kP_r} = \frac{\partial \Pi_k}{\partial P_r}, \quad \text{and}$$
$$f_{kP_r} = \frac{\partial f_k}{\partial P_r}\,.$$

From (10)

$$\Pi_{kP_r} = X_{rk} + \sum_{j=1}^{s_k} P_j \frac{\partial X_{jk}}{\partial P_r}, \qquad r = 1, \ldots, s_k,$$

and

$$\Pi_{rk} = P_r, \qquad r = s_k + 1, \ldots, n.$$

from (11)

$$f_{kP_r} = \sum_{j=1}^{s_k} f_{jk} \frac{\partial X_{jk}}{\partial P_r}, \qquad r = 1, \ldots, s_k.$$

Then the first-order conditions for (12) to be a maximum include

$$\Pi_{kP_r} - \lambda f_{kP_r} = 0, \qquad r = 1, \ldots, s_k,$$
$$\Pi_{rk} - \lambda f_{rk} = 0, \qquad r = s_k + 1, \ldots, n.$$

Utilizing the last of these we may write

$$\lambda = \frac{\Pi_{nk}}{f_{nk}}.$$

Substituting this ratio for λ we may write the first-order conditions for (11) to be a maximum subject to (12) as follows

(13)
$$\begin{cases} \dfrac{\Pi_{kP_r}}{f_{kP_r}} = \dfrac{\Pi_{nk}}{f_{nk}}, & r = 1, \ldots, s_k, \\[2mm] \dfrac{\Pi_{tk}}{f_{tk}} = \dfrac{\Pi_{nk}}{f_{nk}}, & t = s_k + 1, \ldots, n - 1, \\[2mm] f_k[X_{1k}(P^*, \overline{X}^*, R^*), \ldots, X_{s_k k}(P^*, \overline{X}^*, R^*), \\ \qquad\qquad\qquad X_{s_k+1k}, \ldots, X_{nk}] = 0. \end{cases}$$

Supposing that the second-order conditions are met the firm will maximize its profit by choosing those values of the n control variables, $P_1, \ldots, P_{s_k}, X_{s_k+1k}, \ldots, X_{nk}$, which satisfy the n equations (13).

If conditions (9) are satisfied, consumer j will maximize his utility subject to his budget restraint. If conditions (13) are satisfied, firm k will be maximizing its profits subject to the constraint of its implicit production function. It remains for us to establish conditions which insure that markets be cleared. We require nothing more than the statement that firms in the aggregate buy (sell) what consumers in the aggregate sell (buy). Market i will be cleared if

(14)
$$\sum_{j=1}^{L} (X_{ij} - \overline{X}_{ij}) = \sum_{k=1}^{m} X_{ik}.$$

We have now stated conditions necessary for each type of economic unit, consumers, firms, and markets, to be in equilibrium. The general equilibrium of the entire system requires that all such units shall simultaneously be in equilibrium. The equilibrium configurations of the various units must be mutually consistent. Market-clearing equations (14) are nothing more than an assertion that the quantities that consumers in total choose to buy (sell) be consistent with the quantities that firms in total choose to sell (buy). If the conditions for one economic unit to be in equilibrium somehow require one value of a variable while those for another unit to be in equilibrium require that the same variable take on a different value, things will indeed be amiss.

Given the ownership of firms within the economy, prices and sales by firms determine the profit incomes of individuals, $R_1, \ldots,$ R_L. The distribution of profit income in turn determines, in part, the sales that firms will be able to realize. We need a set of equations to establish values for these variables so that the values of $R_1, \ldots, R_L$ on the basis of which firms choose output so as to maximize their profits are the same values that the distribution of those profits will lead to. From equation (10) we have firm k's profit

$$\Pi_k = \sum_{i=1}^{n} P_i X_{ik}, \qquad k = 1, \ldots, m.$$

Similarly we have defined individual j's profit income as

$$R_j = \sum_{k=1}^{m} \lambda_{jk} \Pi_k, \qquad j = 1, \ldots, L,$$

where λ_{jk} is the fixed proportion of firm k owned by individual j. Thus

$$(15) \qquad R_j = \sum_{k=1}^{m} \lambda_{jk} \sum_{i=1}^{n} P_i X_{ik}, \qquad j = 1, \ldots, L.$$

Substituting equation (15) into the conditions for consumer j to be in equilibrium, equations (9), yields

$$U_{ij} = U_{nj} P_i, \qquad i = 1, \ldots, n - 1,$$

$$(16)$$

$$\sum_{i=1}^{n} P_i (X_{ij} - \bar{X}_{ij}) = \sum_{k=1}^{m} \lambda_{jk} \sum_{i=1}^{n} P_i X_{ik}.$$

Equations (16) tie the consumer's purchases of commodities explicitly to the profit income of those firms of which he is part owner.

Supposing that the second-order conditions for maximization

are satisfied for all consumers and all firms, we require that for each consumer, conditions (16) be satisfied; for each firm, conditions (13) be satisfied; and for each market, conditions (14) be satisfied. Consider the system of equations

a)
$$\begin{cases} U_{ij} = U_{nj}P_i, & \begin{aligned} i &= 1, \ldots, n-1, \\ j &= 1, \ldots, L, \end{aligned} \\ \sum_{i=1}^{n} P_i(X_{ij} - \bar{X}_{ij}) = \sum_{k=1}^{m} \lambda_{jk} \sum_{i=1}^{n} P_i X_{ik}, & j = 1, \ldots, L. \end{cases}$$

b)
$$\begin{cases} \dfrac{\Pi_{kP_r}}{f_{kP_r}} = \dfrac{\Pi_{nk}}{f_{nk}}, & \begin{aligned} r &= 1, \ldots, s_k, \\ k &= 1, \ldots, m, \end{aligned} \\ \dfrac{\Pi_{tk}}{f_{tk}} = \dfrac{\Pi_{nk}}{f_{nk}}, & \begin{aligned} t &= s_{k+1}, \ldots, n-1, \\ k &= 1, \ldots, m, \end{aligned} \\ f_k[X_{1k}, \ldots, X_{nk}] = 0, & k = 1, \ldots, m, \end{cases}$$

c)
$$\sum_{j=1}^{L} (X_{ij} - \bar{X}_{ij}) = \sum_{k=1}^{m} X_{ik}, \qquad i = 1, \ldots, n-1.$$

We seek to establish the quantity of each of n commodities consumed (sold) by each of L consumers, Ln variables. We further seek the production (purchase) of each of n commodities by each of m firms, mn variables. Finally, since $P_n = 1$, we seek only $n-1$ prices. This gives us

$$Ln + mn + n - 1 = n(L + m + 1) - 1$$

variables to determine. Equations (*a*) are nL in number, equations (*b*) are mn in number, and equations (*c*) are $n-1$ in number. Thus, we have

$$nL + mn + n - 1 = n(L + m + 1) - 1$$

equations which, according to the untheorem of Chapter 2, is precisely what we need. However, examination of equations (*c*) indicates that one market-clearing equation,

(17)
$$\sum_{j=1}^{L} (X_{nj} - \bar{X}_{nj}) = \sum_{k=1}^{m} X_{nk}$$

has been left out. If the entire economy is to be in equilibrium, *all* markets, including the nth, must be cleared. Then (17) must be satisfied. We shall show that if the last L of equations (*a*) and all of equations (*c*) are satisfied, then equation (17) must be satisfied.

If equations (*a*) are satisfied we may add the last L of them to get

(18)
$$\sum_{j=1}^{L} \sum_{i=1}^{n} P_i(X_{ij} - \bar{X}_{ij}) = \sum_{j=1}^{L} \sum_{k=1}^{m} \lambda_{jk} \sum_{i=1}^{n} P_i X_{ik}.$$

All of each firm must be owned by someone, thus

$$\sum_{j=1}^{L} \lambda_{jk} = 1, \quad k = 1, \ldots, m.$$

Since we may take the sums on the right-hand side of (18) in any order, this yields

$$\sum_{j=1}^{L} \sum_{i=1}^{n} P_i(X_{ij} - \overline{X}_{ij}) = \sum_{i=1}^{n} \sum_{k=1}^{m} P_i X_{ik}.$$

Rearranging these terms once more yields

(19) $$\sum_{i=1}^{n} P_i \sum_{j=1}^{L} (X_{ij} - \overline{X}_{ij}) = \sum_{i=1}^{n} P_i \sum_{k=1}^{m} X_{ik},$$

a form of Walras' Law. If conditions (c) are satisfied then

(20) $$\sum_{i=1}^{n-1} P_i \sum_{j=1}^{L} (X_{ij} - \overline{X}_{ij}) = \sum_{i=1}^{n-1} P_i \sum_{k=1}^{m} X_{ik}.$$

If (19) is true and (20) is true then we may subtract the latter from the former to get

$$P_n \sum_{j=1}^{L} (X_{nj} - \overline{X}_{nj}) = P_n \sum_{k=1}^{m} X_{nk},$$

and dividing both sides of this by P_n yields (17). Thus if the last L of equations (a) and all of equations (c) are satisfied then equation (17) must be satisfied as well. Accordingly, should we establish the values of the $n(L + m + 1) - 1$ variables that satisfy the $n(L + m + 1) - 1$ equations (a), (b), and (c), and should our theories of the economic processes involved be correct, then no economic unit would have cause to change its ways so long as the "economic situation" did not change. More we cannot say.

The Pareto Optimality of Purely Competitive Equilibrium

In Chapter 2, we introduced the concept of Pareto optimality. A situation was said to be Pareto optimal if given the relevant preference orderings, no one could be made better off without someone else being made worse off. We showed that if there are but two persons and two commodities, then a competitive pure exchange equilibrium was Pareto optimal. We *argued* that the same thing would be true if there were n persons and m commodities. We have since developed the theory of production, and the question suggests itself: if one allows for the existence of production, is a purely competitive equilibrium then Pareto optimal? In this section, we shall show that it is. In particular, we shall show that if there are L persons and n commodities, production is possible and all people take prices as given, then the resultant equilibrium configuration is Pareto optimal.

The productive resources of such an economy will consist of whatever capital assets it might contain and whatever skills and abilities the population may possess in transforming existent commodities into more desirable commodities. Let X_{ij} be the quantity of commodity i ultimately possessed by individual j. He may employ this in the production of other commodities. We seek conditions such that no person may be made better off without some other being made worse off. This will be true when each individual's utility is maximized subject to the constraints that each other person's utility be at a fixed level and that the quantities possessed by all individuals be producible by the economy.

Maximize each individual j's utility function

$$\text{(21)} \qquad U_j = U_j(X_{1j}, \ldots, X_{nj})$$

as j goes from 1 to L, subject to the constraints

$$\text{(22)} \qquad \bar{U}_i = U_i(X_{1i}, \ldots, X_{ni}), \qquad i = 1, \ldots, L \neq j,$$

and

$$\text{(23)} \qquad F(X_1, \ldots, X_n) = 0$$

where

$$X_i \equiv \sum_{j=1}^{L} X_{ij}.$$

Constraint (23) is an implicit production function for the entire economy. The identity is not a constraint. It is simply a notational convenience enabling us to write (23) in manageable form. The process here is to first maximize

$$U_1 = U_1(X_{11}, \ldots, X_{n1})$$

subject to

$$\bar{U}_i = U_i(X_{1i}, \ldots, X_{ni}), \qquad i = 2, \ldots, L,$$

and to

$$F(X_1, \ldots, X_n) = 0,$$

and list the necessary conditions for this maximum. Then maximize

$$U_2 = U_2(X_{12}, \ldots, X_{n2})$$

subject to

$$\bar{U}_i = U_i(X_{1i}, \ldots, X_{ni}) , \qquad i = 1, 3, \ldots, L ,$$

and to

$$F(X_1, \ldots, X_n) = 0$$

and list the necessary conditions for this maximum. Then maximize

$$U_3(X_{13}, \ldots, X_{n3})$$

subject to the appropriate constraints, etc. For Pareto optimality it must be true that *no* man can be made better off without some other being made worse off. Accordingly, second-order conditions being satisfied, the conditions for Pareto optimality involve the simultaneous satisfaction of the first-order conditions for all L of these constrained maxima, each one of which insures that a particular individual can be made no better off without some other being made worse off.

To formulate this in terms of Lagrange's method we first recognize that if $\bar{U}_i$ is some constant, then when $U_i(X_{1i}, \ldots, X_{ni})$ is a maximum so will $U_i(X_{1i}, \ldots, X_{ni}) - \bar{U}_i$ be a maximum. We then formulate the L individual maximization processes as follows: maximize the Lagrangian functions

$$(24) \qquad \sum_{i=1}^{L} \lambda_i [U_i(X_{1i}, \ldots, X_{ni}) - \bar{U}_i] + \lambda_{L+1} F(X_1, \ldots, X_n) ,$$

alternatively allowing $\lambda_j = 1$, as j goes from 1 to L. The first-order conditions for *all* these constrained maxima to be simultaneously true so that *no* man can be made better off without another being made worse off are

$$U_{ij} = \lambda_{L+1} F_{ij} , \qquad \begin{aligned} i &= 1, \ldots, n , \\ j &= 1, \ldots, L . \end{aligned}$$

Since the terms X_{ij} enter (23) as they do

$$F_{ij} = F_i , \qquad j = 1, \ldots, L .$$

Thus, eliminating the Lagrangian multipliers, the first-order conditions for Pareto optimality may be written

$$(25) \qquad \frac{U_{rj}}{U_{sj}} = \frac{F_r}{F_s} , \qquad \begin{aligned} r, s &= 1, \ldots, n , \\ j &= 1, \ldots, L . \end{aligned}$$

We shall not discuss the second-order conditions but will suppose that they are satisfied.[2]

Having supposed that the second-order conditions for Pareto optimality are satisfied, we need only show that the conditions for purely competitive equilibrium imply the first-order conditions for Pareto optimality, conditions (25). This will be sufficient to establish the Pareto optimality of purely competitive equilibrium. To this end, we must state the relevant conditions for purely competitive equilibrium. With the variables defined as before, consumer j will choose to become possessed of that bundle of commodities $X_{1j}, \ldots, X_{nj}$ such that $U_j = U_j(X_{1j}, \ldots, X_{nj})$ is maximized subject to the budget restraint,

$$\sum_{i=1}^{n} P_i(X_{ij} - \overline{X}_{ij}) = R_j .$$

The first-order conditions then for consumer equilibrium are the familiar

$$U_{ij} = \lambda_j P_i , \quad i = 1, \ldots, n; j = 1, \ldots, L ,$$

which may be written

(26)
$$\frac{U_{rj}}{U_{sj}} = \frac{P_r}{P_s} , \quad \begin{array}{c} r, s = 1, \ldots, n , \\ j = 1, \ldots, L . \end{array}$$

In principle, each person being possessed of his own particular set of skills and abilities, each person will have associated with him a distinct production function stating how he can transform certain commodities into other commodities. This does not, of course, mean that each man will run his own store. He may maximize his profits

---

[2] See P. A. Samuelson's *Foundations of Economic Analysis* (Cambridge, Mass.: Harvard University Press, 1955), p. 231. Conditions (25) represent a set of $n \cdot L$ simultaneous equations, the solution to which ($n \cdot L$ variables X_{ij}, $i = 1, \ldots, n$, $j = 1, \ldots, L$) will be Pareto optimal. Notice that all these equations must be satisfied. One is sometimes tempted to establish Pareto optimality by proving that a single *typical* consumer, say individual 1, could not be made better off without others being made worse off. Thus one would maximize
$$U_1 = U_1(X_{11}, \ldots, X_{n1})$$
subject to
$$\overline{U}_i = U_i(X_{1i}, \ldots, X_{ni}), \quad i = 2, \ldots, L ,$$
and to
$$F(X_1, \ldots, X_n) = 0 .$$
The conditions for this maximization are
$$\frac{U_{r1}}{U_{s1}} = \frac{F_r}{F_s}$$
which are L in number and do *not* insure Pareto optimality even if the second-order conditions for it are satisfied.

by selling his labor to others. In principle, however, he could run a firm, and it would be different from other peoples' firms. Accordingly, we allow for the existence of L firms, one for each production function. Firm k will maximize

$$\Pi_k = \sum_{i=1}^{n} P_i X_{ik}$$

subject to its implicit production function,

$$f_k(X_{1k}, \ldots, X_{nk}) = 0 .$$

The first-order conditions for this maximization may be written

$$(27) \qquad \frac{f_{rk}}{f_{sk}} = \frac{P_r}{P_s}, \qquad \begin{matrix} r, s = 1, \ldots, n , \\ k = 1, \ldots, L . \end{matrix}$$

Equations (26) and (27) comprise part of a system of equations, the simultaneous solution to which will be a general equilibrium for a purely competitive production and exchange economy. The reader should write out the rest of this system of equations. (In proving the dependence of one equation, utilize the relationship $R_i = \Pi_i$, $i = 1, \ldots, n$.)

Equations (26) and (27) together imply

$$(28) \qquad \frac{U_{rj}}{U_{sj}} = \frac{f_{rk}}{f_{sk}}, \qquad \begin{matrix} r, s = 1, \ldots, n , \\ j, k = 1, \ldots, L . \end{matrix}$$

We now wish to show that conditions (28) imply conditions (25), i.e., that any purely competitive equilibrium of production and exchange is Pareto optimal. Obviously, the left-hand side of conditions (25) is identical with the left-hand side of conditions (28). We must establish the identity of the right-hand sides. The production function for the entire economy is given by

$$F(X_1, \ldots, X_n) = 0 .$$

Suppose that we wish to increase the output of commodity s (or decrease our use of input s) thus,

$$dX_s > 0 .$$

Suppose further that we want to increase X_s at the expense of X_r only, keeping all other

$$dX_i = 0 , \qquad i = 1, \ldots, n \neq r, s .$$

(The reader should write out the various interpretations of this change where X_s is an input, i.e., $X_s = -Y_s$ and X_r an output, etc. We shall refer to both as outputs.) Then,

$$0 = dF = F_r dX_r + F_s dX_s ,$$

so that

$$F_r dX_r = -F_s dX_s$$

and

$$\frac{F_r}{F_s} = -\frac{dX_s}{dX_r}.$$

The right-hand side of (25) is the marginal rate of transformation of commodity r into commodity s for this economy.

By an identical argument, it can be shown that for firm k

$$\frac{f_{rk}}{f_{sk}} = -\frac{dX_{sk}}{dX_{rk}}, \qquad \begin{matrix} k = 1, \ldots, L, \\ s, r = 1, \ldots, n. \end{matrix}$$

Notice, however, that conditions (27) imply that this ratio is the same for all firms. If commodity r is to be converted into commodity s in this economy, then some firm must do it, since any economic unit converting commodities into other commodities is called a firm. Thus,

(29)
$$\frac{dX_{sk}}{dX_{rk}} = \frac{dX_s}{dX_r}, \qquad \begin{matrix} s, r = 1, \ldots, n, \\ k = 1, \ldots, L, \end{matrix}$$

so that

$$\frac{f_{rk}}{f_{sk}} = \frac{F_r}{F_s}, \qquad \begin{matrix} k = 1, \ldots, L, \\ s, r = 1, \ldots, n. \end{matrix}$$

Accordingly, in purely competitive equilibrium

$$\frac{U_{rj}}{U_{sj}} = \frac{F_r}{F_s}, \qquad \begin{matrix} j = 1, \ldots, L, \\ s, r = 1, \ldots, n, \end{matrix}$$

which are the conditions for Pareto optimality. Purely competitive equilibria are Pareto optimal.

The reader may justifiably feel some misgivings about the last paragraph. In particular, our proof is only valid under the assumptions that we have made. At least one such assumption important to the argument, while it has been quite explicitly written into our analysis, has not been discussed. The implicit production restraint for the kth firm was written

$$f_k(X_{1k}, \ldots, X_{nk}) = 0$$

where the variables X_{ik}, $i = 1, \ldots, n$, are the inputs and outputs of firm k. Thus, firm k's production depends only upon firm k's activity; there are no technological external effects on k's production by the production and employment of other firms. It is for this reason that we can write equation (29) without lying.

Before we close our discussion of Pareto optimality, a few

comments are in order. The reader will have noticed that we have referred above to pure, not perfect, competition. This was intentional. Our analysis has not required any entry assumptions. We have supposed that the firm was able to vary all its inputs and outputs so our proof pertains to long-run equilibrium. Entry is quite another thing, however. Suppose that there are technical restrictions on entry into the ith market so that it is not possible for firm k to produce commodity i. Then, the firm's implicit production function will indicate this. Moreover, in the derivation of the implicit production function for the economy, $F(X_1, \ldots, X_n) = 0$, such restrictions will be taken into account and the resultant purely competitive equilibrium will be Pareto optimal, given these constraints.

What we have shown is that a purely competitive equilibrium is (assuming the appropriate second-order conditions to be met) Pareto optimal. We have not shown that a purely competitive *system* is Pareto optimal. The desirability of the disequilibrium configurations of such a system remains to be demonstrated. It has been shown (though not here) that purely competitive equilibria will be stable under certain dynamic adjustment assumptions. It has not been established that such dynamic adjustments are typical of any actual purely competitive economy, nor, for that matter, have purely competitive economies been shown to be particularly thick upon the ground.

The economic systems that we observe appear to be rich in impurities; monopolies seem to exist, as do externalities and exceptions to almost every assumption that we have made. What appear to be attempts to legislate away such impurities have been made, thus, antimonopoly laws, etc. Such legislation is ill supported by economic theory. In an imperfect economy removal of a few imperfections will not necessarily improve things. If hundreds of firms exist which have some control over prices, it will not necessarily take one nearer to Pareto optimality[3] to break up one firm because it happens to be a single seller. Analysis of such situations has been undertaken[4] and it does not indicate the

---

[3] Configurations which are near Pareto optimal configurations would seem to lack attractiveness in any case. All that can be said for a configuration that is Pareto optimal is that no man can be made better off without someone being made worse off. All that can be said for a configuration that is near a Pareto optimum is that someone *can* be made better off without someone else being made worse off which is hardly a recommendation for such configurations.

[4] R. G. Lipsey and R. K. Lancaster, "The General Theory of Second Best," *Review of Economic Studies*, Vol. XXIV (1), No. 63 (December, 1956), pp. 11–32.

existence of quite such simple solutions. We shall not pursue such analysis here, but recommend it to the reader's attention.

In determining the Pareto optimality of purely competitive equilibria, we took as given the distribution of skills and abilities to the population. The man who has managed, perhaps through diligent effort and long self-deprivation, to become highly skilled will be better rewarded, if his skills are highly valued, than will his less able neighbor. It is consistent with pure competition and Pareto optimality to have widely divergent purchasing power among consumers. Thus, some may starve while others grow fat, and one could not aid the destitute without hindering the affluent. Purely competitive equilibria are Pareto optimal; no one has claimed that they are nice.

SELECTED BIBLIOGRAPHY

HICKS, J. R. *Value and Capital.* 2d ed. Oxford: Clarendon Press, 1946.

KUENNE, R. E. *The Theory of General Economic Equilibrium.* Princeton, N.J.: Princeton University Press, 1963.

LANGE, O. "The Foundations of Welfare Economics," *Econometrica* (1942), p. 215.

MISHAN, E. J. "A Survey of Welfare Economics, 1939–1959," *The Economic Journal,* Vol. LXX (June, 1960), pp. 197–265.

SAMUELSON, P. A. *Foundations of Economic Analysis.* Cambridge, Mass.: Harvard University Press, 1948.

WALRAS, L. *Elements of Pure Economics.* Translated by W. Jaffé. Homewood, Ill.: Richard D. Irwin, Inc., 1954.

Chapter 10

SUMMARY AND OVERVIEW

You push the middle valve down,
The music goes round and round
And it comes out here.
—*"The Music Goes 'Round and Around"**

The dictates of tradition require that any economic writing be divisible into three parts. In the first part, one tells what it is that he will be saying; in the second part, he says it; and in the third part, he tells what it is that he has said. In this chapter we shall repeat all we have said above. This chapter will be quite short.

Basically, we have been concerned with three topics: the theory of demand, the theory of supply, and the theory of markets. These three topics assume various names in the literature, but all that we have discussed may accurately be said to lead either to the determination of quantities supplied or of quantities demanded of commodities, or to analysis of how the "market" determines price so as to rationalize such quantities.

In order that the discussion that follows may be more integrated, we recommend to the reader's attention Chart 1, below. This chart is intended to summarize our discussion.

Demand

The theory of demand is dominated by the theory of consumer equilibrium, although, as noted in the text, it properly includes analysis of the firm's demand for factors of production. We shall treat this latter topic, below, in connection with the theory of supply, as is customary. However, we shall be careful to return it ultimately to its appropriate classification.

The consumer, we have supposed, has a preference ordering defined over his commodity space. This ordering has particular monotonicity, continuity, and transitivity properties, which enable

---

* "The Music Goes 'Round and Around," by "Red" Hodgson, Edward Farley, and Michial Riley. Copyright, Anne-Rachel Music Corporation. USED BY PERMISSION.

us to define a continuous cardinal utility function preserving the preference ordering on the commodity space. We take as given to the consumer a set of prices for all commodities traded. He is not able to alter these prices by his own actions. He is also given a fixed amount of purchasing power. This purchasing power may be in the form, simply, of income from unexplained sources or it may be in the form of an initial endowment of commodities (including the consumer's labor) which the consumer may sell as he chooses at the given prices.

The given set of prices in conjunction with the given purchasing power determine the consumer's budget restraint. This restraint constitutes the subset of the commodity space that the consumer is able to afford. We suppose that the consumer purchases that bundle of commodities that he most prefers among those that he can afford. This is equivalent to maximizing his utility function subject to his budget restraint. In this way, the consumer chooses the bundle of commodities that he will purchase, given the set of prices and his purchasing power. By examining the ways in which the bundle varies as prices and purchasing power change, we derive the consumer's demand functions for commodities. If his purchasing power is a given initial endowment of commodities, we are able to derive the same information in the form of excess demand functions which will include information regarding quantities of factors that he will supply to producers. We may summarize the theory of consumer equilibrium as in box 1 of Chart 1 as follows:

CONSUMER
  Given:
    Preferences: Utility function
    Prices
    Purchasing power
  Behavior:
    Maximizes utility subject to budget restraint
  Derive:
    Individual excess demand functions or net
      demand functions and supply functions of
      some commodities and factors

The excess demand functions so derived are aggregated and added to those derived from the theory of the firm (see below) to determine market excess demand functions.

Supply: Competitive Firms

The competitive firm is a price taker. As with the consumer, the set of prices must be included in the initial conditions confronting the firm. These given prices enter its decision process in two ways. They are basic to the definition of the firm's expenditure function which associates with each point in the firm's input space a given expenditure exactly sufficient to purchase the set of inputs represented by the point. In the competitive case, this function will be linear. The given prices also enter the firm's total revenue function which, as well, is linear in the competitive case. This function associates with each possible level of output a given level of revenue received by the firm. The revenue function may be defined for a multiproduct firm as in the appendix to Chapter 5.

The information contained in the firm's revenue and expenditure functions relates to the costs of inputs and the income from outputs. Before the firm can act according to our behavioral assumptions, it must possess information, additional to the above, relating to the possibilities of transforming inputs into outputs. This information is contained in the firm's production function which in the single-product case, associates a given level of output with each possible point in the firm's input space. In the multiproduct case, this function may be written implicitly, as we have done at several points above, or explicitly, associating a given level of production of one commodity with each possible set of inputs and each level of production of all other outputs.

We assume that the firm combines this information in order to choose that output which will maximize its profits. These profits are defined as the difference between the expenditure associated with any level of output and the revenue derived from the sale of that output. The problem of identifying the profit maximizing output may be viewed in several ways. One may define functions associating a certain cost with each level of output and seek that output for which the difference between revenue and this cost is a maximum. Alternatively, one may view the problem as one of input selection, choosing that set of inputs such that the difference between the expenditure associated with them and the revenue associated with what they will produce is maximized. In the latter case, one may derive information governing the firm's demand for inputs. In the former case, this information is still available. However, it is gained when one derives the firm's cost function. By examining the firm's reaction to variations in prices, we are then able to determine supply functions associating with each set of prices the profit-maximizing quantities that the firm will offer for sale of the commodities that it produces. Similarly, we may derive functions associating with each set of prices that set of inputs that the firm will employ in order to produce its profit-maximizing outputs, i.e., the firm's demand functions for factors. Of course, this information could alternatively be stated in the form of excess demand functions.[1]

We may summarize the theory of the competitive firm as in box 2 of Chart 1 as follows:

COMPETITIVE FIRMS
   Given:
      Prices
         That is, expenditure function and
            revenue function
      Production function
   Behavior:
      Maximizes profit subject to its production
         function
   Derive:
      Individual firm's excess demand functions
         or net demand for factors of production
         and supply of outputs

The excess supply functions are aggregated and taken with those of consumers to provide market excess supply (or demand) functions (see below).

Competitive Markets

Since a monopic firm is, in a sense, also a market, we will discuss competitive markets before turning our attention to monopic firms.

The competitive market is the institution through which the actions of competitive firms and competitive consumers confront one another and are rationalized. From the theory of consumer equilibrium, we have, for each consumer, a set of functions showing quantities that the consumer will demand (or supply) of each commodity. Similarly, from the theory of the competitive firm, we have functions showing each firm's demand for factors and supply of outputs. Aggregating all these demand functions for each

---

[1] We could, also, have summarized this information in the form of excess supply functions. The reader will recall that an economic unit's excess supply function is simply minus its excess demand function.

commodity and all these supply functions for each commodity (alternatively, adding together the excess demand functions of all economic units), we derive a set of market supply and demand functions (or of market excess demand functions). The market then determines a set of prices such that the aggregate demand for each commodity will exactly equal the aggregate supply, as in box 3 of Chart 1:

COMPETITIVE MARKETS
  Given:
    Market demand functions from
      consumers and competitive firms
    Market supply functions from con-
      sumers and competitive firms
  Derive:
    Prices such that the market supply of
      each commodity will equal market
      demand

Monopic Firms—Markets

A firm may be monopic in some commodities and competitive in others. For any commodity in which such a firm is competitive, its actions will be as described above. Here we shall confine our attention to those commodities, the prices of which are somewhat under the control of the firm. Such commodities may either be among the firm's inputs so that the firm is monopsonistic or among its outputs so that the firm is monopolistic. The monopic firm differs from its competitive counterpart in that its decision is more complex. It is unable to simply adjust to given prices because its actions will affect prices.

Because prices vary with its actions, the expenditure function of the monopic firm is not linear. This function may, however, be defined. Thus, the monopic firm purchases its inputs from consumers and from other firms, and it is so significant a buyer that the prices of these inputs will vary with its actions. The firm will not be given a set of prices but rather an expenditure function associating a given level of expenditure with each point in the firm's input space.

The firm will, also, be given a nonlinear total revenue function. In the single-product case, this function will associate a given total revenue with each possible level of output. In the multiproduct case, it will associate a given total revenue with each possible output bundle.

In addition to these two functions, the firm will need information regarding the ways in which inputs may be transformed into outputs. Such information is embodied in the firm's production function.

The firm transforms inputs into outputs so as to maximize its profit function. Notice, however, that the monopic firm not only maximizes its profits, it also serves to rationalize the quantities supplied by itself to those demanded by other firms and consumers, as well as those demanded by itself to those supplied by other firms and consumers. We may, for example, view the firm's expenditure function as a group of supply functions, one for each commodity that it employs. These associate with each set of prices those quantities of inputs that other firms and consumers will be willing to supply to the monopic firm. Similarly, the firm's total revenue function will associate with each set of prices a set of quantities that will be demanded of the firm by other firms and consumers. The monopic firm will, then, take over the functions of the market and will set prices so as to rationalize its own profit maximization with the demand and supply functions of others. The firm may be viewed as setting either quantities (as in the single product case of Chapter 6) or prices (as in the multiproduct case of Chapter 9), but the fact is that in determining one set of variables, the firm determines the other set. Thus, we have the final box, 4, of Chart 1, and may complete the chart. The arrows indicate where information derived in one box is taken as initial data in another.

If traditional microeconomic theory were no simpler than the summary in Chart 1 indicates, it would still be an embarrassingly simple subject. The reader will presumably have realized, however, that it is far simpler than that. He need only consider the behavior classifications of boxes 1, 2, and 4 to realize that here are not three different types of analysis, but rather the same analysis repeated three times, those variations on that theme by Lagrange, again.

The consumer maximizes a function

$$U = U(X_1, \ldots, X_n)$$

subject to the linear constraint

$$\sum_{i=1}^{n} P_i X_i = Y$$

where it is assumed that

$$U_i > 0 \quad \text{and}$$
$$U_{ij} = U_{ji}.$$

CHART 1

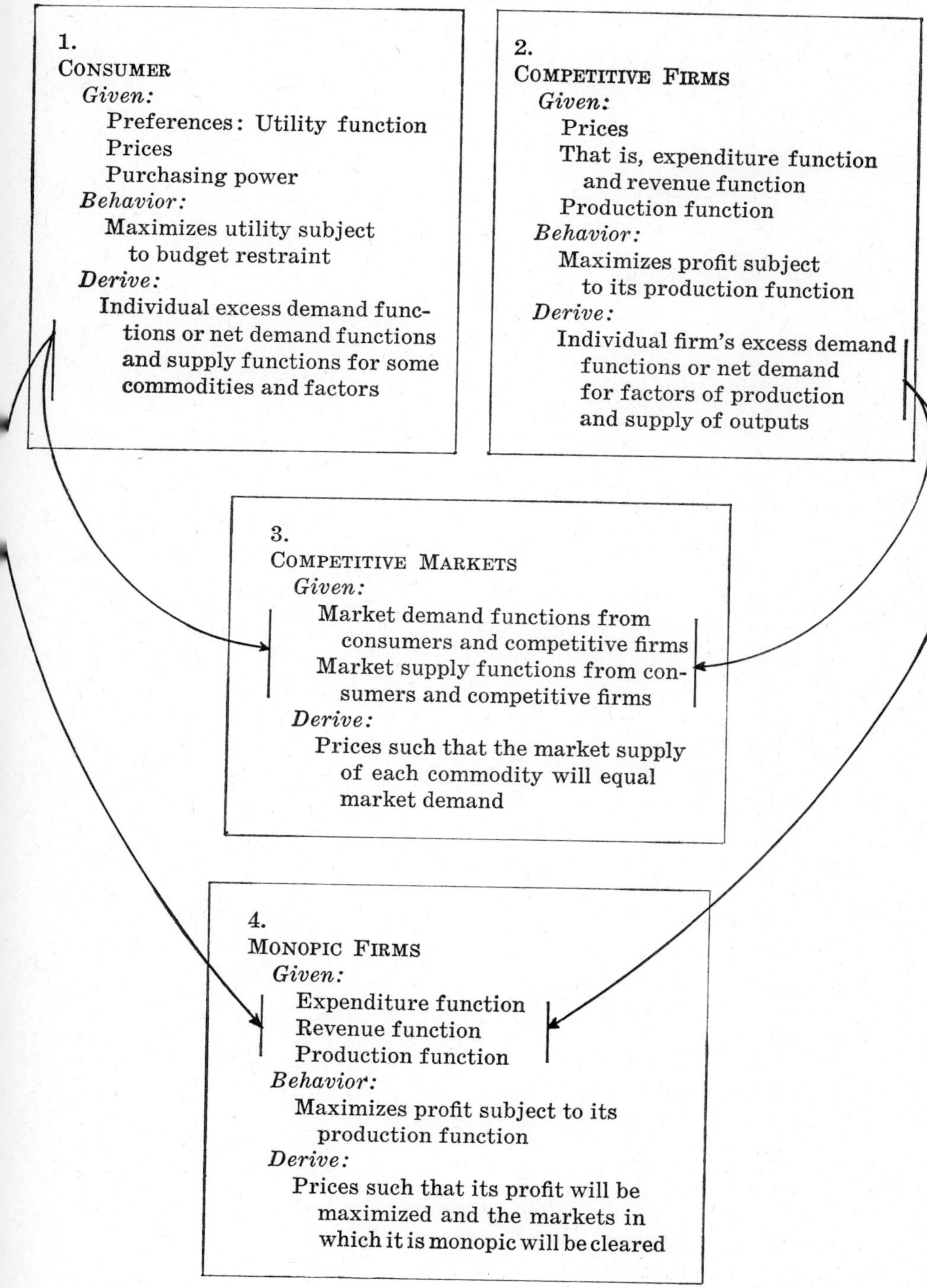

1.
CONSUMER
Given:
  Preferences: Utility function
  Prices
  Purchasing power
Behavior:
  Maximizes utility subject
    to budget restraint
Derive:
  Individual excess demand func-
    tions or net demand functions
    and supply functions for some
    commodities and factors

2.
COMPETITIVE FIRMS
Given:
  Prices
  That is, expenditure function
    and revenue function
  Production function
Behavior:
  Maximizes profit subject
    to its production function
Derive:
  Individual firm's excess demand
    functions or net demand
    for factors of production
    and supply of outputs

3.
COMPETITIVE MARKETS
Given:
  Market demand functions from
    consumers and competitive firms
  Market supply functions from con-
    sumers and competitive firms
Derive:
  Prices such that the market supply
    of each commodity will equal
    market demand

4.
MONOPIC FIRMS
Given:
  Expenditure function
  Revenue function
  Production function
Behavior:
  Maximizes profit subject to its
    production function
Derive:
  Prices such that its profit will be
    maximized and the markets in
    which it is monopic will be cleared

In deriving its cost functions, the firm which purchases its factors competitively minimizes

$$\sum_{i=1}^{n} X_i P_i$$

subject to the constraint

$$\Phi = \Phi(X_1, \ldots, X_n) \, ,$$

where

$$\Phi_i > 0$$
$$\Phi_{ij} = \Phi_{ji} \, .$$

This problem is not only similar to the consumer's utility maximization problem, it is nearly identical. The production constraint is of exactly the same form as the consumer's utility function while the firm's expenditure function is of precisely the same form as the consumer's budget restraint. In fact, the firm's minimization problem is identical in form to the dual of the utility maximization problem.

The competitive firm seeks a maximum for its profit function,

$$\sum_{i=1}^{n} X_i P_i \, ,$$

subject to the implicit production function,

$$f(X_1, \ldots, X_n) = 0$$

which is supposed to have the properties

$$f_i > 0 \, ,$$
$$f_{ij} = f_{ji} \, .$$

Once again, the problem is of the same form. The first-order conditions are identical in form with those of the above extrema problems. The introduction of a minus sign would render the second-order conditions, as well, identical with those above (see the mathematical appendix to Chapter 5).

The monopic firm is, admittedly, slightly different. We have formulated the theory of monopic firms in two ways. The formulation for a multiproduct monopic firm was presented in Chapter 9. We have not pursued the comparative statics of this formulation because such analysis seems, in this case, more complex than rewarding. The theory of the single-product monopoly was developed in the mathematical appendix to Chapter 6. In fact, the formulation there employed is general enough to describe any firm having a defined revenue function. This is of the form

$$\text{Maximize} \qquad R[\Phi(X_1, \ldots, X_n)] - \sum_{i=1}^{n} P_i X_i \,.$$

This maximization problem is *slightly* different from the above in that it is unconstrained. Notice, however, that it is of precisely the same form as the Lagrangians of the above problems with Lagrangian multiplier equal to 1.

Is it any wonder, then, that time and again we have established the same comparative-static results with only the names of the variables changed? For every economic actor (save those oligopolists for whom revenue functions cannot be defined) be he firm or consumer, concerned with profit-maximizing or cost-minimizing, we have established some sort of own substitution effect which must be negative, some sort of symmetry property, some sort of reciprocal determinants property, and in all cases except that of the profit-maximizing monopolist, an alien cofactors property. Moreover, we have been able to derive interesting ramifications from the fact that the Lagrangian multiplier is equal to the rate of change of the quantity being maximized with respect to a change in the constraint.

All of which brings us to the first law of research in traditional microeconomic theory. Whenever *anyone* proves *anything* about one sort of microeconomic unit, check the others.

Index

INDEX

*This book has been set in 10 and 9 point
Century Expanded, leaded 2 points. Part
and chapter numbers and part titles are in
18 point Spartan Medium italic; chapter
titles are in 18 point Spartan Medium. The
size of the type page is 27 by $45\frac{1}{2}$ picas.*